ISBN 978-1-397-88937-9
PIBN 10019220

1 MONTH OF
FREE
READING

at

www.ForgottenBooks.com

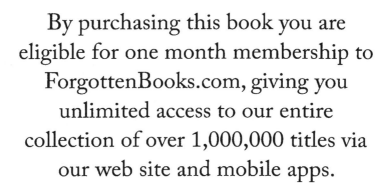

By purchasing this book you are eligible for one month membership to ForgottenBooks.com, giving you unlimited access to our entire collection of over 1,000,000 titles via our web site and mobile apps.

To claim your free month visit:
www.forgottenbooks.com/free19220

THE JOSEPH WILLIAMS SERIES OF HANDBOOKS ON MUSIC
UNDER THE RESPONSIBLE EDITORSHIP OF STEWART MACPHERSON

MELODY AND HARMONY

A TREATISE FOR THE
TEACHER AND THE STUDENT

BY

STEWART MACPHERSON

(Fellow, Professor and Lecturer, Royal Academy of Music;
Author of "Practical Harmony," "Form in Music," "Music and its Appreciation," etc., etc.)

BOOK I.	BOOK II.	BOOK III.
MELODIC MOVEMENT.	ELEMENTARY HARMONIC PROGRESSION.	ADVANCED HARMONY.

(PRICE FOUR SHILLINGS AND SIXPENCE NET EACH)

THE COMPLETE VOLUME, IN CLOTH BOARDS (WITH ANALYTICAL INDEX BY SYLVIA E. CURREY)
PRICE TWELVE SHILLINGS AND SIXPENCE NET

LONDON: JOSEPH WILLIAMS, LIMITED
32, GREAT PORTLAND STREET, W. 1

AUSTRALIA
D. DAVIS & CO. LTD., Sydney

NEW ZEALAND
A. A. CORRIGAN & CO. LTD., Wellington

U.S.A.
THE B. F. WOOD MUSIC CO., Boston

TABLE OF CONTENTS.

PAGE

PREFACE i

DIRECTIONS TO THE TEACHER v

INTRODUCTORY CHAPTER I

CHAPTER

PART I.

I. THE SINGLE MELODIC LINE 4
II. DUAL MELODIC LINES—MAJOR KEY 8
    MINOR KEY 13
III. „ „ „ (continued): FIRST STAGES OF FLORID MELODIC MOVEMENT... 17
IV. „ „ „ „ FLORID MELODIC MOVEMENT (SECOND STAGE) ... 26
V. „ „ „ „ THE USE OF THE TIE 34
VI. „ „ „ „ (1) CERTAIN 'ESSENTIAL' DISSONANCES 40
    (2) FURTHER USES OF THE MELODIC MINOR SCALE... 43
VII. THREE-PART MELODIC WRITING 46
VIII. FOUR-PART MELODIC WRITING 59
    SUPPLEMENTARY EXERCISES ... ... (at end of Book) viii

PART II.

IX. HARMONIC PROGRESSION—THE PRIMARY TRIADS 64
. 74
. 80
. 81
.. 92
.. 104
.. 111
.. 112
.. 120
.. 133
.. 148
.. 158
.. 161
.. 165
.. 179
... 188

ERRATUM. P. 70, F. Ex. 4.

The latter part of the above-named exercise should read as follows :—

|No harmony here.|

(3) SECONDARY SEVENTHS, INVOLVING USE OF MELODIC MINOR SCALE 192
XXII. CHROMATICALLY-ALTERED CHORDS 195
XXIII. CHORDS OF THE NINTH :
    (1) THE CHORD OF THE DOMINANT NINTH 202
    (2) SECONDARY CHORDS OF THE NINTH 212
XXIV. THE CHORD OF THE DOMINANT ELEVENTH 215
XXV. THE CHORD OF THE DOMINANT THIRTEENTH 218
XXVI. CHROMATIC HARMONY :
    (1) THE SUPERTONIC CHROMATIC TRIAD 224
    (2) THE SUPERTONIC CHROMATIC CHORD OF THE SEVENTH ... 226
    (3) THE TONIC CHROMATIC CHORD OF THE SEVENTH 229
XXVII. CHROMATIC CHORDS OF THE NINTH, ELEVENTH AND THIRTEENTH :
    (1) SUPERTONIC AND TONIC NINTHS 232
    (2) SUPERTONIC AND TONIC ELEVENTHS AND THIRTEENTHS ... 238
XXVIII. CHROMATICALLY-ALTERED CHORDS (continued) :
    THE CHORD OF THE AUGMENTED SIXTH 241
XXIX. MODULATION (continued) :
    (1) CHROMATIC PIVOT-CHORDS 247
    (2) ENHARMONIC MODULATION 249

APPENDIX A. CONCERNING SEQUENCES AND PEDALS : (1) SEQUENCES 257
    (2) PEDALS 260
„ B. SPECIAL PIANOFORTE IDIOMS 263
„ C. CONCERNING THE NOTATION OF THE CHROMATIC SCALE 271
„ D. THE ECCLESIASTICAL MODES 277
„ E. THE STRING QUARTET 281
„ F. MISCELLANEOUS EXERCISES (WITH PRELIMINARY NOTE) 285
„ G. GLOSSARY OF TECHNICAL TERMS 295
ANALYTICAL INDEX 298

ERRATUM. P. 70, V. Ex. 4.

The latter part of the above-named exercise should read as follows:—

[No harmony here.]

TABLE OF CONTENTS.

PAGE

PREFACE i
DIRECTIONS TO THE TEACHER v
INTRODUCTORY CHAPTER I

CHAPTER   PART I.
  I. THE SINGLE MELODIC LINE 4
 II. DUAL MELODIC LINES—MAJOR KEY 8
                          MINOR KEY 13
III. „ „ „ (continued) : FIRST STAGES OF FLORID MELODIC MOVEMENT... 17
 IV. „ „ „ „ FLORID MELODIC MOVEMENT (SECOND STAGE)... 26
  V. „ „ „ „ THE USE OF THE TIE 34
 VI. „ „ „ „ (1) CERTAIN 'ESSENTIAL' DISSONANCES 40
                    (2) FURTHER USES OF THE MELODIC MINOR SCALE... 43
VII. THREE-PART MELODIC WRITING 46
VIII. FOUR-PART MELODIC WRITING 59
      SUPPLEMENTARY EXERCISES ... ... (at end of Book) viii

                             PART II.
 IX. HARMONIC PROGRESSION—THE PRIMARY TRIADS 64
  X. FURTHER USE OF THE PRIMARY TRIADS 74
 XI. THE INVERSIONS OF THE PRIMARY TRIADS 80
                   (1) THE FIRST INVERSION 81
XII. THE INVERSIONS OF THE PRIMARY TRIADS (continued) :}
                   (2) THE SECOND INVERSION   } 92
XIII. THE SECONDARY TRIADS OF THE MAJOR OR MINOR KEY }
                   (1) THE SUPERTONIC AND SUBMEDIANT CHORDS } 104
XIV. THE SECONDARY TRIADS OF THE MAJOR OR MINOR KEY (continued) ... 111
                   (2) THE TRIADS UPON THE MEDIANT AND LEADING-NOTE... 112
 XV. THE CHORD OF THE DOMINANT SEVENTH 120
XVI. THE HARMONIC ASPECT OF SUSPENSIONS 133
XVII. (1) THE USES OF THE ACCENTED PASSING-NOTE, OR APPOGGIATURA ... 148
      (2) THE FREER TREATMENT OF PASSING-NOTES—ANTICIPATIONS ... 158
XVIII. THE MELODIC MINOR SCALE IN CHORD-FORMATION ... ... · ... 161
XIX. MODULATION (EXPERIMENTAL STUDIES IN) 165

                             PART III.
 XX. SECONDARY CHORDS OF THE SEVENTH :
                   (1) FIRST OR NORMAL RESOLUTION 179
XXI. SECONDARY CHORDS OF THE SEVENTH (continued) :
                   (2) FREER RESOLUTIONS 188
                   (3) SECONDARY SEVENTHS, INVOLVING USE OF MELODIC MINOR SCALE 192
XXII. CHROMATICALLY-ALTERED CHORDS 195
XXIII. CHORDS OF THE NINTH :
                   (1) THE CHORD OF THE DOMINANT NINTH 202
                   (2) SECONDARY CHORDS OF THE NINTH 212
XXIV. THE CHORD OF THE DOMINANT ELEVENTH 215
XXV. THE CHORD OF THE DOMINANT THIRTEENTH 218
XXVI. CHROMATIC HARMONY :
                   (1) THE SUPERTONIC CHROMATIC TRIAD 224
                   (2) THE SUPERTONIC CHROMATIC CHORD OF THE SEVENTH ... 226
                   (3) THE TONIC CHROMATIC CHORD OF THE SEVENTH 229
XXVII. CHROMATIC CHORDS OF THE NINTH, ELEVENTH AND THIRTEENTH :
                   (1) SUPERTONIC AND TONIC NINTHS 232
                   (2) SUPERTONIC AND TONIC ELEVENTHS AND THIRTEENTHS ... 238
XXVIII. CHROMATICALLY-ALTERED CHORDS (continued) :
                   THE CHORD OF THE AUGMENTED SIXTH 241
XXIX. MODULATION (continued) :
                   (1) CHROMATIC PIVOT-CHORDS 247
                   (2) ENHARMONIC MODULATION 249

APPENDIX A. CONCERNING SEQUENCES AND PEDALS : (1) SEQUENCES 257
                                           (2) PEDALS 260
      „   B. SPECIAL PIANOFORTE IDIOMS 263
      „   C. CONCERNING THE NOTATION OF THE CHROMATIC SCALE 271
      „   D. THE ECCLESIASTICAL MODES 277
      „   E. THE STRING QUARTET 281
      „   F. MISCELLANEOUS EXERCISES (WITH PRELIMINARY NOTE) 285
      „   G. GLOSSARY OF TECHNICAL TERMS 295
ANALYTICAL INDEX 298

. The thanks of both Author and Publisher are due to the following Firms for permission to use extracts from their copyright works, as under :—

Messrs. RICORDI & Co.
PUCCINI'S "Madam Butterfly."

Mons. E. FROMONT, of Paris.
DEBUSSY'S "Prelude" from Suite.
,,   "Sarabande" from Suite.

Messrs. DURAND ET CIE., of Paris.
DEBUSSY'S "Children's Corner" Suite.
RAVEL'S Sonatina.
SAINT-SAËNS' "Le Rouet d'Omphale."

Messrs. SCHOTT & Co.
WAGNER'S "Die Meistersinger."
,,   "Parsifal."
,,   "Die Walküre."
,,   "Tristan and Isolde."

Messrs. AUGENER, LTD.
GRIEG'S Violin Sonata, Op. 8.
,,   Sonata for 'Cello, Op. 36.
,,   Pianoforte Concerto.
,,   "Peer Gynt" Suite.
,,   "Ich liebe dich."
,,   "Lyrische Stückchen," Op. 43.

Mons. J. HAMELLE, of Paris.
FRANCK'S Symphony in D minor.

Jos. AIBL-VERLAG, of Leipzig.
STRAUSS' "Nachtgang." (Universal Edition.)

Messrs. NOVELLO & Co.
DVORAK'S "Stabat Mater."
GOUNOD'S "Redemption."
MACKENZIE'S "Rose of Sharon."
ELGAR'S "In the South" Overture.
,,   "Dream of Gerontius."

Messrs. ALFRED LENGNICK & Co.
BRAHMS' Variations in Bb, for Orchestra.
,,   Symphony in D (No. 2).
DVORAK'S String Quartet in F, Op. 96.
,,   Pianoforte Quintet, Op. 81.
BRAHMS' "Vergeblicher Ständchen," Op. 84.
,,   Sextet in G.
DVORAK'S "New World Symphony."

Messrs. J. & W. CHESTER.
FIBICH'S "Stimmingen," Op. 41.

PREFACE.

1. The present volume is an attempt to solve certain practical difficulties connected with the education of the musician. Of recent years views concerning the actual value of Harmony-study and the method of its presentation, have undergone a wholesome and very welcome change. Instead of being regarded solely as a preparation for the work of the would-be composer, it is beginning to take its rightful place in the musical development of the average student, as a natural corollary of his elementary aural training, both melodic and rhythmic.

2. It has gradually been forced upon the minds of teachers that the real object of the study of Harmony is to help the student whose ear is as yet undeveloped, to hear and to think in terms of sound-combinations and progressions—a work of real practical difficulty to many—and that, in order to achieve this end, he must from the very outset learn to make experimental, first-hand use of his material. This has led to the conviction that the usual figured bass (which, of course, *can* be worked by the student in such a way that no actual harmonic thinking is done by him in the process) is, save in a very limited degree, of little or no real value as the actual basis of his studies. It has thus come about that the harmonization of melodies and unfigured basses has assumed an importance that it formerly did not possess, and much progress has been made in this direction to stimulate the pupil's harmonic perception. Although a few figured basses will be found amongst the exercises in this book, the scheme of teaching developed in it depends very little upon them.

3. But in the earliest stages of the study, at the point where constructive harmony-work should link up with the pupil's previous aural training, a very distinct and unfortunate *lacuna* has existed. Instead of being taught from the very first how to make experimental use of the limited vocabulary at his command in the early stages of his study—a vocabulary, it may be at the time, of only a couple of chords—and to express something musical by their means, his first work in melody-harmonization has too frequently required a knowledge of chord-effect and chord-progression far beyond his powers at the moment. It has thus been necessary to precede his attempts in this direction by the learning of a great many purely intellectual facts relative to a variety of chords, and to commit to memory a number of rules as to their treatment. In other words, he has had to learn *about* chords, rather than to learn the musical value of the chords themselves from practical experience of their habits and functions.

4. It is obvious that the successful harmonization of a melody (either for voices or for instruments) depends, first and foremost, upon the character of the bass. To form a really good bass, a fairly comprehensive range of harmonies is necessary, and this involves not a little aural perception and knowledge of musical effect, a knowledge hardly to be expected of the average beginner.

5. In order to deal with this very practical difficulty, not a few musicians have advocated that the study of Counterpoint should precede that of Harmony, rightly feeling, first, that a *melodic* conception of the bass is of paramount importance, and secondly, that it is easier to begin to imagine the effect of merely two parts running side by side than to grasp that of a continuous progression of fuller harmonies. Both of these facts are indubitably true; but, while recognizing this, it seems that we need to take certain other matters into consideration. It will be convenient to set these out in order :—

(a) To start the young pupil—perhaps little more than a child—upon what is known as Strict Counterpoint, on the usual unrhythmical and not very inspiring *Canto Fermo*, would in all probability soon have the effect of making the eager beginner disgusted with music and all its works. Such a procedure would omit any provision for that exercise of the imagination which (especially in the case of the young pupil) needs to be called into play by means of definitely rhythmical tunes possessing a degree of spring and of life.

(*b*) Counterpoint, as it is usually taught to-day, presumes the realization of a harmonic basis in the case of even the simplest two-part exercise ; therefore, unless some change of method is admitted, the pupil is again face to face with the necessity of learning facts *about* chords before he can successfully begin his experimental work. Moreover, the aural perception of implied absent sounds is more than he can usually be expected to possess at this elementary stage, and when it comes to a case such as the

following [musical notation] which he is asked to recognize as an incom-

plete version of [musical notation] the point is far too subtle for a be-

ginner, unless he be gifted with an abnormally acute ear.

(*c*) The young pupil is usually attracted by the rich and sonorous effect of full harmonies, and it interests him to hear them and to experiment with them. Indeed, in some instances, his harmonic instinct is perceptibly in advance of his power of grasping the elaborate kind of "line-drawing" which is represented by what is (usually) known as Counterpoint. When such is the case it would seem to be sound common-sense not to neglect the early cultivation of that side of his nature where there is the greater likelihood of response.

(*d*) Strict Counterpoint is far too hedged-in by arbitrary rules formulated by a succession of theorists, to be dreamt of as a help towards the spontaneous development of a young pupil's musical sense, and its perpetual " Thou shalt not " prevents it from being in any way an inspiring adventure into which he would be likely to throw himself with any degree of ardour or enthusiasm.

6. What, then, is to be done ? Is not a possible solution to be found, not by teaching Harmony before Counterpoint, or Counterpoint before Harmony, (as separate, and even at times conflicting, subjects), but by dealing with the melodic and harmonic elements *pari passu*, from the very outset ? The author of the present volume has during the last few years been led irresistibly to this conclusion, and the scheme set forth in the succeeding pages is therefore planned so as to present these two aspects of the matter to the pupil *concurrently*, as complementary factors of one comprehensive whole.

7. Although it will be observed that the book is divided for the sake of convenience into two main parts, viz. : (i) Melodic movement, and (ii) Harmonic progression, these parts are not to be studied separately, but in the closest relation to each other throughout. The general idea aimed at is sufficiently indicated by the title *Melody and Harmony*.

8 As melody naturally precedes harmony; the student's first exercises take the form of the invention of original melodies. From this he proceeds to the addition of *one* other melodic part to one already given, thus arriving at a point at which the need for the melodious bass is impressed upon him. Obviously, this is also one of the aims of the ordinary Strict Counterpoint exercise in two parts ; but the type of "subject" presented to him at this stage differs widely from the usual *Canto Fermo* (i) in being always of a rhythmical and melodious character, and (ii) in being designed for working upon an *interval*-basis, without any previous knowledge of harmony being necessary. (That the intervals he has been using are merely incomplete chords becomes clear to him as soon as he understands the triad and its inversions, and can aurally realize their constituent parts.) By this means the hampering and needless complication (for a beginner) of thinking of implied chords and absent notes is avoided, and the author is of opinion that the pupil may thus be given the right orientation from the first, and may have some chance of avoiding the common pitfall of thinking merely in dull processions of " chord-blocks."

9. When once these first simple exercises have been accomplished and the principle of melodic movement (especially that of a bass-part) has been to some extent grasped, the student is at once called upon to turn his attention to the realization of complete chords and easy chord-progressions. These are brought to his notice gradually, so that he may perceive with some degree of accuracy their habits and their special musical effects, and may thus recognize what may be described as their individual personality. Every chord, as soon as it is aurally perceived, has at once to be used in the course of little musical phrases, which he has to play at the Pianoforte and to write as a test of memory. Simple melodies and unfigured basses are then given him to harmonize with the actual material at his command, so that every new harmony may have the chance of becoming for him a means of self-expression, not a mere abstraction of whose sound he has little or no idea. The plan thus initiated, of studying melodic movement and harmonic progression concurrently, is continued throughout the present volume, the interdependence of the two in all music worthy the name being thus constantly impressed upon the pupil's mind.

10. The various types of unessential notes (the Passing-note, the Suspension and the Appoggiatura), are dealt with at the first possible moment, in accordance with their import-ance. As a consequence of their introduction at an elementary stage of the study, it has been possible for many of even the earliest exercises to be planned in the form of little instrumental pieces, in which, moreover, the chords are often presented in "broken" and ornamented forms, such as are to be found in most of the examples of Pianoforte music with which the student is likely to be familiar. In this way it is hoped that he may reasonably gain a clearer idea of the close connexion of his Harmony-study with the music he plays or hears than is usually the case.

11. The unessential notes to which reference has been made are introduced to his notice first in the course of his two-part writing, their purely melodic nature being thus brought home to him more vividly, and their use and treatment divested of many of the initial "part-writing" difficulties usually encountered when they are first studied in relation to com-plete harmonies.

12. It will be noticed that the author, differing from the plan pursued in his *Practical Harmony*, has preferred to treat the 9th, 11th and 13th (when resolved upon notes of their own harmony) as "unessential," and to introduce them in a simple and practical form, as decorations of the Dominant 7th, in an early chapter dealing with "the uses of the Appog-giatura." Moreover, he has—since the publication of his former work—become convinced that the practice of regarding many obvious chords of the 7th as 11ths and 13ths, with certain notes (usually the more fundamental ones) omitted, is not only cumbersome and complicated, but from the aural standpoint makes demands upon the imaginative powers of the student's ear which he is often very naturally unable to cope with, even if it be admitted that we are dealing with verifiable acoustical facts—which is extremely doubtful.

13. As a consequence of what has just been said, the subject of "Non-Dominant," or "Secondary" 7ths has assumed a far greater degree of importance, and the majority of (so-called) inverted 11ths and 13ths are presented in what the author considers to be a more direct and aurally-realizable form, as examples of Secondary 7ths—with or without what is known as "Chromatic alteration," a matter which is dealt with in some detail.

14. Far less space in the volume has been given to the question of the treatment of the more elaborate and recondite harmonies, than to that of the more elementary and founda-tional branches of the study; the author feels strongly that *these* are really the things that matter most. In the case of the gifted student, what is needed is merely that his feet shall be set in the right direction; his own growing harmonic perception, gained by general musical experience and observation, will soon teach him the rest; while in the case of the pupil of average ability, or of one who may even be described as dull of hearing, it is obviously the simpler and more familiar chords and progressions that are of the greater moment as the basis of his aural development, and of any practical use he may be called upon to make of the idioms of the language he is learning. It is most lamentably true that the lack of the power to assimilate even the simplest of such idioms is responsible for the utter

inability of the majority of even professed music-students to play half-a-dozen chords in a rhythmical way, " off their own bat," to say nothing of extemporizing in the higher sense of the word.

15. Although the author indulges the hope that the melodic work (chiefly included in Part I) may prove to be a not altogether unsuccessful substitute for a great deal of so-called Strict Counterpoint, it goes without saying that there is nothing to prevent the student from gaining a knowledge of the particular restrictions and conventional formulæ of such Strict Counterpoint from one of the many existing text-books on the subject. He will find that the course of melodic writing in the present volume will in no sense act as a hindrance, but that it may conceivably lighten his task in a material degree.

16. In conclusion : the author realizes that, as the book in certain directions breaks fresh ground, and as he has (perhaps with a degree of temerity !) cast a modicum of doubt—by inference at least—upon the supposed efficacious virtues of that cherished British institution, Strict Counterpoint, he cannot hope for an unanimous welcome from all his colleagues of the teaching profession ; of that he must take the risk. He has, however, endeavoured—and for this he would fain be credited—to shew the student that the melodic and the harmonic aspects of the musical fabric should be realized from the first as having equal claims on his attention, and that success in constructive work can only be truly achieved by the union of the two. Moreover, his great aim, from start to finish, has been to drive home the fact that, unless Harmony-study is, all along the line, a real education of the ear and an actual development of the musical sense, it is merely time wasted, and involves an expenditure of effort which would be far more profitably diverted into other channels.

₊ The cordial thanks of the author are due to Miss Sylvia Currey, Dr. A. J. Greenish and Dr. H. W. Richards for much valued assistance in the revision of the proof-sheets of this volume.

London—1920.

DIRECTIONS TO THE TEACHER.

1. As the plan of the present volume differs in many respects from that of most treatise on Harmony, it is of the first importance that the following directions should be observed in its use. Although it is divided for the sake of convenience into two separate parts dealing respectively with (i) Melodic Movement, and (ii) Harmonic Progression, it is imperative that these parts *should be studied concurrently.* The order in which the several topics should be brought to the pupil's notice is set forth below:—

PART I.			**PART II.**	

Introductory Chapter.

Chapter I. The single Melodic line.

„ II. Dual Melodic lines. *To be followed by* ——>Chapters IX and X. The Primary triads.

„ III. First stage of Florid Melodic movement. *To be worked with* { „ XI and XII. The Inversions of the Primary triads.

{ „ XIII. Secondary triads.

„ IV. Florid Melodic movement (second stage.) *To be worked with* { „ XIV. Secondary triads (*cont^d.*).

{ „ XV. The chord of the Domt. 7th.

„ V. The use of the Tie. *To be followed by* „ XVI. The Harmonic aspect of Suspensions.

*** From this point onwards the two Parts of the book should be studied side by side at the teacher's discretion, according to the needs of the individual pupil.

2. Unless, or until, the pupil can mentally hear the sound of the examples given in the course of the text, the teacher should insist on his playing them, in order that they may be aurally realized in connexion with the remarks to which they refer.*

3. In order further to stimulate the pupil's aural perception, dictation exercises should be given, in the recognition both of the movement of two or more simultaneous melodic lines and of progressions of harmony regarded as *chords.* For this purpose any of the examples given in the text may be used by the teacher (with or without transposition into other keys).† In dictating two independent melodic lines, it will be necessary for him to make the movement of the parts particularly clear ; to this end it will often be found advisable to play the two parts with different qualities of tone. The lower of the two, being as a rule the less easily recognized, will often need to be played rather more prominently than its companion. In dictating progressions of complete chords, three different courses may be adopted ; the pupil may be asked (i) merely to describe the chords (as I_b, IV_c, ^7V, etc.); (ii) to describe the chords and write the notes of the outer parts (treble and bass) ; (iii) to write *all*

---

* Mr. Frederick Corder, in his *Modern Musical Composition* (Curwen & Sons), says truly : "In default of [systematic aural training in childhood] there is only one alternative. Dispense with writing as much as possible and force the generally reluctant pupil to play all [examples and] exercises on the Pianoforte. *In learning music the eye is no help; only a hindrance.* One does not realize the truth of this until one has taught the blind."

† The chord-progressions in Roman numerals, given in the course of the exercises throughout the volume, may also be used with this object.

the parts of the harmony as played.* Unless he possesses what is usually called "absolute" pitch," the key should be named in every instance, and the Tonic chord carefully impressed upon his ear and mind. It need hardly be said that if he loses his hold upon the key-centre, his task is rendered practically impossible.

4. The exercises intended to be played at the Pianoforte are an extremely important feature of the present volume, and however slow the beginner may be at first in conquering the difficulties of this part of his work, he must on no account be allowed merely to write these exercises.† Their object is (i) to drive the pupil to *hear* the progressions he is studying, and (ii) to help him to form a vocabulary of his own—so to speak—a collection of every-day idioms and expressions, the possession of which will at any rate prevent him from being "tongue-tied" when called upon to frame a sentence or two in the language he is learning (in other words, to play—as so few students can—two or three chords "out of their own head," in a musical way.)‡

5. In the first stages of the pupil's work at the keyboard it will be found best for him to play the three upper parts of four-part harmony with the right hand, the *bass only* with the left. As soon as he obtains some degree of facility in doing this, he should play the exercises with the chords spaced more widely (*i.e.*, with two parts in each hand).

· 6. In cases of special aptitude it may not be necessary for the pupil to work all the earlier melodies and basses in Part II, at any rate as *written* exercises.

7. Appendix B, upon Special Pianoforte Idioms, should be carefully studied by the pupil, especially when reference is made to it in the course of the exercises. He should be encouraged (when he can play and write fairly easily in four-part harmony) to experiment at the keyboard in the manner suggested in this Appendix.

8. Special attention is drawn to the remarks upon the construction of rhythmical sentences, in the final section of the volume, "Miscellaneous Exercises" (page 285). The teacher should stimulate the pupil by every means in his power to improvise at the Pianoforte, and to write little pieces of his own.

REMARKS UPON THE USE OF THE NUMERAL NOTATION.

9. The teacher will notice that most of the exercises to be worked at the keyboard are given in each chapter in the form of chord-progressions indicated by Roman numerals. The advantage of having these progressions set forth in this way, instead of in actual musical notation, is that they may be thought of and played *in any key* at will. This is a most vital matter, for it is of the first consequence that the musician shall be able to think, both melodically and harmonically, in all keys with equal ease.

10. Throughout the present volume Roman numerals always indicate the *harmonies* of the key (*e.g.*, V = the Dominant triad, $^{7}\text{II}_{b}$ = the first inversion of the Secondary 7th of the Supertonic, etc.), forming therefore a convenient and rapid "shorthand" method of describing such harmonies. The signs / and \ through a figure imply respectively a note produced by raising or lowering the normal diatonic degree of the major or *Harmonic* minor scale by a chromatic semitone, *e.g.*,—(in key C major) $^{♭}\text{V}$ indicates (*i.e.*, the Dominant

---

* To the majority of pupils the order of difficulty is as has been set forth above.

† They should be written down subsequently—*away from* the Pianoforte—as a test of his power of correlating sound, symbol and locality.

‡ The grasping of the material of the musical language, as of any other language, is in reality the assimilation and memorization of its phrases and idioms which, in the first stages of conscious study, are of necessity the simpler and more usual ones.

triad with its 5th raised) ; ^{9}V signifies (*i.e.*, the chord of the Dominant 9th with

a lowered, or *minor*, 9th. In key C minor, also, Ħ similarly implies (*i.e.*, the

Supertonic triad with its *root* chromatically lowered) ; ^{9}V representing

(*i.e.*, the raised, or *major*, 9th from the Dominant, used in ascending to the 3rd of its own root), and so on.

11. When Arabic numerals stand alone in an exercise, thus :—2 5 4 3, they invariably refer to *melody*-notes, and represent the degrees of the scale counted from the key-note. Thus, the above series would (in key F) imply , (in key D) etc.

THE "FIGURED-BASS."

12. The figures in the conventional type of Figured-Bass represent, it should be remembered, merely the intervals of any particular chord *counted from the bass-note.* By reason of this, many chords are necessarily figured alike (*e.g.*, the Dominant 7th, the various Secondary 7ths, certain positions of chords of the Ninth, etc.); the degrees of the scale upon which the chords are indicated, and the context generally, must of course determine their nature.

13. Whenever the figures 7, $\begin{smallmatrix}6\\5\end{smallmatrix}$, $\begin{smallmatrix}4\\3\end{smallmatrix}$, and $\begin{smallmatrix}4\\2\end{smallmatrix}$ occur, they imply respectively $\begin{pmatrix}7\\5\\3\end{pmatrix}$, $\begin{pmatrix}6\\5\\3\end{pmatrix}$, $\begin{pmatrix}(6)\\4\\3\end{pmatrix}$, and $\begin{smallmatrix}(6)\\4\\2\end{smallmatrix}$ and the harmony should be filled up accordingly, (*see*, however, Chapter XVI, Sec. 11). An accidental against a figure signifies that the note represented by that figure should bear a similar accidental.

14. A figure *over* a bass-note, thus (3), indicates the interval (counted from that bass-note) which should be placed in the highest part of the harmony. This applies also in the case of Unfigured Basses (*see*, for example, Sec. H on p. 79).

MELODY AND HARMONY.

INTRODUCTORY CHAPTER.

1. MODERN music depends for its full effect upon a combination of three distinct factors, Melody, Harmony, and Rhythm. These are so closely woven together in our thoughts about music that it is somewhat difficult to think of them apart. Underlying these three factors are the two elements of Time and Pitch : these form the bed-rock of all musical experience and are so obvious as to need no further explanation here.

2. By Melody is understood, technically, the idea of a succession of single sounds—that and nothing more ; but in actual music the expression includes enough of the related ideas of Time and Rhythm to give the impression of shapeliness and order. Viewed in this light, therefore, Melody may be said to signify a succession of single sounds *with a musical purpose*—in other words, a succession possessing the essential characteristics of *tune*. Each of the following examples represents Melody in the technical sense referred to, but it is only in (*b*) that a musical effect is produced, sufficient to satisfy our instinctive desire for some kind of design and shape:—

3. Similarly, in speaking of Harmony in a purely technical sense, it is customary to imply merely the thought of sounds in combination ; but again, from a musical point of view, any such combination must be based upon artistic principles, and bear definite relationships to others that precede and follow it. For instance, the following group of sounds ⟨♪⟩ taken by itself, has little or no point or meaning ; but when placed in relation to its context :—

GOUNOD.—" Faust."

it is felt to be part of a clear purpose or plan in the composer's mind, with a very distinct beauty of its own.

4. Rhythm, the third factor spoken of in Sec. 1, is the element that imparts not only shape and symmetry to a succession of sounds (whether those sounds are taken singly or in combination), but endues them with life. Implied in Rhythm is the principle of *movement* towards certain points of climax or repose in the music, where that movement is itself broken or arrested—producing thereby the idea of " phrase."

5. The principle of movement or progression spoken of above lies **at the root of all musical** thought, and the simplest musical idea involves the movement from one sound (or combination of sounds) to another,* *e.g.*—

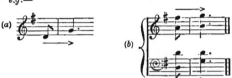

6. In any passage of harmony, two distinct kinds of movement or progression are observable; there is not only (i) the progression from chord to chord but also (ii) the *melodic* movement of the separate parts or "voices" of which the passage consists. The following well-known extract will illustrate this:—

*** The two aspects of the matter will be readily grasped if the above example is first played as it stands, and if each single melodic line is afterwards played or sung separately. It will then be found that, apart from the strong and musical succession of *chords*, each of those "lines" is melodious in itself, even without direct reference to the rest of the harmony.

7. It almost goes without saying that the actual amount of melodic interest possessed by the individual parts varies largely with the character of the music itself. It is greatest in those compositions which are *polyphonic* (*i.e.*, many-voiced) or contrapuntal in style, *e.g.*, in a Fugue; it is least in evidence where a melody is supported by some conventional form of accompaniment, such as the following:—

where the only part possessing much intrinsic melodic value is the so-called "tune" in the right hand.†

It is of the highest importance that the learner should realize the necessity of keeping the two aspects of progression now under consideration, (viz., the melodic and the harmonic) steadily in view throughout his Harmony study, otherwise there is a danger that his exercises and his attempts at original work will be little more than successions of dull and uninteresting "chord-blocks."

* "When two contrasted and balancing beats are associated, the single entity so formed . . . . is capable of being employed as the medium for the expression of a definite musical thought."—J. B. McEwen: *The Thought in Music.*

† Even in the above example, although the interior parts of the harmony are—as in a good deal of pianoforte-music, and in most dance-accompaniments—more or less left to take care of themselves in the matter of melodic interest, it will be seen that the *bass* at any rate possesses the characteristics of a good melodic line:—

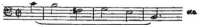

8. The history of music shews us that the composers of the 14th, 15th and 16th centuries, who were striving after a pure style of vocal writing, knew little or nothing of *chords*, as we understand the term to-day; they concerned themselves principally with the setting of one voice against another in such a way that the melody of one would combine more or less pleasantly with the melody of the other, while at the same time each kept its own independence of movement. They thus gradually found out that certain intervals sounded well together, and others less well, or even altogether unsatisfactory. Such a passage as the following from a Mass by William Byrd (1538–1623) would have been imagined purely in this light:—

9. The musician of to-day would naturally think of such combinations as those in the above extract as representing chords—complete or incomplete, direct or inverted—and it would be difficult for him to free his mind altogether from the harmonic side of the matter even in those cases where melodies run the most independently. It is not desirable that he should do so; for he has to remember that this independent flow of the parts must not only produce pleasant melodies but good, strong harmonic progressions as well.

10. The task of the student is, therefore, two-fold; (i) he has to learn by experience to distinguish good chord-progressions from weak or bad ones, and (ii) he has to acquire the power of hearing and *imagining* two or more melodies moving in combination side by side. The course of study in the succeeding chapters will have in view the attainment of both these ends.

PART I.

MELODIC MOVEMENT.

CHAPTER I.

THE SINGLE MELODIC LINE.

1. THE student's first task in his constructive work should be the invention of short rhythmical melodies. At first these melodies should be thought of as designed for voices; if the limitations of the human voice are kept in view, there is the greater chance of their being smooth, vocal, and natural.

2. The two following passages well illustrate most of the characteristics of good vocal melody* :—

MOZART.—"Don Giovanni."

WAGNER.—"Die Meistersinger."

*** It will be noticed that in the above extracts there is a considerable amount of "conjunct" (*i.e.*, step-wise) movement which greatly aids the flow of the melody, the occasional larger leaps securing the necessary degree of contrast and helping to provide what is often spoken of as a good "melodic curve."

* A melody intended to be sung by a voice will often differ materially from one written for an instru. ment. This arises from two facts, viz., (i) that the compass of any single voice is necessarily limited, (ii) that a singer must *think* a sound before he is able to sing it, and certain melodic intervals are more awkward to conceive than others. On an instrument such as the pianoforte, the organ, or the violin, these difficulties are for all practical purposes non-existent. For example, the following succession of sounds would be virtually impossible for the average soprano voice, but perfectly easy on the violin :—

Again, a passage such as this from Chopin's Ballade in G minor

although offering no special obstacles to the pianist, would be next to impracticable for the human voice— at any rate, at the requisite speed.

3. In the construction of his own melodies, the beginner will be materially assisted by the following directions :—

(a) Use "scale-wise" movement (*i.e.*, movement by step) frequently ; whenever a *leap* is made, avoid one that is specially dissonant (*e.g.*, the interval of a major 7th, a major or minor 9th, or any augmented interval) :—

N.B.—A *diminished* interval is, however, quite musical in effect, if the next note lies *within* the interval :—

(b) A succession of large leaps is awkward and unmusical :—

but a leap of a 6th or an 8ve is effective and strong, provided that the note preceding and following the leap is one *within* it,† *e.g.*—

(c) The leading-note of the key has a strong upward tendency, and when it occurs as the final note but one in a melody, it usually rises a semitone to the key-note.‡ At other times it is generally better for it *not to fall*, unless in the midst of a descending scale-passage, as in the following instance :—

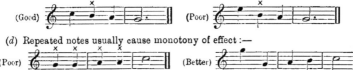

(d) Repeated notes usually cause monotony of effect :—

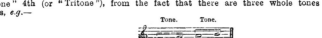

---

* The interval of augmented 4th between the Subdominant and the Leading-note is known as the "Tritone" 4th (or "Tritone"), from the fact that there are three whole tones between the two degrees, *e.g.*—

† Occasionally a *minor* 7th may be used, particularly if the upper note returns in this way *by step* within the interval :-

‡ It is interesting to note that certain degrees of the major or minor scale possess, in greater or less measure, the character of *movement* or *activity*, which manifests itself in a tendency to rise or fall to others possessing a greater feeling of *rest*. The latter are the 1st, 3rd, 5th, and 8th degrees of the scale, to which the adjacent sounds naturally fall or rise by step, *e.g.*—

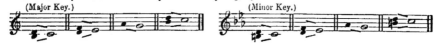

EXERCISES.

A. Write several melodies (vocal) upon the following rhythmic schemes.* At this stage each melody should either (i) remain in the same key throughout, or (ii) move only to one of the nearly-related keys (see page 165), ending in the original Tonic.

B. Construct further melodies upon time- and rhythm- schemes of your own.

* On page 7 will be found a few suggested "openings," based upon the above schemes, to which the student may add the responsive phrases. After using these, he should invent openings of his own.

MELODY AND HARMONY.

SUGGESTED OPENINGS FOR RHYTHMS IN SEC. **A.**

CHAPTER II.

DUAL MELODIC LINES.

1. The next stage of the student's work should be that of adding a second melody under-neath (and, subsequently, above) one that is given.* This second part should not only har-monize with its companion, but possess independent melodic interest, as in the following example from Handel :—

2. In the above extract the notes of both parts are of identical length ; when one part moves more quickly than the other, their independence is obviously more marked :—

3. If the parts move in the same direction, *e.g.*—

they are said to proceed in *Similar Motion ;* if in opposite directions, *e.g.*—

by *Contrary Motion ;* when one part moves while another remains, *e.g.*—

Oblique Motion is produced. The three kinds of Motion are seen combined in the succeeding example :—

---

* The power of imagining a bass to a melody is really the first step towards musicianship, and is akin to that possessed by the painter or draughtsman who, on being shewn—it may be—the outline of the roof of a building, is able to see in his mind's eye the completed structure. Melody and Harmony are so intimately connected that anyone calling himself a musician should be able, on hearing a fragment of tune, mentally to supply some kind of harmony suitable to it. Until this power is to some extent acquired, real progress is impossible.

, **4.** In order to obtain the independence of melodic line to which reference has been made, Contrary (or, occasionally, Oblique) Motion is more valuable, generally speaking, than Similar Motion ; but the best effect is achieved by a judicious use of all three varieties.

5. The possibilities of the simplest form of "Two-part harmony," in which—as in the extract from Handel in Sec. 1—the notes are of the same length in both parts, will be seen from the following illustrations, where a second melody has been added to the ascending scale of *D* major :—

** The following, though *correct,* are feeble and uninteresting, for the reason that there is no independence in the added part, which merely duplicates the given melody at the distance of a 3rd and a 6th :—

6. From examples (i) to (iv) above may be gathered the general principles which should guide the learner at this early stage of his work :—

    (i) *Only concordant intervals should (at present) be used.*

    These are the 3rd, 6th, unison, 8ve, and perfect 5th.

    (ii) *Of these, only 3rds* and 6ths should be used with any frequency.* In order to preserve independence, not more than three 3rds or three 6ths should, as a rule, follow one another in similar motion.†

    (iii) *It is best to confine the employment of the Unison to the initial and final notes of an exercise.*

    (iv) *The 8ve generally has a " thin " effect,* unless used in one of the following ways :—

        (*a*) In the same manner as the Unison ; •

        (*b*) If approached and quitted *in both parts* by step, in contrary motion. *See* (*x*) in Exs. (i) and (iii) in Sec. 5.)

    (v) *The 5th, being bare and empty, should be almost entirely excluded.*

    Occasionally, however, the 5th over the Tonic or the Dominant may be used happily in such "horn-like" passages as the following :—

(See also (*y*) in Exs. (iii) and (iv) in Sec. 5.)

---

  * The 10th is considered for all practical purposes as a 3rd.   .

  † The two major 3rds on the fourth and fifth degrees of the major scale, taken in succession, almost invariably sound rough, and had better be avoided :—

7. The only intervals that can occur twice—or more often—in succession at any time are the 3rd and the 6th. If two octaves are taken successively, thus :—

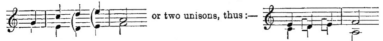

the musical effect may not be actually *disagreeable*, but the passage is reduced for the moment from one in *two* parts to one in which—strictly speaking—there is no harmony at all, but only an ineffective duplication of a single part.

*** This fault is usually described as *Consecutive 8ves*, or *Consecutive Unisons*.

8. Two or more perfect 5ths in succession between the parts are usually crude and ugly and should be rigorously avoided in two-part writing :—

*** This fault is described as *Consecutive 5ths*.

9. The parts should not cross one another in the type of exercise to which these remarks chiefly apply :—

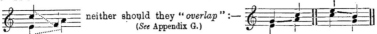

10. In order to make a satisfactory termination to an exercise in two parts, one part should rise from Leading-note to Tonic. The accompanying part should then proceed to the Tonic from either the 2nd of the scale, thus :—

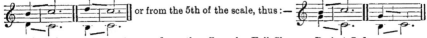

Either of these progressions produces the effect of a Full Close, or Perfect Cadence.

11. In writing for voices, it is well not to exceed the following compass in each case :—

ELEMENTARY EXERCISES IN TWO-PART MELODIC MOVEMENT.

A. Add a melodious part *underneath* the following passages.* Use notes, throughout, of the same length as those in the given part, unless otherwise indicated.

*** The particular voice for which the added part should be written is indicated at the commencement of each exercise. The treble clef should be used for the Alto voice : the bass clef for the Tenor and Bass voices. The figure below any note signifies the interval required at that point. A dash underneath a figure, thus :—(8,), implies a note in the *second octave* below the given note.

---

* Do not separate the two parts at such a distance from one another that the result seems like a 4-part exercise, with the two middle parts missing, *e.g.*—

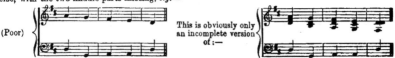

N.B.—Observe that the passage marked $\lfloor a \quad a \rfloor$ is a repetition or reproduction, at a different pitch, of the previous section of the melody. Such a reproduction is termed a *Sequence*, and should be carried out strictly in the added part also. The following extract from Bach's 1st "Two-part Invention" furnishes a familiar instance of a Sequence in two parts :—

* See Sec. 6 above, as to use of the interval of 5th in "horn-like" passages.

† This Exercise might be thought of as planned for a Violin and a Viola. The Viola part should be written on the Alto staff, and the lowest note available is :—

N.B.—Treat passages (*a*) and (*b*) sequentially.   (*See* Supplement, page viii, for further exercises.)

B. Add a melodious part *above* the following passages, in a manner similar to that indicated in Section **A.** A figure above any note signifies the interval required at that point. A dash *above* a figure, thus : (3'), implies a note in the *second octave* above the given note.

C. Write several original melodies, similar in style and scope to those given in Sections **A** and **B.** After these have been criticized by the teacher, a second part should be added, above or below, as the case may be.

TWO-PART WRITING IN THE MINOR KEY.

12. The Minor key presents not a few difficulties to the beginner, prominent among which is that of maintaining the idea of a clear and definite tonality. The fact that the Minor scale exists in three distinct forms, viz.—

(i) Harmonic Minor scale.

(ii) Melodic Minor scale (ascending form).

(iii) Melodic Minor scale (descending form).*

and the common mistake of thinking of the Leading-note of the key as a "raised" (or chromatically-altered) note—due largely to the anomalous signature in common use to-day—causes many a student to be in considerable doubt whether he is actually playing or writing in a minor key or its so-called "Relative" major.†

* Identical with the Æolian Mode of mediæval use.

† The following example, taken from a recent work on Counterpoint, will shew exactly the sort of thing that many an inexperienced pupil would write, without the faintest idea that he was oscillating between A minor and C major:—

The passage is, of course, perfectly correct; the important point, however, is that the student should feel the changes of tonality in its course, and not imagine that it remains in the key of A minor throughout—which, for some curious reason, is actually the view taken by the author of the work in question.

13. His first aim, therefore, must be to distinguish carefully between these two tonalities, and to acquire the power of *thinking* easily in each.   To this end, the exercises in the present chapter will be founded entirely upon scale (i), *i.e.*, the *Harmonic* Minor Scale, by which confusion with the "Relative" major will be rendered practically impossible.

N.B.—When he has had sufficient practice in the use of the Harmonic Minor Scale, the many beautiful effects obtainable by the employment of the other two forms of scale will be considered.

14. In the minor key, special care needs to be taken (particularly when writing for voices), to avoid augmented intervals in the melody of any part.   (*See* Chap. I., Sec. 3.)

The following diagram will show that there are four such intervals, and that in every case either the 6th or 7th degree of the scale is involved :—

Particular attention should therefore be paid to the approaching and quitting of these degrees, *e.g.*—

15. The two following rules are useful in connexion with this matter :—

(i) Avoid using the 6th and 7th degrees of the Harmonic Minor scale in succession, unless they stand from one another at the distance of a diminished 7th.

(ii) Always approach the Leading-note *from above* (unless it follows the 5th or 2nd of the scale) :—

* The inversion of each of these intervals is good :—

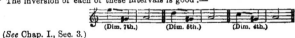

(*See* Chap. I., Sec. 3.)

EXERCISES IN TWO-PART MELODIC MOVEMENT IN THE MINOR KEY.

D. Add a melodious part *underneath* the following passages, in notes of the same length as those of the given part, unless otherwise indicated. (For further directions *see* p. 10.)

E. Add a similar melodious part *above* the following :—

(*See* Supplement, page viii.)

F.   Write several melodies of your own, afterwards adding a part above or below (as the case may be), or compose the two melodies simultaneously.

CHAPTER III.

DUAL MELODIC LINES—(Cont⁴.).

FIRST STAGES OF FLORID MELODIC MOVEMENT.

1. IT is obvious that when two melodies are written in such a way that the notes of one differ in length from those of the other, a further degree of independence and contrast between them is produced, and the interest correspondingly increased :—

(*See also* Ex. from Bach in Chap. II., Sec. 2.)

2. The above passage illustrates the use of notes which do not belong to the harmony against which they are sounded, and are dissonant * with it. These are termed *Unessential notes,* and instances will be seen at (*a*), (*b*), (*c*), (*d*), (*e*), (*f*), (*g*) and (*h*).

3. In the student's first exercises in florid movement, any Unessential note should be approached and quitted *by step* of a 2nd (as shewn in the foregoing example). It then forms what is known as a *Passing-note.* The use of such passing-notes materially aids the flow of the music, adds point and zest, and prevents stiffness of effect :—

N.B.—In example (*a*) from Mendelssohn's "Italian" Symphony it will be observed that in several places the quicker part moves, not by step but by leap. In every instance the leap is made to a *concordant* interval (*i.e.*, to a note of the prevailing chord). The student will perceive from his exercises on triads, that the two quavers, C♯ and A, in the bass part at (*x*), both form part of the Dominant triad in D minor, the F, A and C at (*y*) part of the Tonic triad in F major, and so forth. All such leaps are, in the best examples, judiciously alternated with step-wise movement which, however, for the most part should prevail in this kind of florid writing.

---

* Under the heading of *Dissonant* intervals are included all 2nds, 7ths and 9ths, all augmented and diminished intervals, and also the *perfect* 4th (provided that there is no consonant note below it).

DIRECTIONS FOR THE FIRST STAGES OF FLORID MELODIC MOVEMENT.

4. The first exercises in florid writing will take the form of "decorating" simple two-part passages with Passing-notes. The following points should be carefully observed :—

(*a*) *All* passing-notes should for the present be approached and quitted *by step*. In this way, a passing-note may either return to the harmony-note from which it sprang (on the principle of the ornament known as the *Mordent*), thus :—

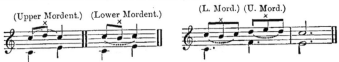

(Upper Mordent.)   (Lower Mordent.)   (L. Mord.) (U. Mord.)

or it may go on in the same direction to *another* harmony-note, thus :—

|One harmony. | | Two harmonies. |

** If the "Mordent" type of passing-note (sometimes called an Auxiliary-note) is used *below* a harmony-note, it is usually (though not invariably) best at the distance of a semitone from it:—

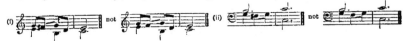

The older writers frequently used the whole-tone, but modern ears have grown accustomed to the more euphonious semitonic step. Good taste must decide which is better at any particular moment.

(*b*) A passing-note, if carelessly introduced, may cause trouble, *e.g.*—

(*c*) Subject to the above remark, the insertion of a passing-note is usually possible and effective if harmony-notes stand at the distance of a 3rd from one another, *e.g.*—

could obviously be decorated as follows :

EXERCISES.

A. By introducing passing-notes (taken in every case by step) in the *upper* part of the following exercises, maintain (as far as possible) a movement in quavers.

N.B.—Where the given part itself moves in quavers, leave it exactly as written.

B. In a similar manner, maintain (wherever possible) a movement in quavers in the *lower* part of the following :—

C. In a similar manner "decorate" the following passages, but break up the melodic lines by introducing the quaver passing-notes *in either upper or lower part*, as may be from time to time possible and effective :—

D. In the following exercises each ♩. or ♩. should be accompanied by three quavers or three crotchets, as the case may be, in the companion voice. Two forms of "decoration" are then readily available, viz., (i) a movement along the scale-line (up or down) as shewn in the first half of bar 1 in Exercise 1 below ; or (ii) the figure described as the "Mordent," as indicated in the second half of the same bar. The passing-note in this figure, it should be remembered, may be taken either *below* the harmony-note from which it springs or *above* it ; thus :—

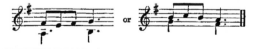

(a) "Mordent" figure here.

N.B.—If two passing-notes (*i.e.*, be it remembered, notes *not* belonging to the prevailing harmony) occur in succession, it is better for the second one to go on in the same direction, and *not* to return, *e.g.*—

In a passage such as the following, the note marked ($_x$) is *not a passing-note*, although it moves by step; but is part of the prevailing chord of C :—

It is, therefore, free in its movement, and may leap if necessary.

(Decorate *upper* part in quavers.)

(*a*) Leave this note as a crotchet.

(Decorate *lower* part in crotchets throughout.)

(Decorate *either* part in quavers, as suitable and effective.)

(*a*) In working this Exercise, the bass part of bars 1 and 2, and of bars 9 and 10, should run in the following rhythm :—♪♪♪♩. | ♪♪♩ ♩. |

(*b*)—(*b*) Do not decorate the notes of the *upper* part within the ⌐────⌐.

E. Add a melodious *upper* part, entirely in "pulse-notes" (with the exception of the final note), to the following :—

F. Add a similar melodious *lower* part to the following :—

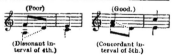

* When the given part (in quicker notes) *leaps*, as here, take care that the accompanying note is concordant with *both* notes of the leap. If this precaution is not observed, the effect will be bad; particularly will this be the case when the added **part** is *below* the given melody, *e.g.*—

(Poor)

(Dissonant interval of 4th.)

(Good.)

(Concordant interval of 5th.)

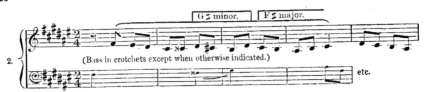

3. Add a part in crotchets *below* example 2 in Section **E**, for a Bass voice.

G. Add a melodious *upper* part, entirely in dotted crotchets, to the following :—

N.B.—Take account of the opportunities for Sequence in the above exercise.

H. Add a melodious *lower* part in dotted quavers, to the following :—

FLORID MELODIC MOVEMENT IN THE MINOR KEY.

THE USE OF THE 'MELODIC' MINOR SCALE.

5. In florid melodic movement in the minor key, the two forms of the so-called *Melodic* minor scale (shewn in Chapter II., Sec. 12), play an important part in securing a smooth and flowing effect, for by their means it is possible to avoid the somewhat unvocal interval of augmented 2nd between the 6th and 7th degrees of the Harmonic minor scale, and thus to increase the possibilities of step-wise movement in the upper tetrachord of the key.

6. The principles with regard to the use of the notes of the Melodic minor scale at the present stage are very simple ; they are as follows :—

(*a*) The major 6th and the minor 7th (the notes not found in the Harmonic minor scale) are to be used (as yet) solely as passing-notes—*not* as harmony-notes.

(*b*) The passing-note taken *below* the Leading-note of the key should be the major 6th of the Melodic minor scale, *e.g.*—

(*c*) The passing-note taken *above* the Submediant * should be the minor 7th of the Melodic minor scale, *e.g.*—

(*d*) In filling-up the gap of a 4th between *Dominant* and *Tonic* (when these are successive harmony-notes), the usual forms of the ascending and descending Melodic minor scale should be followed respectively, according to the direction of the passage, thus :—

8. The following passage will illustrate the above-named uses :—

---

* The Submediant, that is, of the *Harmonic* minor scale.

EXERCISES ON FLORID TWO-PART MOVEMENT IN MINOR KEYS.

I. Decorate the *upper* part of the following, by maintaining a quaver movement where possible. (*See* directions for Section **A** in major keys, on page 18.)

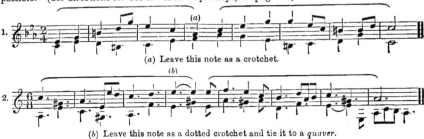

(*a*) Leave this note as a crotchet.

(*b*) Leave this note as a dotted crotchet and tie it to a *quaver.*

J. In a similar manner, maintain a quaver movement (wherever possible) in the *lower* part of the following exercises :—

(*a*) Whenever the lower part has the following pattern :— the dotted crotchet should be tied to the first of a group of three quavers, thus :—

K. In a similar manner, maintain a quaver movement (wherever possible) in the following passage. Introduce the quavers in *either* upper or lower part, as may be from time to time effective :—

L. Add a melodious upper part, entirely in crotchets (with the exception of the final note), to the following passages :—

M. Add a melodious *lower* part, entirely in crotchets, to the above two melodies.

N.B.—No. 1 should be transposed an 8ve higher. In this case the suggested small notes will, of course, be disregarded.

N. Add a similar part, entirely in *dotted* crotchets, *above* the following :—

O. Transpose the above passage an 8ve higher, and add a *lower* part entirely in dotted crotchets.

CHAPTER IV.

DUAL MELODIC LINES.—(Cont^d.)

FLORID MELODIC MOVEMENT—SECOND STAGE.

1. In the preceding chapter the student's exercises in connexion with florid melodic writing were confined to (i) the embellishment, by means of passing-notes, of simple two-part passages, and (ii) the addition of a melody (in longer notes of a fixed value) to a given florid part.

2. The next step will be the addition of a florid part to a melody in slower notes, and also the combination of two melodies, *each* of which is to a greater or less extent florid in character (*i.e.*, in which the notes vary in length, and in which a flowing style is preserved by the introduction of unessential notes.) The two following examples illustrate both forms of exercise : —

(*a*) Melody entirely in crotchets, to which a part in quavers is to be added.*

(Given melody.)

(*b*) Florid melody, to which another melody of a similar character is to be added :—

(Given melody.)

DIRECTIONS FOR THE ADDITION OF A FLORID PART.

3. From the foregoing examples, certain conclusions may be drawn which will serve as directions for the kind of work next to be attempted.

(*a*) Whenever the two parts are *struck together*, they should (as heretofore) form a concordant interval, and all passing-notes should be approached and quitted *by step*.

(*b*) An occasional leap may be made in the quicker-moving part, *but only to a concordant interval* (*i.e.*, to a 3rd, 6th, perfect 5th,† 8ve, or unison).

---

* This form of exercise will be familiar to the teacher, in all probability, as " Counterpoint of the Second Species."

† The leap to the perfect 5th over the Mediant of the major key is usually rough in effect, and is best avoided by the beginner. The Mediant should usually be thought of as bearing the 1st inversion of the Tonic triad, and the leap made accordingly, *e.g.*—

N.B.—A leap will therefore be satisfactory if it is made from one note of a concordant triad (either in its root-position or its 1st inversion *) to another note of the same chord, the quicker part thus moving in "arpeggio," *e.g.*—

(*See also x, y,* and *z* in Examples in section 2 above.)

The following leaps are clearly bad:—

N.B.—In any case, leaps should be sparingly used, as they check the flow of the music if introduced frequently.

(*c*) In writing a florid part of *two* notes to each one of a given melody (*i.e.*, in writing quavers against crotchets, crotchets against minims, etc.), it is most important—in order to secure a flowing part—to remember that if the given melody proceeds by two or more steps in "scale-wise" movement (as, for example, in the first two bars of exercise (*a*) in Sec. 2 above), the florid part should go in *contrary motion* to it. On the other hand, if the given melody skips a 3rd, the florid part can usually proceed by step in *similar motion* to it. (*See* bars 3, 5, and 6 in the same exercise.)

(*d*) Consecutive 5ths and 8ves are not rendered less objectionable by the introduction of passing-notes, *e.g.*—

N.B.—5ths taken upon successive *unaccented* beats (or *unaccented* portions of beats), are perfectly good in effect, if they are formed by passing-notes taken by step, *e.g.*—

Two or more successive *leaps* to a 5th or an 8ve will usually give the impression of "consecutives," *e.g.*—

* Any leap suggestive of a 2nd inversion is usually of doubtful effect, and needs great care;

The beginner will be well advised to avoid this particular form of leaping bass. (*See* Chap. XII, Sec. K).

† The leap to a 4th from a 6th (in the *lower* voice, as here), may be permitted if the note making the 4th moves afterwards *by step downwards*, thus:—

BACH.—Two-part Inventions, No. 1.

(*e*) A passing-note should not proceed from a 2nd into a unison, as in the following instances :—

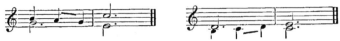

The effect is usually " smudgy."*

(*f*) To obtain an agreeable movement along the scale-line (particularly the descending scale), it is permissible occasionally to sound a passing-note *with* a note of the chord, *upon the accent*, and not (as usual) after it. In this way the resolution of the dissonant note takes place at the succeeding weaker part of the bar, as in the following instance :—

The upward resolution is much more difficult to introduce successfully, and usually requires that *both* parts move " scale-wise " in contrary motion : —

The following, however, shews a further possible use :—

Accented passing-notes † are usually much more appropriate and effective in the upper, than in the lower, of the two parts.

N.B.—The occasional use of the *accented* dissonance prevents the somewhat insipid effect produced by an extended passage in which there is nothing but a stream of consonances on the accented beats. It is, however, often difficult to make Accented passing-notes sound well in two-part writing, and their employment at this stage of the learner's work should be somewhat exceptional. To *skip* to an Accented passing-note is usually very harsh if there are only two parts ; and such a proceeding should be rigorously excluded from the present exercises.

---

* This rule is not so binding when the parts are written for instruments of contrasted qualities of tone (*e.g.*, for a horn and a violin). The following extract from Haydn's Symphony in D (Peters' Edition, No. 2), will shew a perfectly correct use of an effect which, in vocal writing at least, is best avoided :—

† Fully discussed in Chapter XVII.

EXERCISES IN FLORID TWO-PART MOVEMENT—SECOND STAGE.

A. Add a melodious part, as specified, *above* the following melodies.

> *N.B.*—Begin each exercise with a concordant interval, *after a rest* corresponding to the prevailing notes of the added part; this makes the entry of the florid part clearer. The final note should be of the same value as that in the given melody. The Roman numerals introduced in the course of the exercises signify the harmonies that should be implied where they occur.

(*See* Supplement, page viii.)

B. Add a similar part *below* the following melodies:—

(*b*) Move down the scale, using an accented passing-note against the B.

3. Add a bass part in quavers below No. 1 in Section **A.**

4. Transpose No. 4 in Section **A** an 8ve higher, and add a bass part in crotchets below it.

(*See* Supplement, page ix.)

NOTES ON THE WORKING OF FUTURE EXERCISES.

4. (i) In the exercises that follow, the added part will occasionally have *four* notes to each one of the given melody, and it is important to note that a good effect may be obtained by carrying on, here and there, some little melodic fragment by sequence : for example, the opening bars of Exercise (i) in Sec. **C** below might well run as follows :—

Care should be taken, however, not to overdo the sequential movement, which easily becomes trite and mechanical.

(ii) When four notes go to one of the given melody, the mixture of leaps with step-wise movement may be more freely employed than in the case of two notes to one, *e.g.*—

(All good)

The following, however, are faulty :—

(Bad leap to a 4th.)　　　　(Bad leap from an　　really
　　　　　　　　　　　　　implied ⁶₄ chord.)

(iii) It is possible to make occasional use of the melodic figure known as " Changing-notes," (which is in reality a development of the " Mordent" figure already met with) :—

Here, it will be seen, in every instance a passing-note, before resolving, *skips a 3rd* to the passing-note on the other side of its resolution-note. The lower of the two passing-notes should usually be at the distance of a *semitone* below its resolution.*

---

* Compare the above examples of Changing-notes with the following " Mordent " figures :—

EXERCISES.

C. Add a melodious part, entirely in quavers, *above* the following :—

D. Add a similar melodious part *below* the following :—

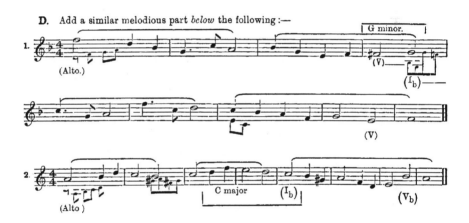

---

5. The succeeding exercises are intended to afford practice in adding to a melody in which the notes vary in length, another part of a similar character. As the aim in this type of exercise is to produce an agreeable degree of contrast of movement between the two parts, it will be well to remember that notes (in the given melody) which move more quickly than the pulse, or beat, should (usually) be accompanied by slower ones; a longer note in the given part, however, often affording scope for a more florid treatment of its companion.

*** Example (*b*) in Sec. 2 of this chapter should be carefully analysed.

6. The following directions should be observed :—

(*a*) Notes quicker than the pulse, or beat, usually sound smoother and more flowing when they are taken on the *weaker* parts of the bar, *e.g.*—

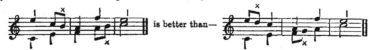

If both strong and weak pulses are broken up into shorter notes, the effect is, however, good :*—

(*b*) An occasional rest, of comparatively short duration, especially at a strong beat (or the stronger *part* of any beat), is frequently of the best possible effect. (*See* Example (*b*) in Sec. 2.)

EXERCISES.

E. Add a melodious part (of similar character to that of the given part) either above or below the following melodies, as indicated.

** Do not introduce notes quicker than quavers. Quavers in the given melody should, unless otherwise specified, be accompanied by longer notes.

(Add Treble.)

(Add Alto.)

** Begin this exercise as indicated by the figure over the A, and then let the Alto "imitate" the Bass exactly, half a bar later (at the distance of a 6th) until the point marked (*a*).

* If carried on for some time in sequence, thus :—

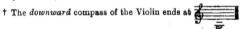

the breaking up of the strong beats only is not objectionable.

† The *downward* compass of the Violin ends at

(*See* Supplement, pages ix and x.)

F. Write original melodies on the above plan, and after criticism by the teacher, add a second florid part above or below each. Also endeavour to compose the two florid melodies simultaneously.

---

* When a rest occurs in the given melody a note (or notes) should be given to the accompanying part.

† The *downward* compass of the Viola ends at ▣▣▣▣. Use the *Alto* staff, with C clef; do not write higher than ▣▣▣.

‡ The lowest note of the Violoncello is ▣▣▣.

CHAPTER V.

DUAL MELODIC LINES—(Cont^d.).

THE USE OF THE TIE—SYNCOPATIONS AND SUSPENSIONS.

1.   A MOST valuable means of obtaining individuality of movement in independent melodic writing is afforded by the use of the Tie.   It may be employed in two ways; it may prolong a concordant note occurring upon a weaker part of a bar (i) so as to form *another concord* on the following stronger accent, *e.g.*—

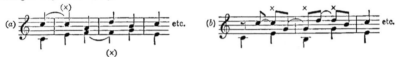

or (ii) so as to form a *discord* needing to resolve by step (usually downwards), *e.g.*—

2.   Little requires to be said in reference to (i), save that it can often be used where the *repetition* of the same note would be dull and monotonous.   Compare the syncopation in (*a*) above with the following :—

3.   The tying of a note so as to produce a *dissonance*, however, gives us the important element of musical effect known as the Suspension.   This may be simply illustrated by taking a passage of 6ths or 3rds, such as :—

and delaying one or other of the parts so that it moves, not *with* its companion but *after* it, in syncopated fashion, thus :—

The " suspended" note is marked x in each case.

4.   The examples in Sec. 3 shew that a Suspension forms no part of the harmony against which it is sounded ; it is therefore another instance of an *Unessential discord.**   Like the accented passing-note, or Appoggiatura, it occurs upon a normally stronger part of the bar than the real harmony-note it delays.

* The actual harmony of the two passages at (*b*) is clearly identical with that of those given at (*a*).

5. Theoretically, any note that can descend by step may be delayed to form a Suspension, but in two-part writing the only effective ones are those which resolve upon the intervals of 3rd and 6th, and occasionally the 8ve,* *e.g.*—

(*a*) *Suspensions in upper part.*†

(*b*) *Suspensions in lower part.*†

N.B.—The 6th over the Mediant of the key is occasionally delayed by the note a semitone *below*, forming an upward suspension (or, as it is sometimes called, a Retardation):—

(*See* Chapter XVI, Sec. 3.)

6. A suspension resolving upon a bare 5th should be avoided in two-part writing :—

7. The following examples illustrate the use of tied notes in the course of a melody in quavers, written against a slower part in crotchets :—

(Given part.)

⁎ The above is merely a " decorated " form of the following :—

---

* *See* Chap. II., Sec. 6.

† As the intervals upon which all the above suspensions resolve are either 3rds, 6ths, 8ves, or 5ths, it is clear that a triad (or an inversion of a triad) is implied in every case. It will not require more than a moment's thought, therefore, to realize that the suspensions themselves are merely incomplete versions of the combinations shewn in Chap. XVI, Secs. 2 and 8.

‡ These two Suspensions should be used only where the notes of the 8ve can be approached and quitted by step in contrary motion, *e.g.*—

(Given part.)

⁎ The harmonic outline of this passage is as follows :—

N.B.—Whenever a leap is made in the course of the quicker-moving part—as at (*x*) in Exs. (*a*) and (*b*)—it must be to a *concordant* interval, as in previous exercises in florid writing.

DIRECTIONS AS TO THE USE OF THE TIE.

8. Whenever a Suspension is used, it stands for the time being *in place of* the note upon which it is going to resolve ; consequently, where that note would cause an unsatisfactory progression, it is impossible for the Suspension to be taken either, *e.g.*—

(All bad)

(oonseo. 8ves.)   (consce. 5ths.)   (similar motion to a 5th.)

N.B.—Passages such as the following, where a 6th is delayed each time by a 5th, are justifiable, for the reason that in (*a*) *two* separate chords are implied in every bar, and in (*b*) the tied note in each case is not the real harmony-note at all, but merely an "unessential" Suspension delaying the appearance of that harmony-note ;—

Neither of these proceedings can be said to be very satisfactory in two-part writing ; with three or more parts the effect would be quite good, *e.g.*—

9. The tie does not materially improve the implied consecutive 8ves and 5ths in passages such as the following :—

(Not to be recommended.)

10. In the student's first exercises, the tie should always be made from a concordant interval (*not* from a passing-note), thus :—

N.B.—Remember in this connexion that a 4th is *not* a concordant interval in two-part writing :—

(Bad)

(4th.)

A single possible exception to the prohibition of the use of the tied 4th occurs when the bass moves in arpeggio *up* to it from the 3rd of the chord, to prepare a Suspension in the lower part, *e.g.*—

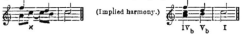

11. *Occasionally, a rest may be substituted for the tie, with excellent effect, e.g.*—

EXERCISES ON THE USE OF THE TIE.

SYNCOPATION AND SUSPENSION.

A. By the frequent use of tied notes (as shewn in the foregoing portions of this chapter), and the occasional introduction of passing-notes, maintain a continuous movement in quavers throughout the *upper* part of the following :—

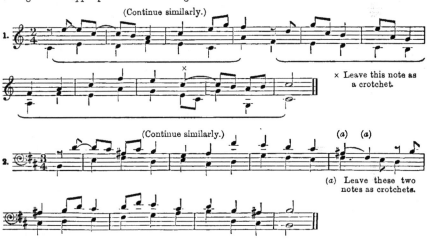

B. In a similar manner maintain a crotchet movement throughout the *lower* part of the following :—

(continue similarly.)

N.B.—Do not *tie* the suspensions in the following exercise where a x is indicated, but strike them afresh, as shewn in bar 1.

C. In a similar manner maintain a movement entirely in crotchets in the following, but distribute the crotchet movement (in the form of syncopations, suspensions or passing-notes) between the two parts, as you deem the effect to be good :—

D. Add a melodious part entirely in crotchets *below* the following * :—

E. Add a similar part in minims *above* the following :—

(*x*) Accented Passing-note.

---

* Treat the tied notes as Suspensions in all cases, except at (*a*).

F. Add a part entirely in quavers, illustrating the use of syncopations and suspensions, *above* the following :—

(Tied notes throughout, except at (*b*).)

(*See* Supplement, page **x**.)

2. A Violin part in quavers to be added; use frequent ties, varied by occasional passing-notes.

| C minor. | | A♭ major. |

G. Add a similar part in quavers *below* the following :—

| G major. | | E minor. | | C major. | | E minor. |

2. A 'Cello part in quavers to be added; use passing-notes freely, varied by an *occasional* tie. (Write the 'Cello part on the Bass staff.)

(*a*) An ornamental resolution of a suspension (*see* page 135).

H. Add another melodious part (in which the notes vary in length), similar in style to the one given, below the following. Introduce tied notes and rests where suitable.

(*See* Supplement, pages x and xi.)

CHAPTER VI.

DUAL MELODIC LINES—(Cont*d*.).

1. THE EMPLOYMENT OF CERTAIN "ESSENTIAL" DISSONANCES.
2. FURTHER USES OF THE MELODIC MINOR SCALE.

1.　It is not often that "essential" discords, such as chords of the 7th, can be made effective in two-part writing. Such discords usually require at least three, and sometimes four, parts to render them intelligible to the ear. One or two exceptions must, however, be mentioned, and amongst these by far the most frequently met with is the interval of the diminished 5th, (with its inversion, the augmented 4th).

2.　In the following familiar progressions :—

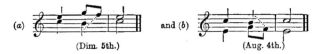

the passing-note, F (taken against *Dominant* harmony), produces in Ex. (*a*) a diminished 5th with the accompanying B, and in Ex. (*b*) an augmented 4th. The F resolves to E in both cases. From this it is only a step to the following :—

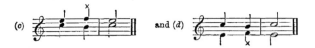

where the passing-note is in each instance *substituted* for the harmony-note from which it originally sprang. An incomplete chord of the *Dominant* 7th is thus formed, the B and the F being respectively its 3rd and 7th.

3.　In "note against note" writing, the above intervals are practically useless unless they resolve immediately as part of the *Dominant* 7th chord, as in these examples from Beethoven :—

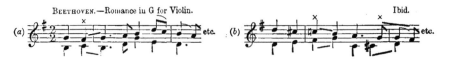

The following would be intolerable :—

4. When, however, one of the parts moves more quickly than the other, a momentary delaying of the resolution of one of the notes of the interval may occur with good effect :—

(Dim 5th.)

(Aug. 4th.)

N.B.—In every case the 8rd or 7th of the Dominant 7th harmony moves to one of the other notes of that same chord, before resolving.

Familiar examples of this procedure are to be found in the two succeeding extracts :—

BACH.—Two-part Inventions (No. 1).

(*a*)

etc.

^7V_b I

BEETHOVEN.—Sonata (Op. 2, No. 3).

(*b*)

etc.

^7V_d I_b

5. The intervals of 2nd and 7th can also be occasionally used as unprepared "essential" dissonances, provided that they resolve as parts of a chord of the 7th. It is rarely, however, that the *major* 7th (or its inversion, the *minor* 2nd), occurs acceptably in two-part writing :—

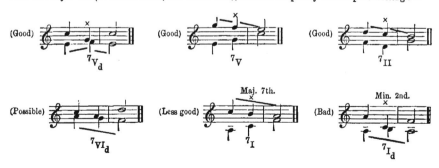

(Good) ^7V_d

(Good) ^7V

(Good) ^7II

(Possible) ^7VI_d

(Less good) Maj. 7th. ^7I

(Bad) Min. 2nd. ^7I_d

A certain amount of care is needed in their introduction, and it is in the majority of cases better that the 7th of the implied chord should be taken by step (as in the previous examples) ;—

The next two extracts, from Handel, shew both intervals in florid two-part writing :—

HANDEL.—Harpsichord Suite in F (No. 2).

HANDEL.—Harpsichord Suite in E minor (No. 4).

6. The striking of the interval of perfect 4th (without previous preparation as in the case of a Suspension), is possible under the following conditions :—

(i) When one part is treated as an accented passing-note resolving by step (*see* p. 28).

(ii) When the interval is formed by an unaccented passing-note moving step-wise, against a harmony-note taken in the midst of an arpeggio, thus :—

*** It will be noticed that this is an inverted form of the " horn-like " passage referred to on p. 9 in which the perfect 5th is similarly used, *e.g.*—

EXERCISES.

A. Beginning as under, write about sixteen bars of music in two parts, including examples of the "essential" dissonances spoken of in this chapter :—

B. Continue the following similarly :—

C. Write about sixteen bars in the key of E flat major, (touching upon F minor and A flat major, and concluding in the Tonic key), and introduce the dissonances given below :—

(*a*) *See* Chapter XX.

FURTHER USES OF THE MELODIC MINOR SCALE IN TWO-PART WRITING.

7. The major 6th and the minor 7th from the key-note of the minor scale may be used, not only as passing-notes (as already shewn in Chapter III), but as "essential" notes of the harmony, under the following conditions :—

(i) That the major 6th shall always *rise* to the Leading-note, and the minor 7th *fall* to the Submediant, each being preferably approached by step also ;

(ii) That they form with the accompanying part the interval of either 3rd or 6th *, *e.g.*—

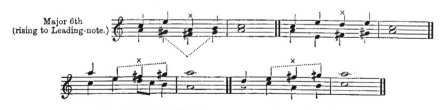

Major 6th
(rising to Leading-note.)

---

* *See* Chapter XVIII on "The Melodic Minor Scale in chord-formation."

Minor 7th
(falling to Submediant.)

N.B.—As there is some risk of the minor 7th of the Melodic minor scale suggesting the "relative" major key, and thus unsettling the tonality, it should be followed as soon as possible by the *major* 7th (*i.e.*, the Leading-note of the minor scale). This, it will be noticed, has been done in the above examples. (See Chapter XVIII, Sec. 3.)

8. In all other instances than those given above, the sixth degree should be minor, and the seventh major, as in the Harmonic minor scale, *e.g.* —

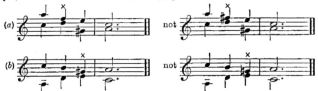

This is due largely to the desire of the ear to approach the Dominant of the Scale by semitone from above, and the Tonic by semitone from below. (*See*, however, Chapter XVIII, Sec. 4.)

9. The two following passages should be carefully analysed :—

EXERCISES.

D. Beginning as under, write about sixteen bars of music in two parts, including examples of the use of the major 6th and minor 7th of the Melodic minor scale as " essential " notes :—

E. Continue the following similarly :—

(i)
(Canon.)

(ii)

CHAPTER VII.

THREE-PART MELODIC WRITING.

1. The importance to the musician of being able to *think* two or more simultaneous "tone-lines," whose melodic movement is independent, is very great; in the first place it is an absolutely essential foundation for success in listening to music of a contrapuntal (or polyphonic) nature, and secondly it is this alone that will enable him in his own writing to avoid the pitfall of considering his harmony merely as a series of dull, lifeless "chord-blocks."

2. The degree of independence possessed by the various parts (or "voices") in a musical composition naturally varies greatly with the character of the music itself; in a Pianoforte accompaniment in broken-chords it is obviously slight, and in simple songs and dance-tunes the opportunities for independent melodic movement in the part-writing are, of necessity, also somewhat restricted. But, in compositions such as trios and quartets for voices, in music written for strings, etc., it would be the last stage of weakness and of dulness for the inner parts to contribute a succession of sounds like the following :*—

Violin I.
Violin II.

Viola.
'Cello.

3. Although the harmony of the above passage is absolutely *correct*, it is nevertheless a supreme example of "how not to do it." The bass is tolerable, but monotonous and rhythmically uninteresting; the 2nd Violin and Viola parts as dreary as could well be imagined

Compare the whole effect with that of the succeeding version in which, though the music is in three parts only, the absence of the fourth part is more than compensated for by the increased melodic interest :—

Violin.

Viola.

'Cello.

4. In "line-drawing" such as this, where every part is a *real* one, three-part harmony is usually more valuable than four-part. Not only does the harmony become uncomfortably crowded where four or more parts are moving independently for long together, but the difficulty of making them flow melodiously is often very great, and the task at times becomes practically impossible.

⁎ Mr. F. Corder says,† "Even Bach cannot always bring it off successfully . . . . Not every note in a chord can be doubled with good effect, so when there are four parts to provide for there is so little choice that the freedom of movement, which is the essence of counterpoint, vanishes, and we have to write mere Harmony." [*i.e.*, chords.]‡

---

* The first Violin part is the melody of Ex. (*a*) on page 26. The four parts are compressed upon two staves to save space.

† "The Commonsense of Counterpoint." (*The Music Student*, March, 1912.)

‡ A careful study of the Fugues in Bach's "48" will shew that, even in the case of those nominally in four parts, the writing is very largely in three parts only.

5. For the reasons stated it is recommended that the student should give a good deal of attention to three-part melodic writing.

The exercises that immediately follow are in the nature of preliminary studies in which one florid melodic part is to be added to two given parts in slower-moving notes. No harmonies beyond triads and the chord of the Dominant 7th are necessary.

(See Supplement, page xi, before proceeding to the succeeding exercises.)

PRELIMINARY EXERCISES IN 3-PART WRITING.

A. (*a*) Add a melodious *Treble* part in quavers to the following passages. Conjunct movement should prevail, and (where suitable) an occasional accented passing-note may be taken, if the diatonic scale-line can be thereby preserved, and an awkward leap avoided.

N.B.—Indicate the harmonies by Roman numerals under the bass part.

* Write a crotchet here.

N.B.—In this next exercise, wherever three quavers are written in the bass, add a *dotted crotchet* in the Treble.

x *See* Appendix A, for remarks on the use of augmented intervals in Sequence.

(*b*) Add a melodious *Alto* part in quavers :—

x x Be careful to avoid consecutive 5ths here.

* Write a crotchet only at each pause.

(c) Add a melodious *Bass* part in quavers :—

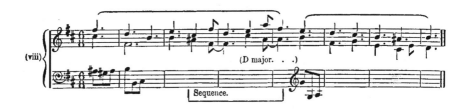

B. The exercises throughout this Section are intended to afford practice in the use of tied notes, in the form of syncopations and suspensions. Before attempting them, the remarks on pages 133–137 should be carefully read by the student.

(a) Add a melodious *Treble* part in quavers to the following passages; the added part should be chiefly in syncopated form, but occasional passing-notes should be used.*

---

* Do not tie passing-notes.

(*b*) Add a similar florid part in the *Alto* to the following :—

Key G major.

(ii)

(^I_c)

(*c*) Add a similar part in the *Bass* to the following :—

(iii)

(C minor.

Sequence.

(*See* Supplement, page **xii.**)

6. The next step in three-part melodic writing will be the addition of *two* independent parts to a given subject, one (or both) of these being of a florid character. Two important points will then deserve careful notice :—

(i) As three parts are sounded together, it is possible in most cases for complete harmonies to be written (that is, in the case of triads and their inversions) ; this is desirable, but as the great aim in this type of exercise is to produce a good, flowing *melody* in each part, it sometimes happens that one of the notes of a chord must be omitted and one of the others doubled, in order that the melodic line may be made as interesting and musical as possible.*

N.B.—Although, therefore, the student must rightly think of sound, pure chord-progressions, his chief care should be to write three flowing, singable melodies which, in their onward movement side by side, form three-part harmony.

(ii) The two *upper* parts—save momentarily—should not be separated too widely from one another; the interval of an 8ve should rarely be exceeded, *e.g.*—

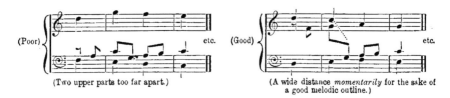

(Poor) ... etc.   (Good) ... etc.

(Two upper parts too far apart.)   (A wide distance *momentarily* for the sake of a good melodic outline.)

A wider distance may be permitted between the *bass* and the part next above it, *e.g.*—

etc.

7. Three types of exercise now present themselves for consideration :—

I. Subject proceeding mainly in pulse-notes; one quicker part, and one part also in pulse-notes, to be added.

II. Subject proceeding mainly in pulse-notes, (as in I); two florid parts to be added.

III. Florid subject, to which two other florid parts are to be added.

Each type of exercise is extremely valuable, and patient work at all three will give the student a command over his resources which will amply repay him for the time and effort spent in mastering their special difficulties. An illustration of each will now be given.

---

* The effect of a *complete* discord of four notes (*e.g.*, a chord of the 7th) may often be simulated by making the quicker part move in "arpeggio," thus :—

(a) ... etc.   (b) ... etc.   (c) ... etc.

(^{7}V$_b$)   (^{7}V$_c$)   (^{7}II$_b$)

I. "*Choral*" (*in Treble*) *in minims*; a bass in half-pulse notes (*i.e.*, crotchets); an alto mainly in notes of the same value as those in the given subject.

Notes on the foregoing Exercise. (1) Although the Alto part is written chiefly in minims, it will be observed that it occasionally proceeds in half-pulse notes, like the bass. Provided that this is not done in such a way as to produce the effect of rapidly-changing harmony (*i.e.*, provided that step-wise movement predominates), the effect of the two *moving* parts is frequently of extremely good effect. It is obvious that, if passing-notes occur in two parts simultaneously, they will move quite naturally in parallel 3rds or 6ths :—

(*See* also bars 2, 4 and 12 in the above exercise.)

In order to preserve the requisite degree of independence of movement, however, it is often necessary for a certain amount of contrary motion to be used in the two moving parts ; (*see* the latter half of bars 10 and 12). In any case, these two quicker-moving parts should—in this type of exercise —always form *concordant* intervals between them.

(2) At (*a*) in bar 1 an accented passing-note is used effectively in the bass-part, which here moves by step in contrary motion to the treble.

(3) The first chord in bar 13 provides an instance of the use of the "Added 6th " at a cadence.

EXERCISES.

C. Take the following Subjects from Chapters II, III, and IV, and work in 3 parts, as shewn in the foregoing example :—

Chapter II **(A)** Exercises 1, 2 and 6.
     „   „   **(B)**   „   1 and 6 (*not* as a Canon).
     „   „   **(D)**   „   1, 2 and 3.
     „   „   **(E)**   „   1 and 2.
Chapter III **(A)** Exercise 1 (lower part).
     „   „   **(E)**   „   3 (taking the ♩ as the pulse).
Chapter IV **(A)** Exercises 1, 2 and 4.
     „   „   **(B)** Exercise 1.   (*See* Supplement, page xiii.)

Give three versions of each exercise, by treating the Subject (in turn) as a Bass, a Treble, and a middle part (Alto or Tenor). Transpose it in every case to suit the compass of the particular voice. The quicker-moving part should be a different one in each instance.

N.B.—" Chorals" such as those given on pages 57 and 58 of the Author's *350 Exercises in Harmony, Counterpoint, and Modulation,* are eminently suitable for this type of study.

II. *Subject (chiefly in crotchets), placed in turn in Treble, Alto, and Bass.* Two florid parts added in each case, mainly in crotchets and quavers.

(Subject in Treble.)

(Subject in Alto.)

(Subject in Bass.)

Notes. (1) It will be seen that the great object in this form of exercise is to break up the melodic line, and to pass the chief interest from one part to another from moment to moment. Thus it comes about that when one of these moves more rapidly, the other (or others) will usually exhibit less activity, and *vice versâ.*

(2) A point of imitation carefully introduced often creates interest and imparts zest to the music (*see* particularly the second of the foregoing examples, especially bars 1–2 and 4–5).

(3) The use of tied notes and Suspensions should be specially noticed; in music for voices or for sustaining instruments their employment is often of the highest value, and tends to reduce any possible feeling of rigidity or squareness.

(4) The importance of the use of occasional *rests* in the various parts must never be overlooked. They lighten the effect, and materially help the realization of the phrasing of the music.

In this connexion, it should be remembered that phrases or musical figures frequently *begin* more effectively on an *unaccented* note, after a short rest (*see* foregoing examples, especially the opening bars of Nos. 2 and 3). On the other hand, a phrase or figure usually concludes best *upon* an accent, when it can often be immediately followed by a rest. (*See* especially No. 1, bar 4 of Alto ; No. 2, bar 4 of Bass ; No. 3, bar 4 of Treble.)

EXERCISES.

D. Take the Subjects named on page 53, and work them according to Plan II. In addition to these, the following will be found suitable :—

Chapter II (**B**) Exercise 2 (treat this as a Bass-part only).

    ,,   IV (**C**) Exercises 1 and 2 (the latter as a Bass-part only).

    ,,   V (**F**) Exercises 1 and 2.

    ,,   ,,   (**G**) Exercise 1.

III. *Florid Subject ; two other florid parts added.*

Example 1.
(Subject in Bass.)

Notes. (1) Imitational effects (such as have been mentioned in connexion with the examples in (II) are here used extensively, in order to impart a degree of unity to the whole piece. It will be observed that the figure of four notes, occurring first in the Alto of bars 1 and 2 ; is imitated by the Treble in bars 2 and 3, and that the figure itself recurs several times in the course of the exercise, either in its original form (as in the Treble of bars 7-9 and elsewhere), or by "Inverse movement" (as in the Alto of bars 4 and 5, the Bass of bars 9 and 10, the Treble of bars 10-12, etc.). The sequential use of the figure in the Treble, it will be noticed, helps the music to reach the climax at the *forte* in bar 9 with increased animation and zest.

(2) Accented passing-notes are effectively introduced in bars 7, 10, 11, 13 and 16 ; in every case they enable the more florid part to move more smoothly along the "scale-line." In connexion with the use of dissonances between two moving parts, it is well to remember :—

(*a*) That if both parts approach and quit the dissonance *by step*, in contrary motion to one another, the effect is often quite good, *e.g.*—

This proceeding, however, needs care, or it may easily produce painful results, such as the following :—

(*b*) That a slower part moving in *arpeggio* may be accompanied by a dissonance in a quicker part, provided that the dissonant note is approached and quitted by step (preferably in contrary motion), *e.g.*—

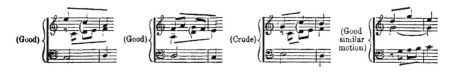

N.B.—Growing aural perception and taste must be the guide in all cases ; the student should *use his ears*, and not rely upon there being a *rule* to fit every case. The above directions should, however, form the basis of his experiments in this direction.

Example 2. For String Trio : Subject in Viola part.

Note. The above example needs little comment. The use of free imitation between the parts will hardly escape observation (*e.g.*, in bars 1 and 2 ; 6 and 7 ; 8 and 9). The Violin and Viola cross one another in bars 5 and 6 ; occasional crossing of the parts for the sake of a better melodic movement is often of the best possible effect. The question of the bowing of stringed-instruments, and also of double-notes (as in the final bar) will be found discussed in Appendix E.

Example 3. Also for String Trio : Subject in Violin part.

Note. In this exercise crossing of the parts is still more freely employed. Two melodic figures form the staple of the whole example, viz. (i) the descending scale first announced by the Violin in bar 1, and (ii) that heard first in the Viola in bars 4 and 5  which re-appears from time to time, either in its original form, or by "inverse movement." (*See* Appendix E for the meaning of "pizz." and "arco.")

EXERCISES.

E. 1. Add two independent vocal parts (Treble and Alto *or* Tenor) above the following :—

2. Add parts for Second Violin and Viola below the following. Take especial care to make the added parts in this and the succeeding exercises melodically interesting. Use rests freely (where effective), mark the bowing, and insert expression-marks.

3. Add parts for Violin and Violoncello to this Viola part :—

4. Add parts for Violin and Viola above the following :—

5. The Subjects named below are also suitable for Florid treatment in the foregoing manner :—

Chapter II (**A**) Exercise 7. (Subject in Soprano voice.)

    ,,   ,, (**B**) ,,   4. (S. for Viola.)

    ,,   ,, (**D**) Exercises 4, 5 and 6.

    ,,   ,, (**E**) Exercise 6. (S. for Viola.)

    ,,   III (**E**) Exercises 1 and 2.

    ,,   ,, (**F**) Exercise 1. (S. for Violin.)

    ,,   IV (**D**) Exercises 1 and 2.

    ,,   ,, (**E**) ,,   1 to 6 inclusive.

    ,,   V (**G**) Exercise 2.

    ,,   ,, (**H**) ,,   1.

N.B.—Further material will be found in the Author's *350 Exercises in Harmony, Counterpoint, and Modulation* (pages 55-57, Sec. B) ; also in the Supplement to the present volume, page xiv.

CHAPTER VIII.

FOUR-PART MELODIC WRITING.

1. The difficulty involved in writing four flowing and independent parts is considerable, and the danger of producing an overcrowded effect in the music is one which it needs great skill to avoid. It therefore becomes increasingly necessary (as was pointed out on page 54, Note 1) to pass the chief melodic interest from part to part, and—in order to prevent heaviness and thickness of effect—to use *rests* still more extensively than in three-part writing, *e.g.*—

Mozart.—Quartet in D major, No. 8).

This breaking-up of the melodic line is especially noticeable in string-quartet writing, where something of the kind is usually necessary unless it is desired that one or more of the parts shall stand out in melodic prominence against a simple background of harmony or accompaniment, *e.g.*—

Schubert.—Quartet in A minor (Op. 29).

2. Two types of exercise may profitably be undertaken by the student at this stage of his work. The first of these consists of the addition of three florid parts to a subject moving mostly in pulse-notes (*e.g.*, a " choral " or hymn-tune) ; the second in the writing of three florid parts against a *florid subject*.

The following are examples of each :—

I. " *Choral* " *chiefly in crotchets :* three florid parts added, mainly in pulse-notes and half-pulse-notes.

***** The treatment by Bach of the foregoing Choral deserves careful analysis. It will be observed that a movement in half-pulse notes (quavers) is maintained throughout, this movement being effectively distributed among the several parts. In bar 6 will be seen a point at which Bach has made them *all* move simultaneously in half-pulse notes ; but it should be noted that the use of more than two quicker-moving parts in this way as a rule causes a certain heaviness and a sense of over-elaboration which the student must be careful to avoid. The effect usually produced is that of too rapidly-changing *harmony, e.g.—*

N.B.—Compare this with bars 5 and 6 above.

In working exercises of this kind, the Choral should be placed in each of the voices in turn, and florid parts added. The following example shews the opening of the Choral " Es ist das Heil " transposed a 5th lower for the Alto voice :—

EXERCISES.

Take the Chorals given on pages 57 and 58 of the Author's *350 Exercises in Harmony, Counterpoint and Modulation,* or in Frederick Corder's *Exercises in Musical Composition* (Forsyth Bros.), and work them according to the foregoing directions. The subjects given on page ix of the Supplement (for Chapter VII) are also suitable, as are any of the Chorals or Hymn-tunes in the present volume.

II.   *Florid Subject·: three other florid parts added.*

    Example I.

    (Subject in Bass.*)

---

* This is the same subject as that worked in 3 parts on page 54.   Compare the differences in treatment.

Example II.

(Subject in Viola part.) *

N.B.—In addition to the frequent use of free imitation in the above example, attention should be paid to the crossing of the parts in several places for the purpose of (i) a better melodic line, or (ii) the employment of some special " register " of one of the instruments concerned.

Example III.

(Subject partly in Violin I. and partly in Viola.)

* Compare this example with that on page 56, where the same subject is used for String Trio.

Notes on Example III.

(a) When a melody begins with an Anacrusis,* it is often advisable not to harmonize it, and even not to harmonize the first metrically-accented note, but to bring in the other parts at the following *weaker beat.* Especially is this effective when the opening figure of a melody can be imitated (as in the foregoing example).

(b) An initial figure may also frequently be treated as a means by which an organic connexion may be maintained between the various sections of a whole piece, and thus produce a certain feeling of unity. The degree of importance given to the little rhythmic figure ♫ ♪ occurring first in the opening bars, will hardly escape observation.

(c) The judicious employment of rests, especially before the introduction of such a rhythmic figure, always gives point, and prevents thickness in the harmony (*see* Sec. 1). It almost goes without saying that rests should not be introduced simply because the writer cannot think of any note or notes to put in their place !

EXERCISES.

(a) Work the exercises given on pages 57 and 58 in four parts, instead of three. Be careful to avoid *thickness* of harmony, by the judicious use of rests.

(b) The Subjects named in Sec. 5 on page 58 are also suitable for Florid treatment in four parts, and further material will be found in the Author's *350 Exercises in Harmony, Counterpoint, and Modulation* (pages 56, 57), and also in *Unfigured Harmony,* by P. C. Buck, (Clarendon Press, Oxford).

(*See,* moreover, the Supplement to the present volume, page xiv.)

Final Note.—The subject of Melodic writing in more than four parts cannot, for reasons of space, be considered in the present volume. The student is referred to the Author's *Practical Counterpoint,* especially to the chapters on " Free Counterpoint."

* See Glossary.

PART II.

HARMONIC PROGRESSION.

CHAPTER IX.

1. To form the simplest *complete* chord, the combination of three different sounds is needed, viz. a bass-note (or root), its 3rd and its 5th., *e.g.*— Such a chord is termed a *Triad* (*Gr.* τριάς = the number three).*

2. There are four kinds of Triads, viz.—

    (i) The Major triad (or Major Common chord), containing a major 3rd and perfect 5th above its root,   *e.g.*—

    (ii) The Minor triad (or Minor Common chord), containing a minor 3rd and perfect 5th,   *e.g.*—

    (iii) The Diminished triad, containing a minor 3rd and diminished 5th, *e.g.*—

    (iv) The Augmented triad, containing a major 3rd and augmented 5th, *e.g.*—

3. Major and Minor triads (or common chords) are termed *Concordant* triads, and Diminished and Augmented triads *Dissonant* (or discordant) triads.

    A *concordant* combination is one which is satisfactory in itself, and which possesses a certain degree of repose ; whereas by a *dissonant* (or discordant) combination is to be understood one which clearly demands a progression to some other chord, in order to complete its effect,† *e.g.*—

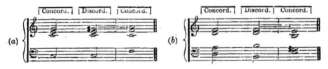

---

    * Compare the formation of this word with others derived from the same source, *e.g.* — *Tripod, Trident, Triangle,* etc.

    † The term Discord is applied in two ways: (i) to the whole combination, (ii) to the special note in that combination which needs to move in a particular way, (*e.g.* the G ♯ in Ex. (*a*), and the F in chord 2 in Ex. (*b*).

EXERCISE.

Play and write Triads of every kind upon various bass-notes, carefully noting the differences in mental effect between them.

---

4. It is possible to form a triad upon every degree of the major or minor scale :—

At present, however, we shall confine our attention to the principal (or *Primary*) triads of the key, viz. those upon the Tonic, Subdominant, and Dominant.

*** These are printed in open notes in the above examples.

5. It will be seen that these three triads, in the major key, are all *Major triads*, the effect of each being, however, wholly different from that of the others, owing to its special position in the key. In the minor key, the triads upon the Tonic and Subdominant are *minor*, the effect of each being similarly quite distinct. *The Dominant triad in both forms of key is a Major triad.*

6. The student should now endeavour to familiarize his ear with the sound of the Subdominant and Dominant triads in relation to that upon the Tonic. The two Cadences which produce the impression of conclusion or repose illustrate this relationship very clearly :—

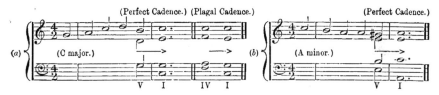

The expectant, inconclusive sound of the Dominant triad,* as contrasted with the restfulness of that on the Tonic—heightened by the relative rhythmic strength of the two chords—will hardly escape observation. The Subdominant triad, while less expectant than that of the Dominant, contains sufficient of the quality of *movement* for it to be impossible as the final chord in any important section of a composition, and shares with the Dominant the desire ultimately to reach the Tonic, *e.g.*—

"Ye banks and braes."

---

* Largely due to the presence of the " active " Leading-note in the chord.

7. The foregoing examples will have shewn that the notes of a triad may be arranged in several different ways—in other words, that it is not desirable (or possible) for them always to be placed in the order of $\left\{\begin{array}{l}\text{5th.}\\\text{3rd.}\\\text{root.}\end{array}\right.$

The following are a few of the forms in which the Tonic triad in the key of C major, in direct (or "root") position, (*i.e.*, with its root in the bass or lowest part), may appear :—

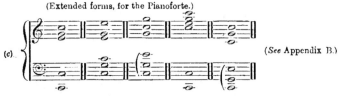

(*See* Appendix B.)

8. In order to secure the smoothest and most musical progression from chord to chord, it is necessary that the parts of which they consist should move as easily and naturally as possible. The following examples indicate the simplest connexions between (*a*) Tonic and Dominant, (*b*) Tonic and Subdominant, harmonies.*

N.B.—The chords are here arranged in four parts for the pianoforte, in what is usually known as "Close position." For ease and convenience, the three upper parts are given to the right hand, the bass only to the left. Each example should be played many times, and transposed into other keys.†

(*a*) Tonic and Dominant triads.

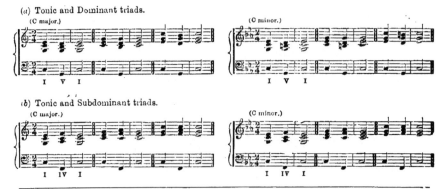

(*b*) Tonic and Subdominant triads.

---

* Notice, in these progressions, that no part save the bass moves by more than the step of a 2nd.

† It is of the first importance that this transposition should be carried out at the pianoforte. The purely notational act of *written* transposition should be used solely as a means of memorizing the effect of any particular progression in various keys, and thus of aiding the connexion between "sound" and "symbol" in the pupil's mind.

9. In four-part harmony it is clearly necessary for one of the notes of a triad to be *doubled* (*i.e.*, used more than once in the same chord.) The best note to double, in the great majority of cases, is the *root*.* (See above examples.)

> *N.B.*—The Leading-note of the key, owing to its sensitive nature, and its special tendency to rise to the key-note, should not be doubled. (See Chapter 1. Sec. 3 (c).)

10. It will also be seen that each pair of chords in the examples in Sec. 8 possesses *one note in common*, and that this note is given to the same part (or voice) in each chord, as a connecting link, (or " binding-tone ") between the two. By this means the danger of faulty progression is minimized, and the smoothest movement of the parts secured. Compare the following examples :—

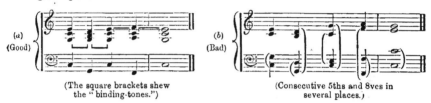

(*a*)
(Good)

(The square brackets shew the " binding-tones.")

(*b*)
(Bad)

(Consecutive 5ths and 8ves in several places.)

₊ Note that, although there is a 5th and an 8ve in each chord in Ex. (*a*), they do not occur between *the same two parts* of the harmony in any two succeeding chords, and so do not cause " consecutives."

EXERCISES ON THE CONNEXION OF (*a*) TONIC AND DOMINANT, (*b*) TONIC AND SUBDOMINANT, TRIADS.

A. (i) Play the Tonic triad in various major and minor keys, in the form shewn in Sec. 8 above (*i.e.*, with the *bass* only in the left hand, and the three upper parts in the right hand). Place at various times the root, 3rd and 5th at the top.†

(ii) Play the Subdominant triad similarly, in various keys.‡

(iii) Play the Dominant triad similarly, in various keys.‡

B Play, in various major and minor keys, the following successions of chords, arranging the upper parts in the several ways shewn in Sec. 8 above :—

(i) **I**   **V**;   **I**   **IV**;   **IV**   **I**;   **V**   **I.**

(ii) **I**   **IV**   **I**;   **I**   **V**   **I**;   **IV**   **I**   **V**   **I**;   **V**   **I**   **IV**   **I.**

---

* Exceptions to this rule will be met with later on. For the present it should be strictly observed.

† The student should aim at executing these first three exercises (i), (ii), and (iii) with readiness and confidence. Such facility at the key-board is of the highest importance to the musician.

‡ In order to feel the true relationship of these chords to their key-centre, it will be well to precede the playing of each by sounding either (i) the notes of the Tonic chord in arpeggio, *e.g.* (Key D):—

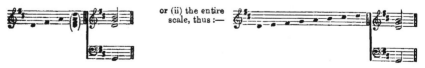

or (ii) the entire scale, thus :—

C. Harmonize these melody-notes (in major or minor keys), with Tonic, Subdominant, and Dominant triads; use various times, letting the last chord fall upon a strong accent in each case.

   (i) 8   2   3 ;   3   4   3;   5   6   5 ;   8   7   8 .

   (ii) 4   3   2   3;   5   6   5   5;   8   8   7   8;   2   3   4   3 .

N.B.—Whereas Roman numerals will always be used in the present volume to imply the *harmonies* of a key, melody-notes will be indicated by Arabic figures, representing the various degrees of the scale, as here. The following examples shew two different arrangements, as regards time, of Ex. (i) in Sec. **C** :—

The bass-part may be played in 8ves, in the manner often found in Pianoforte music, *e.g.*—

In such a case the harmony is complete without the doubling of the bass-part, which is merely strengthened by this means. Such 8ves do not constitute a case of "consecutives."

THE RELEASE OF THE "BINDING-TONE."

11. Although the retaining of a common note, or "binding-tone," in one of the parts of the harmony usually produces the smoothest connexion between any two successive chords, this plan is not always possible when they are placed in "close position," *e.g.*—*

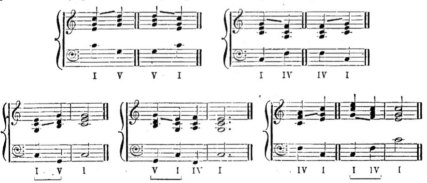

N.B.—The impossibility of using the "binding-tone" arises, as will be seen from the above passages, when the 1st and 2nd degrees of the scale occur in succession in any part, in passing between Tonic and *Dominant* harmonies ; also wherever the 4th and 5th degrees so occur, in passing between Tonic and *Subdominant* harmonies.

---

* The Examples given here are equally available in **the Minor key.**

12. If, at a Perfect Cadence, the melody ends with the 2nd of the scale falling to the 1st,
thus : 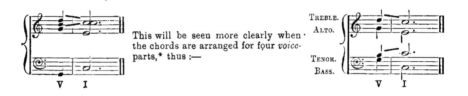 the *5th of the Tonic chord has to be omitted*, if the Leading-note is to
proceed correctly to the Key-note, *e.g.*—

This will be seen more clearly when·
the chords are arranged for four *voice-parts*,* thus :—

V   I   TREBLE.
                ALTO.
                TENOR.
                BASS.
                      V   I

13. Although the 5th of any triad may thus be omitted, and the root used thrice, the 3rd
should always be present, otherwise the result is bare and empty :—

N.B.—This rule, like many others, is sometimes set aside by experienced composers for some
special effect of colour or "atmosphere." Beethoven, for instance, creates a feeling of dim vastness
in the opening of his 9th Symphony, by omitting the 3rd from the Dominant triad of D minor :—

---

* Bach and other writers sometimes allow the Leading-note to fall, even in a vocal cadence, thus :—

BACH.—"Christmas Oratorio."

in order to obtain the fuller effect of the complete Tonic chord. The student is advised not to use this
licence at the present stage of his work, as it is most important for him to get into the habit of *listening*
carefully for the natural melodic tendencies of those degrees of the scale which are more essentially
sounds of movement or activity, (See Chap. I. Sec. 3. f.n.)

FURTHER EXERCISES ON THE CONNEXION OF (*a*) TONIC AND DOMINANT, (*b*) TONIC AND SUBDOMINANT, TRIADS.

D. PLAY, in various major and minor keys, and in four parts, the following successions of chords, in a manner similar to that in preceding exercises.

N.B.—The small Arabic figures above the Roman numerals indicate the required melody-notes. Use various time-schemes.

(i)   I V I;   I IV I;   I IV I;   I V I.

(ii)   I V I IV I;   I IV I V I;   IV I IV I V;   V I IV IV I.

E. Harmonize these melody-notes at the pianoforte (in major and minor keys,) with Tonic, Subdominant and Dominant triads. Use various time-schemes.

(i)   3   4   5;   5   4   3;   8   6   5;   7   8   6;   3   2   1
                                                             | Perf. Cadence.* |

(ii)   3   2   1   2   3;   5   4   5   6   5;   1   2   3   4   5;

  5   4   3   2   1:   5   6   8   6   5;   5   3   4   3   5   2   3.
   | Perf. Cadence.* |

F. Add two inner parts to the following passages, at the Pianoforte. Play the three upper parts with the right hand, the bass only with the left (as in previous exercises). Afterwards write out each exercise, as a test of memory, placing the three upper parts on the Treble staff.

CHOPIN (paraphrased).

No harmony here.

---

* Be careful as to the progression of the Leading-note.

G. Add harmonies at the places indicated. Arrange the chords as in previous exercises.

(a) Finish with a *major* chord of the Tonic. When the Plagal cadence (IV—I) is met with—as here—at the conclusion of a piece in a minor key, the 3rd of the Tonic chord is far more often than not *major*, instead of minor. This major 3rd is, for some unexplained reason, often spoken of as the "Tierce de Picardie," (or "Picardy 3rd ").

(b) Shift the position of the two inner notes of this chord, when the treble moves up to the E, sustaining the bass note.

H. Using only the chords of the Tonic, Subdominant and Dominant (I, IV and V) in root-position, harmonize the points marked |___| in the following melodies. (*N.B.* —Do not use IV and V in succession.)

* Remember that the Dominant chord (V) in a minor key is a *major* triad, whose 3rd (the leading-note) requires an accidental. This will not be specially indicated in future exercises; the student's feeling for "key " *must* be his guide, and be sufficient to prevent his playing or writing a minor triad in such cases.

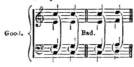

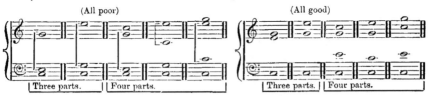

(*a*) Repeat the chord taken upon the first beat of the bar.   The *repetition* of an 8ve or 5th does not constitute a case of " consecutives,' *e.g.*—

ON WRITING HARMONY FOR VOICES.

14.   In arranging the notes of a chord for *voices*, it is important to avoid uncomfortable gaps between the upper parts.   As a rule, the distance of an 8ve should not be exceeded between any two adjacent voices, save between the *Bass* and the part next above it :—

15.   If a chord is arranged for three parts only, these voices* will be :—
$\begin{cases} 3. \text{ Treble.} \\ 2. \text{ Alto (or Tenor).} \\ 1. \text{ Bass.} \end{cases}$

If four are used, the following order is observed :—
$\begin{cases} 4. \text{ Treble.} \\ 3 \text{ Alto.} \\ 2. \text{ Tenor.} \\ 1. \text{ Bass.} \end{cases}$

In the latter case, it is customary (when writing in what is known as " short score,") to place the .Treble and Alto on the upper of two staves, and the Tenor and Bass on the

lower, thus :—

---

* *See* Chap. II., Sec. 11 for compass of each voice.

PREPARATORY EXERCISES IN VOCAL WRITING.

I. Transcribe for four voices (Treble and Alto on the upper staff, and Tenor and Bass on the lower), several of the preceding exercises.

J. Add the Alto and Tenor parts to the following passages, making as smooth and "singable" a connexion between the various chords as possible :—

CHAPTER X.

FURTHER USE OF THE PRIMARY TRIADS.

1. Although it is comparatively easy to obtain a smooth and musical connexion between (i) Tonic and Dominant, (ii) Tonic and Subdominant harmonies, a good deal of care is needed when the Subdominant and Dominant chords occur in succession. These two triads possess no "common" note, or "binding-tone," and there is always considerable danger of crude consecutive 5ths and 8ves, in passing from one to the other,* *e.g.*—

(Consecutive 5ths and 8ves.)   (Consecutive 5ths.)

₊ The above passages should not be merely looked at, but played many times, so that the effect of the "consecutives" may be realized aurally. The examples should also be played in C minor, by substituting A flat and E flat for A natural and E natural.

2. To remedy the faulty part-writing, it is best to make the parts above the bass (at any rate, the 5th and the doubled root) *move in contrary motion* to it, thus :—

---

* The same difficulty arises (as will be seen later) whenever the roots of two successive triads lie a 2nd apart.

The following is a familiar instance of the use of the Subdominant and Dominant harmonies taken in succession :—

Hymn-tune.—"Rockingham."

3. In the minor key, extra care needs to be used in connecting the above chords, in order to avoid the leap of an augmented interval in any of the parts (*see* Chap. I, Sec. 3), *e.g.*—

It is useful to notice that, in producing such augmented intervals, either the 6th or 7th degree of the scale is concerned. Therefore, remember (i) that each of those degrees requires attention as to the manner in which it is approached and quitted, and (ii) that it is a safe general rule to reach the Leading-note of a minor key *from above*, rather than from below :—

Compare with Ex. (*a*) in Sec. **3**.

4. It is obvious that, with the chords of the Tonic, Subdominant and Dominant at our disposal, it is possible to harmonize the whole of the diatonic scale :—

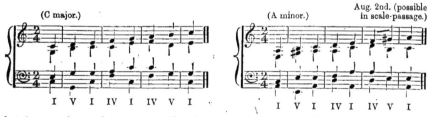

but the above harmonization must not be taken as an ideal, or even a desirable, one. The bass, which (as has been seen in the two-part melodic work) should be melodious in its movement, is far from satisfactory from that point of view ; and the passage must be taken merely as an illustration that the three harmonies under consideration—the Primary triads, as they are termed—include all the sounds contained in the diatonic scale.

1 ¸ *⁎*⁎ Compare the bass of the foregoing examples with that of the two-part harmonization of the · ascending scale given in Chap. II., Sec. 5.

EXERCISES ON THE USE OF THE THREE PRIMARY TRIADS.

A. Play the examples given in Sec. 2 above *in all keys*, and memorize them.

B. Complete the following passages as indicated. The parts necessary to complete each exercise should first be *written*, for practice in correct part-writing. The exercises should afterwards be *played*, and their effect on the ear carefully noted.

** Remember that, in order to obtain a smooth and flowing movement of the parts, it is well to *avoid large leaps.* In four-part harmony the best course usually is (*a*) to make use, where possible, of the idea of the "binding-tone" between successive chords* ; (*b*) to let the remaining notes of the first chord move to the *nearest* notes of the next chord that may be possible, *e.g.*—

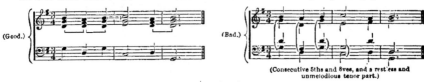

(Good.)   (Bad.)

(Consecutive 5ths and 8ves, and a rest·ess and unmelodious tenor part.)

N.B.—The "binding-tones" are indicated by a ⎿⎾ .

(i) Add two middle parts (on upper staff)꞉

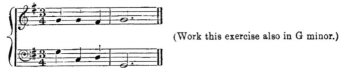

(Work this exercise also in G minor.)

(ii) Add two middle parts (on upper staff).

(iii) Add two middle parts (on upper staff):

---

* This recommendation is to be thought of as applying to the early stages of the student's work, and as being likely to prevent awkwardness of part-writing. Later, as he gains experience, it will be possible (and most desirable) for his parts to move more freely, for the sake of increased interest. Even at the stage represented by the present chapter he should endeavour to bring to bear upon his four-part exercises the idea of *melodic* movement, especially as regards the outside (*i.e.*, the highest and lowest) parts of the harmony

(iv) Add an Alto *voice-part* on upper staff, and a Tenor on lower staff:

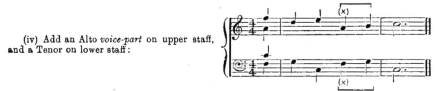

(×) The part-writing here needs great care ; (*See* Ex. (*d*) in Sec. 2 above).

(v) Add two middle parts (both for the right hand) on upper staff.

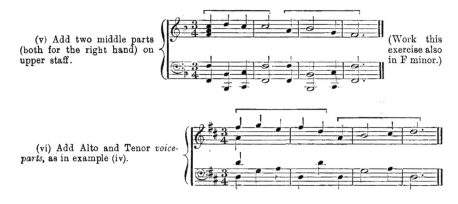

(Work this exercise also in F minor.)

(vi) Add Alto and Tenor *voice-parts*, as in example (iv).

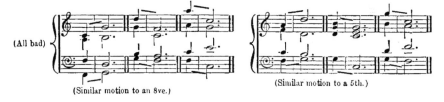

5. In the exercises that now follow, the student will have to construct the outside parts of the harmony, as well as the inner ones. He must, therefore, carefully bear in mind the following points, which refer to the production of a good melody and a good bass :—

(*a*) It is usually not advisable for the " extreme " (*i.e.,* the highest and lowest) parts of the harmony to approach an 8ve or a 5th *by similar motion, e.g.*—

(All bad)

(Similar motion to an 8ve.)   (Similar motion to a 5th.)

(*b*) If, however, the highest part *moves by step*, the above restriction does not hold good between—

(i) Tonic and Dominant chords, *e.g.*—

(Good)

(ii) Tonic and Subdominant chords, *e.g.*—

(Good)

EXERCISES—(*Cont^d.*).

C. Play (in four parts) the following progressions in various major and minor keys. Play the three upper parts in the right hand, the bass only (which may be strengthened in octaves) with the left.* Arrange the examples in different times.

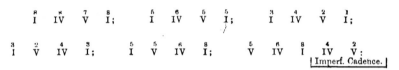

D. Harmonize these melody-notes (in major and minor keys) with the Primary triads :—

$$3 \quad 4 \quad 2 \quad 3; \qquad 5 \quad 6 \quad 5 \quad 8; \qquad 8 \quad 8 \quad 7 \quad 8;$$

$$\cdot 8 \quad 4 \quad 5 \quad 6 \quad 5 \quad 5; \qquad 3 \quad 2 \quad 4 \quad 3 \quad 1 \quad 1 \quad 7, \quad 1.$$

E. Arrange the exercises in (**C**) for four *voice-parts*, writing the Treble and Alto on the upper staff, the Tenor and Bass on the lower.

F. Harmonize the following melodic succession for four *voice-parts*, in the key of E flat major :—

$$5 \ , \ 6 \ , \ 7 \ , \ 8 \ .$$

N.B.—Write this out in various other major keys.

G. Harmonize these melodic phrases, using only the three Primary triads, as in previous exercises.

---

* For the description of the various numeral signs, see page 68.

N.B.—In the next three melodies, harmonize only those notes within the ⌐⎯⎯¬.

(Key B♭....)

(a) Only one chord for these two quavers.

(Key G......) (Key C, to end.)

H. Harmonize these basses, using only the Primary triads. Make the highest part as melodious as possible. *(See p. vii for meaning of (5), (8), etc. over the bass-notes.)*

(a) Shift the position of the three upper parts.

N.B.—The ♯ under the Dominant bass note indicates that the 3rd of the chord (the Leading-note of the minor key) needs a similar accidental.

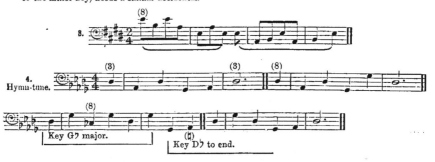

Key G♭ major. Key D♭ to end.

I. Endeavour to improvise short rhythmical phrases at the Pianoforte, using the chords and progressions thus far studied. The main object in doing this should be to obtain a necessary degree of fluency, therefore niceties of part-writing need not be considered too closely *at first;* but as soon as the student can think fairly easily at the key-board, such matters should, of course, receive careful attention.

CHAPTER XI.

THE INVERSIONS OF THE PRIMARY TRIADS.

1. THE student's exercises in two-part melodic writing will have shewn him that, to produce a really musical result, the movement of the bass is of paramount importance. If this bass-part does not possess the feeling of *purpose*, if it wanders aimlessly and unmelodiously from note to note, even the most beautiful and artistically-conceived tune it may accompany will be weakened and impoverished beyond belief. A comparison of the two succeeding examples will afford ample proof of this :—

BEETHOVEN.—Sonata (Op. 14, No. 2.) (with bass as written by the Composer).

(a)

(The same—with altered bass.)

(b)   etc.

After the general effect of each of the above passages has been carefully noted, the *bass only* should be played. Two conclusions will follow :—

  · (i) That in (a) it is melodious, smooth and natural (owing to the happy mixture of leaps and " step-wise " movement) ;

  (ii) That in (b) it is awkward, ungainly and purposeless (owing to the constant leaps and meaningless repetitions).

2. It will be noticed that all the chords in example (b) are direct triads, (*i.e.*, triads having their root in the bass), and the effect is decidedly heavy. In order to produce a flowing bass-part it is usually necessary for some of the chords to be *inverted*. A chord is said to be inverted when any other note than its root is placed in the bass (or lowest) part, *e.g.*—

(Triad in direct, or " root," position.)
                             (The same in inverted positions.)

(a)   (b)

3. It is obvious that the number of inversions possible to a given chord will be one less than the number of different notes in the chord itself. A triad, having three such notes, will therefore have *two* inversions, described as its first and second inversions respectively. When the 3rd of a chord is placed in the bass, that chord is said to be in its *first inversion* (*See* Ex. (*a*) in Sec. 2); when the 5th is in the bass, it is spoken of as being in its *second inversion* (*See* Ex. (*b*) in Sec. 2).

4. The following extract will illustrate the use of the three Primary triads in an inverted form :—

"On the banks of Allan water."

V_b I_b IV_b I_c V

*** The letters (*b*) and (*c*) below the Roman numerals indicate that the chords are in their first and second inversions respectively, *e.g.*— V_b signifies the *first* inversion of the Dominant triad, I_c the *second* inversion of the Tonic triad, and so on.

The mental effect of these inverted chords should be carefully realized, and the example compared with the following, in which the clumsy and unmusical use of direct triads in corresponding situations will readily be felt :—

V   I   IV   I   V

THE FIRST INVERSION OF THE PRIMARY TRIADS.

5. It is possible to use all the triads of the major or minor key in the first inversion, *e.g.*—

For the present, however, the student's exercises will deal only with the first inversion of the three Primary triads, viz. those of the Tonic, Subdominant and Dominant (indicated in the above examples by "open" notes).

---

* Compare these examples with the tables of triads in Chap. IX, Sec. 4).

6. The introduction of " first inversions " is often advantageous—

(i) When the melody moves from one note to another of the same harmony :—

(ii) For the purpose of avoiding ungainly skips or monotony in the bass part :—

₊ The student should study carefully the two examples in Sec. I. in connexion with the above remark.

N.B.—When two positions of the same chord are used in succession, *the first should not occur upon a weaker part of the bar (or beat) than the second,* as the rhythmic flow of the music is usually checked if a chord that is to be heard on a stronger beat is thus anticipated, or forestalled, on the previous weaker one, *e.g.* :—

₊ Compare this with Ex. (*b*) above.

The two positions of the chord should always run from " strong " to " weak," thus : ♩ ♩, not from " weak " to " strong," thus : ♩ ♩.

It may be taken as a useful hint that, if two melody-notes moving thus : ♩ ♩ can be regarded as belonging to the same harmony, it is often good (in order to avoid " fussiness " of effect), *not to change the harmony* at the weaker beat, but to use another position of the same chord—the direct position or the first inversion, as the case may be.

---

* Compare the movement of the bass in Ex. (c) with the following :—

7. The bass-note of the first inversion of a *major* triad should not be doubled, in the great majority of cases ; the effect is nearly always rough and uncouth, *e.g.*—

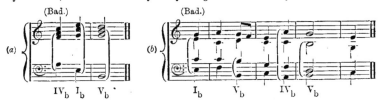

Either the 3rd or the 6th from the *bass-note* * (*i.e.*, the 5th or the root of the original triad) may, however, be freely doubled, and—save in the instances mentioned in Secs. 11 to 13—the first inversion of these chords will sound equally well with either the 3rd or the 6th at the top :—

₊ Compare this example with Ex. : (*b*) above.

8. A *minor* triad may have the bass-note of its first inversion doubled at times, but this doubling needs care, and for the moment the student is advised to avoid it. (See, however, Chap. XIII, Sec. 6.) The following passage shews two instances of such doubling :—

9. The first inversion of a triad is frequently called a "chord of the sixth," or a "chord of the six-three." This of course arises from the fact that the intervals of the chord counted from its bass-note are respectively a 6th and a 3rd.†

---

* Not from the *root*.

† The student will now begin to realize the harmonic significance of the *interval of 6th* which he has used from the first in his two-part melodic work. It really implies—in almost every instance – an incomplete *chord* of the 6th, and could be effectively filled up with a 3rd from the bass-note, as will be seen if we arrange Ex. (iii) of Chap. II, Sec. 5 for three parts instead of two :—

The remaining intervals of the original passage (viz., the 5th, 3rd, and 8ve) imply *direct* triads. The chord-basis of two-part writing will be increasingly evident as the various triads of the key are progressively studied in the following chapters.

10.   Figures are often added under the bass-part of an exercise, and indicate the harmonies required from time to time, by specifying the intervals of the chords counted from that bass⁻part, which is then described as a *Figured Bass.* The figures $\frac{6}{3}$ (usually abbreviated into 6) therefore signify that a bass-note is to bear the first inversion of a triad, *e.g.*—

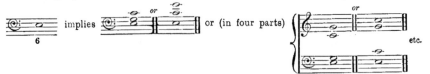

N.B.—An *unfigured* note in the course of a Figured Bass implies a triad in its direct (or root) position.

PROGRESSION OF PARTS.

11.   When two or more "chords of the sixth" occur in succession (especially on adjacent degrees, as in the well-known examples from Beethoven given below), it is necessary—in order to avoid "consecutives"—to place the 6th from the bass in the highest part (that is, above the 3rd from the bass)* :—

BEETHOVEN.—Sonata Op. 2, No. 3.

Compare the above examples with the following :—

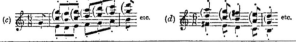

---

* It will be noticed that the two upper parts in the chain of "chords of the 6th" move in parallel 4ths.   Although in two-part writing the interval of a 4th is dissonant and, as a consequence, a succession of bare 4ths such as the following would be exceedingly crude— 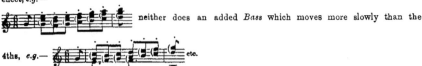 the crudity entirely disappears if a bass (moving at least as rapidly as the 4ths) is placed below them, as in the examples in Sec. 11.   The addition of a similar part *above* the 4ths does not remove the bad effect, *e.g.*—

neither does an added *Bass* which moves more slowly than the

4ths, *e.g.*—   etc.

† **Note that** the harmony here is in three parts only, in spite of the strengthening of the top part in 8ves.

12. In three-part writing (which is often employed in music for the Pianoforte) there is little or no difficulty involved in a succession of chords of the 6th, provided that the above direction is followed; in four-part harmony the 6th should still be placed at the top, and the 6th and 3rd (or 3rd and 6th) doubled alternately in the middle parts. Thus, if example (*b*) were to be arranged for four *real* parts, the passage would conveniently take this form—

Lack of care in this matter of doubling will almost inevitably cause faulty part-writing, *e.g.*—

13. As for the present we are concerned only with the inversions of the three Primary triads, the progression that will need the most care in these respects is that between the first inversion of the Sub-dominant and Dominant chords of the major key,* *e.g.*—

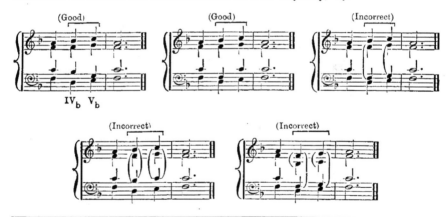

* Obviously this progression cannot so well be taken in the minor key, owing to the augmented 2nd between the 6th and 7th degrees of the scale :—

N.B.—The faults, it will be seen, arise in every instance from neglect of the directions given in Sec. 12. The following is, however, good :—

V$_b$ IV$_b$

14. The following succession of chords, viz., V$_b$ to IV, should be avoided ;—

(Bad)   (Good)   (Good)

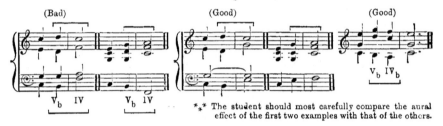

V$_b$ IV   V$_b$ IV   V$_b$ IV$_b$

⁎ The student should most carefully compare the aural effect of the first two examples with that of the others.

EXERCISES ON THE FIRST INVERSION OF THE PRIMARY TRIADS.

A. Play, as isolated chords, the first inversion of any of the three Primary triads in various keys—first in *three* parts, *e.g.*—  and afterwards in *four* parts, *e.g.*—

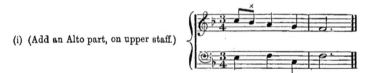

B.. Complete the following passages, as directed.

⁎ Where any doubt could exist as to the use of a direct chord or of a 1st inversion, the latter is indicated by a Roman numeral followed by (b), *e.g.*— I$_b$ = 1st inversion of Tonic triad.

(i) (Add an Alto part, on upper staff.)

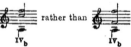

N.B.—When harmony is in 3 parts only, the inner part may leap more freely than in the case of 4-part writing. A chord in its first inversion usually sounds best when all its notes are present, *e.g.*—

rather than

IV$_b$ IV$_b$

(ii) (Add an Alto part, on upper staff.)

(iii) (4 vocal parts.)

N.B.—An accidental under a bass-note signifies that the 3rd from that bass-note is to have a similar accidental.

(iv) (3 parts.)

(v) (4 parts.)

(vi) (3 and 4 parts, as indicated.)

No Tenor here.   Add Tenor.

C. Write a melodious treble to the following figured and unfigured basses. Introduce occasional passing-notes.

(i) (3 parts only.)

6   6
6

× Passing-note, not to be harmonized.

(ii) (4 parts.)

(iii) (4 parts.)

D. Insert suitable first inversions at the asterisks. Take care that the bass moves smoothly and melodiously.

(i) (3 parts.)

(ii) (4 parts.)

₊ Play each of the above exercises also in the Tonic minor key.

E. Improve the following passages, modifying the position of some of the chords by the use of 1st inversions, so as to produce a more melodious bass-part. Do not alter the melody of the top part.

(Example.)   (Improved version.)

(i)   (ii)

F. Harmonize the following melodies, using the three Primary triads (either in "root position" or in their first inversion, as you deem suitable). Take care that the bass runs melodiously.

(i) To be played in 4 parts, for the Pianoforte, and in various keys and times :—

$3 \quad 4 \quad 3 \quad 2 \quad 3$; $3^{1} \quad 2^{1} \quad 3^{1} \quad 8 \quad 8 \quad 7 \quad 8$; $3 \quad 2 \quad 4 \quad 3$;

$5 \quad 4 \quad 6 \quad 5$; $3 \quad 5 \quad 2 \quad 3$; $1 \quad 2 \quad 3 \quad 4 \quad 5 \quad 6 \quad 5$.

(ii) *In 3 parts only.* Try to make not only the bass but the middle part melodically interesting :—

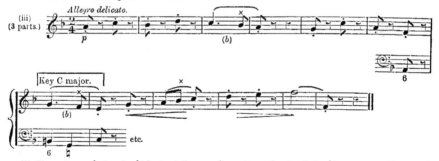

(a) Use the Tonic chord in root-position for both these notes, changing the position of the middle voice, so as to complete the final chord.

(b) The notes marked ✕ should be treated as passing-notes, and a chord should occur upon the second beat of the bar as well as upon the first, in order to maintain the necessary movement during the time that the melody-note on the first beat is prolonged into the second. The dot in each case produces somewhat of the effect of a syncopation, the two passages being equivalent to

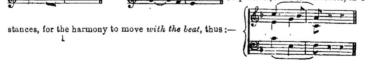

and respectively. It is advisable, in such in-

stances, for the harmony to move *with the beat*, thus :—

x Passing-note.

N.B.—Think of this exercise as written for the Pianoforte (mostly in 4 parts). Use *one* harmony in each bar, shifting the position of the middle notes of the chords when necessary. Remember that the modern Valse is virtually in $\frac{6}{4}$ time, two bars as written really making *one* bar as heard in performance, thus :—  etc. The varying weight of the *written* bars is indicated by the signs — and ⌣, respectively signifying a stronger and a weaker bar.

Begin the harmonization like this :—

maintaining the Valse-like accompaniment in the R.H. part throughout. Take care to make the bass smooth and melodious ; the middle parts should move as quietly as possible, it is not necessary that they should possess definite melodic interest in a case such as this.

(v.) Harmonize the following in broken chords (as indicated in the first bar), using the harmonies implied by the Roman numerals :—

G. Play and write the following progressions (in four parts). Work each exercise in more than one key, and change the melody in so doing. Try to invent broken-chord formations upon the harmonic schemes.

I V_b I ; I IV_b I ; I I_b IV IV_b I ;

V_b I IV I_b ; I IV_b V_b I ; I V_b IV_b I IV V I .

(In major key only.)

H. Harmonize these basses (figured and unfigured), using Primary triads and their 1st inversions. Make the treble as melodious as possible, and work in both 3-part and 4-part harmony.

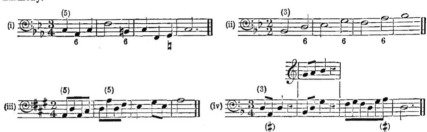

N.B.—Work the following exercise in the form of a Waltz for the Pianoforte, keeping to one harmony in each bar, but endeavouring to ornament the melody with occasional passing-notes. The figure described as the "Mordent" in Chapter III., Sec. 4, will be found useful (*see* bar 3). The indications given above the staff as to the length of the melody-notes should be adhered to:—

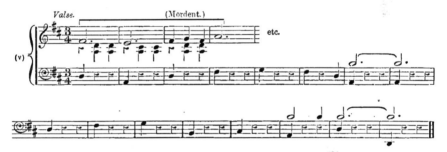

I. Improvise rhythmical sentences at the Pianoforte, using the material already studied. Try to decorate the melody of the top part by means of "arpeggio" figures and occasional passing-notes.

** In working the "numeral" exercises in succeeding chapters, any chord may be repeated (if necessary), in order to produce a successful rhythmic scheme. The order of the chords must, however, not be altered. Examples of such repetition will be afforded by the following renderings of the last exercise in Sec. G on page 90:—

When a chord is thus repeated, the repetition should occur upon a *weaker* beat (*see* page 82, Sec. 6).

CHAPTER XII.

THE INVERSIONS OF THE PRIMARY TRIADS—*(Contd.).*

THE SECOND INVERSION.

1. THE second inversion of a triad differs materially in its effect from the root position or the first inversion of that triad. If the following passage be played, and a pause made on each of the chords marked respectively (*a*), (*b*), and (*c*), it will be noticed that, whereas the ear rests comfortably at (*a*) and (*c*), the chord at (*b*) seems imperatively to demand some other chord to succeed it :—

This impression is strengthened the longer this chord is dwelt upon, or the oftener it is repeated, *e.g.*—

THE CADENTIAL "SIX-FOUR" CHORD.

2. The desire of the second inversion of a triad to move onward in this way, renders it specially suitable for certain situations in the course of a phrase, and the most familiar of these is found where the Tonic chord is taken in the second inversion, just before the Perfect cadence, and where it gives the necessary feeling of impulse forward, and keeps the interest alive. Compare the good effect of the second inversion at (*a*) with the halting lameness of the *direct* Tonic triad at (*b*) ;—

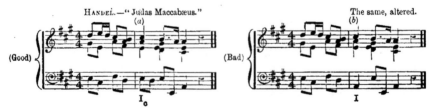

3. The following extract from Beethoven illustrates the use of the same chord at an Imperfect (or Half) cadence * :—

₊ See also "On the banks of Allan Water," (page 81).

4. A second inversion is frequently spoken of as a "chord of the six-four," from the fact that the intervals of the chord counted upwards from its bass-note are respectively a 6th and a 4th, (compare Chapter XI, Sec. 9); and when it is used at or near a cadence, the second inversion of the Tonic chord † is usually termed a "cadential $\frac{6}{4}$."

N.B.—In a figured-bass, the figures $\frac{6}{4}$ therefore indicate the 2nd inversion of a triad.

5. The best note to double in any $\frac{6}{4}$ chord is its *bass-note*. The doubling of either of the other notes of the chord is not satisfactory in four-part writing :—

(Good)   (Poor)

6. As the "Cadential $\frac{6}{4}$" is very frequently followed by a direct common chord on the same bass-note or its octave, the smoothest progression is usually produced by doubling the bass-note

---

* This form of Imperfect cadence is usually described as a "Feminine ending," and is produced when a note of the Dominant chord in the melody is delayed in its appearance, and thrown on to a weaker part of the bar, by a note of the Tonic harmony being taken *upon* the accent. The two notes are then usually slurred, thus :

(Feminine ending.)

(1)

The above progression is virtually a "decorated" form of :—

(Masculine ending.)

(2)

If I, or I_b, be substituted for I_c in Example No. 1 above, it will be noticed that the special "persuasiveness" of the Feminine ending will be completely ruined.

† The "six-four" upon the Dominant *bass.*

of the $\frac{6}{4}$ (as stated above), and by allowing the other two parts to proceed downwards by step The doubled bass-note of the $\frac{6}{4}$ then remains to form part of the next chord, *e.g.*—

7. The "Cadential $\frac{6}{4}$" should not be placed at a weaker part of the bar than the chord that follows it :—

PRELIMINARY EXERCISES ON THE "CADENTIAL $\frac{6}{4}$."

A. Play, as isolated chords, the second inversion of the Tonic triad in various keys—first in three parts, *e.g.*—(Key C.)  and afterwards in four parts, *e.g.*—

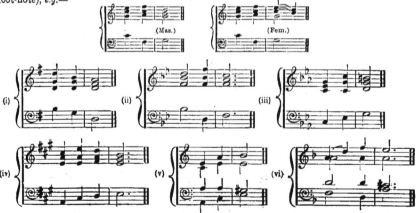

(Key C.)

B. Convert the following "Masculine" Imperfect cadences into "Feminine" ones, by the use of the "Cadential $\frac{6}{4}$" upon the strong beat of the second bar, as described on page 93 (foot-note), *e.g.*—

C. Harmonize the following phrase-endings in various keys and times, introducing the " Cadential $\frac{6}{4}$ " at the suitable places. (*N.B.*—These are indicated, in the first two exercises, by a *). Bear carefully in mind the direction in Sec. 7 above.

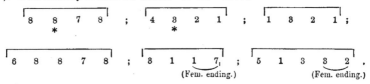

D. Harmonize the following melody for the Pianoforte, continuing as indicated, and introducing the " Cadential $\frac{6}{4}$ " where suitable.*

---

* It will be seen that the harmony in this exercise is arranged in a " broken " form, the middle part (in quavers) virtually supplying the place of *two* voice-parts in vocal writing. The first two bars are clearly another version of:—

In Pianoforte-music such " broken-chord " formations are very frequent, as will readily be perceived on reference to any standard works. The movement of the chords should be carried out for the present just *as accurately as if the parts were written in unbroken harmony;* such a progression as the following should not be tolerated on any account:—

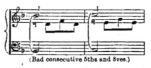

(Bad consecutive 5ths and 8ves.)

In the treatment of the concluding cadence, however, the Leading-note may fall, in order to preserve the shape of the accompaniment figure, thus:—

E. Harmonize the following phrase-endings for the Piano. Arrange each example in some suitable time and rhythm, especially bearing in mind the direction as to the rhythmic position of the $\frac{6}{4}$ chord, mentioned in Sec. 7 above. Play each exercise in various major and minor keys, and make the highest part as melodious as possible.

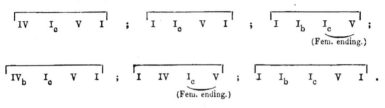

IV I_c V   I   ;   I I_c V   I   ;   I I_b I_c V   ;

(Fem. ending.)

IV_b I_c V   I   ;   I   IV I_c V   ;   I I_b I_c V   I   .

(Fem. ending.)

THE PASSING "SIX-FOUR" CHORD.

8. Second inversions may be taken otherwise than cadentially, as will be seen from the following examples:—

MOZART.—Sonata in C (No. 2).

Andante. ×

(1)

V_c etc.

Grave. BEETHOVEN.—Sonata in C minor (Op. 13).
×

(2)   etc.

V_c

MENDELSSOHN.—Variations in B flat (Op. 83).
Andante.

(3) (Key F.)   etc.

I_c I_c

In each of the above instances, it will be noticed, the bass-note of the $\frac{6}{4}$ chord is quitted *by the step of a 2nd.* The chord is then usually termed a "Passing $\frac{6}{4}$."

9. The "Passing $\frac{6}{4}$" is perhaps most frequently found upon the 2nd degree of the scale, forming the second inversion of the *D*ominant triad* (*see* Examples 1 and 2 in Sec. 8 above), but is also met with upon the 5th degree, producing the second inversion of the Tonic triad (*see* Example 3 above). In either case, the student is for the present advised to restrict its use to those cases where both the bass and the top part move by step to and from it *in contrary motion to one another, e.g.*—

N.B.—Unlike the "cadential $\frac{6}{4}$" "the Passing $\frac{6}{4}$" may occur at either a stronger or a weaker part of the bar than the chord which follows it (*see* particularly the examples in Sec. 8).

10. It is not good to approach any $\frac{6}{4}$ chord *by leap* :—

except (i) from a chord in its *root* position :—

(ii) from the *first* inversion of its own chord, *e.g.*—

---

* The second inversion of the Dominant triad cannot be followed by a chord on the same bass-note with good effect :—

† Note that the use (as here) of the $\frac{6}{4}$ chord on the strong accent, after another position of the same chord on the preceding weaker beat, constitutes one of the rare exceptions to the rule in Chap. XI, Sec. 6.

PRELIMINARY EXERCISES ON THE "PASSING $\frac{6}{4}$."

F. Memorize the following progressions, and play them in all keys, major and minor:—

N.B.—Arrange the above progressions also in Open Vocal harmony in four parts, thus:—

G. Complete the following passages, by adding two middle parts as indicated. *N.B.*—The use of the "Passing $\frac{6}{4}$" is, in the first two exercises, denoted by a Roman numeral.

(i) Add Alto and Tenor voice-parts.

(ii) For Piano; add two parts in R.H.

(iii) (For Piano; add one part in each hand.)

(iv) (Add one part in each hand.)

(Play this also in *D* minor.)

(Play also in E minor.)

H. (i) Play, and write from memory, the following progressions in various keys, arranging them in different times and rhythms. Use both "close" and "extended" positions :—

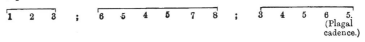

(ii) Harmonize the following melody-notes in a similar manner, introducing the "Passing $\frac{6}{4}$" where suitable :—

MELODIES AND BASSES INCLUDING "CADENTIAL" AND "PASSING" SECOND INVERSIONS.

I. Harmonize the following melodies, introducing examples of both "Passing" and "Cadential" second inversions, where you deem the effect would be good.

(i)  (Also in C minor.)

(ii) (Also in F minor.)

(iii) (Also in *D* major.)

(iv)  (Also in B major.)

(*a*) The rule in Sec. 6 as to the movement of the parts cannot be observed here.

(**v**)

N.B.—The chords in this exercise should not move more rapidly than the beats (*i.e.*, in crotchets). At (*b*) consecutive 8ves (by *contrary* motion) between the Treble and the Bass will be necessary. They are always of good effect when the melody of the Cadence proceeds from Dominant to Tonic, as here.

---

x Passing-note : not to be harmonized.　　　‡ Use one chord (minim) for these two slurred notes.

For String Quartet.

Begin the above exercise as follows, and make occasional use of the little melodic figure at (*x*) ;—

(*See* Appendix E.)

(vii) Harmonize the following for the Pianoforte, continuing as indicated in the opening bars. (*See* note to Exercise *D* on page 95).

N.B.—In the following melody, harmonize in 4 parts only where indicated by the small notes under the staff.

J. Harmonize the following Basses (figured and unfigured), using only the Primary triads and their inversions. Insert occasional Passing-notes in the Melody.

₊ Exercises (i) to (iv) should be worked for four *voice-parts.*

(*a*) and (*b*) The second quaver of these groups is to be regarded as a passing-note. In a Figured Bass, lines of continuation (as here) signify that the same harmony is to be retained or repeated as long as the lines last, *e.g.*—

(v) Complete this exercise as indicated, using sometimes 3-part and sometimes 4-part harmony. Do not harmonize with chords shorter than crotchets :—

---

* One of the comparatively rare uses of the Subdominant chord in the second inversion, forming a Feminine ending somewhat similar in construction to that produced by the progression I$_c$ V. In the present case the 6th from the bass should be slurred down to the 5th, and the 4th to the 3rd, while the key-note is held in the Treble and Bass. It is worthy of note that the only case in which one second inversion can, as a rule, follow another successfully is found where V$_c$ proceeds to IV$_c$, thus :—

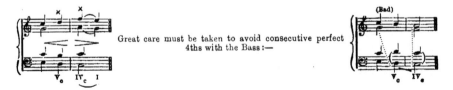

Great care must be taken to avoid consecutive perfect
4ths with the Bass :—

(vi) Harmonize the following Bass as indicated, endeavouring to continue the melody in the style suggested by the opening bars :—

K. Improvise rhythmical sentences at the Pianoforte, illustrating the use of both "Cadential" and "Passing" six-fours. Decorate the melody of your examples with occasional Passing-notes and broken-chord formations.

$*_*$ Remember that the only *leap* possible to the bass of a $\frac{6}{4}$ chord is that of an 8ve. (*see* conclusion of Ex. ii of Sec. J), unless it is followed by another position of the same chord.

---

* The A and F♯ are accented passing-notes.

CHAPTER XIII.

THE SECONDARY TRIADS OF THE MAJOR OR MINOR KEY.

1. THE triads hitherto considered (viz., I, IV and V) form, so to speak, the staple or back-bone of the key, and many comparatively straightforward melodies may be harmonized effect-ively with these chords alone (either in root position, or inverted). In many cases, however, their exclusive use produces a certain squareness of effect, and other chords whose character dominates the key rather less strongly are needed for variety and relief.

2. These chords—Secondary triads, as they are frequently called—occur upon the 2nd, 3rd, 6th and 7th degrees of the scale, as will be seen by the following examples :—

*** The Secondary triads are printed in black-headed notes.

Of these four, those on the Supertonic and Submediant are by far the most important and useful, and for the present the employment of these will be considered exclusively.

THE SUPERTONIC TRIAD.

3. The Supertonic chord (II) is most valuable in harmonization. In the major form of the key it is a *minor triad*, and in the minor form of the key a *diminished triad*, and as the effect of both of these is vaguer and less direct than that of the Primary triads, it will be found that in both cases the Supertonic triad most usually *leads up to* one of the stronger chords, *e.g.* that of the Dominant :—

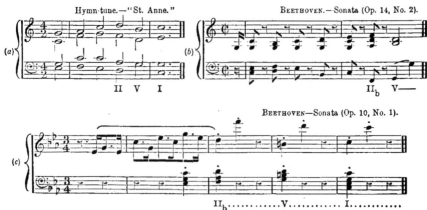

4. The fact of the Supertonic chord leading so well to the Dominant chord causes it to be particularly appropriate *just before a Cadence*, as in the foregoing extracts. In such a case, it may be used equally well to precede the " Cadential $\frac{6}{4}$ " *e.g.*—

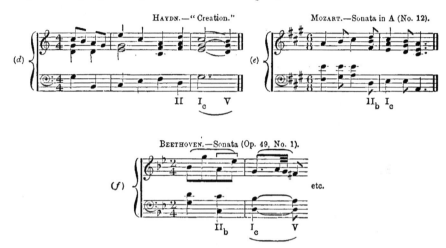

5. The examples in Secs. 3 and 4 above shew that the Supertonic triad in a major key may be used either in root-position (as in Exs. (*a*) and (*d*)), or in its first inversion (as in Exs. (*b*) and (*e*)). In the minor key, however, it is seldom taken in any other form than the first inversion (Exs. (*c*) and (*f*)), the effect of a Diminished triad in root-position being rarely satisfactory.*

6. When the Supertonic triad (in either form of a key) is taken in the first inversion, its *bass-note* may be freely doubled, particularly when it leads to a cadence (*see* above examples). In this connexion, the following general directions as to doubling in the case of chords of the 6th may prove useful :—

(*a*) The bass-note of the first inversion of a *major* triad should *not* be doubled ; †

(*b*) In the case of a *minor* triad, the bass-note of its first inversion may often be doubled with good effect (especially in the case of II_b in a major key) ;

(*c*) The bass-note of the first inversion of a *diminished* triad (*e.g.* II_b in a minor key) is usually the *best* note to double.

---

* Compare the good effect of :—  with the crudeness of —

† Exceptions to this will be considered at a later stage.

THE SUBMEDIANT TRIAD.

7. The Submediant chord is far more frequently found in root-position than in an inverted form. It is particularly useful for the purpose of avoiding the monotony of too much Tonic harmony, and the 1st or the 3rd degree of the scale can often be harmonized effectively by its means, instead of by some position of the Tonic chord. It then frequently forms the final chord in an "Interrupted Cadence," (*i.e.*, a cadence in which some other chord than that of the Tonic follows the Dominant at the end of a phrase), *e.g.*—

BEETHOVEN.—Sonata (Op. 10, No. 3).

The following example illustrates the use of the Submediant chord to harmonize both the 1st and 3rd degrees of the scale :—

MENDELSSOHN.—"Elijah."

8. In the great majority of instances the Submediant chord sounds best with its 3rd (and not its root) doubled * (*see* the two preceding extracts), and it is often difficult to obtain a smooth and musical movement of the parts in any other way :—

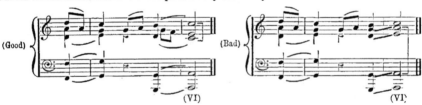

In the minor form of the key, the need for this doubling of the 3rd instead of the root is virtually imperative when VI follows, or is followed by, V, to avoid some bad fault of part-writing :—

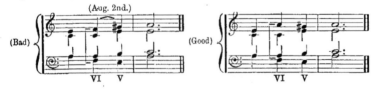

---

* The 3rd is the strong (Tonic) note of the scale.

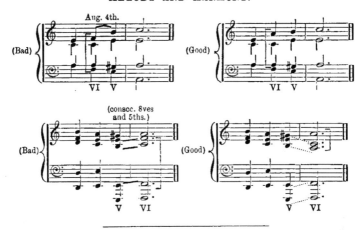

PRELIMINARY EXERCISES UPON THE USE OF THE SUPERTONIC AND SUBMEDIANT CHORDS.

A. Play, as isolated chords, the Supertonic and Submediant triads (in root-position and in first inversion), in various major and minor keys. Play these chords both in 3 parts, *e.g.*—

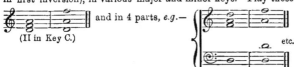

and in 4 parts, *e.g.*—

B. Play the following passages, inserting a suitable chord at each asterisk :—

C. Introduce the Supertonic chord (either in root-position or 1st inversion, as you deem suitable) at (*a*), and the Submediant chord (in root-position) at (*b*), in each of the following exercises :—

D. Play (and write from memory) the following progressions, in various major and minor keys. Make the treble part melodious, and give more than one version of each :—

$$\text{II}_b \quad \text{V} \quad \text{I} \quad ; \quad \text{II}_b \quad \text{I}_c \quad \text{V} \quad \text{I} \quad ; \quad \text{II}_b \quad \text{I}_c \quad \text{V} \quad \text{VI} \quad ;$$

$$\text{I} \quad \text{II}_b \quad \text{I}_c \quad \text{V} \quad ; \quad \text{I} \quad \text{VI} \quad \text{II}_b \quad \text{V} \quad \text{I} \quad .$$
(Fem. ending.)

N.B.—The following are to be worked in the major form of the key only :—

$$\text{I} \quad \text{I}_b \quad \text{IV} \quad \text{II} \quad \text{V} \quad ; \quad \text{I} \quad \text{VI} \quad \text{II} \quad \text{I}_c \quad \text{V} \quad \text{I} \quad .$$

MELODIES AND BASSES INCLUDING THE SUPERTONIC AND SUBMEDIANT CHORDS.

E. Harmonize the following melodies, introducing the Supertonic * and Submediant chords where suitable. (Use the Submediant chord, as yet, only in its root-position.)

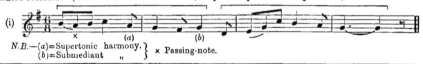

N.B.—(a)=Supertonic harmony.⎫
(b)=Submediant „ ⎬ × Passing-note.

---

* Observe that the presence of the 2nd degree of the scale in a melody does not usually imply Supertonic *harmony*, unless it comes just before a cadence (where it is frequently indispensable). Otherwise, some form of Dominant harmony is needed, *e.g.*—

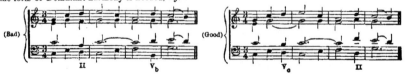

x Passing-note.

Note.—In the next two exercises passing-notes are more freely employed, and several instances of the "Mordent" figure are introduced.

* The apparent "consecutive 5ths" in the Left hand part of the two final chords are quite justifiable in Pianoforte writing, (*See* Appendix B.)

F. Harmonize the following Figured and Unfigured Basses. Make the highest part of the harmony as melodious as possible.

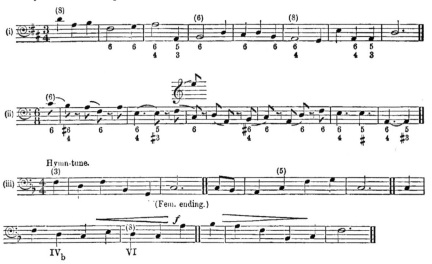

Hymn-tune.

(Fem. ending.)

Add two upper parts for the Right hand (in crotchets) to the following Left-hand part :—

(iv)
(For Piano.)

G. Improvise rhythmical sentences, illustrating the use of II and VI. Decorate the melody with passing-notes and broken-chord formations.

CHAPTER XIV.

THE SECONDARY TRIADS OF THE MAJOR OR MINOR KEY (*Cont*^d.).*

1. In the preceding chapter the more familiar and obvious uses of the Supertonic and Submediant harmonies have been considered, and it is most essential that a clear grasp of these should be obtained at this stage. There are, however, many other ways in which these chords may be introduced ; but as they are the weaker chords of the key, their indiscriminate employment tends to produce a certain vagueness of tonality :—

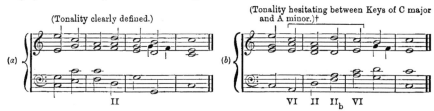

In most cases the best effect is obtained where the Secondary triads are judiciously blended with the stronger Primary chords (I, IV and V) and their inversions (*see* Ex. (*a*) above).

2. The following extracts will shew some further typical and effective uses of the Supertonic and Submediant harmonies :—

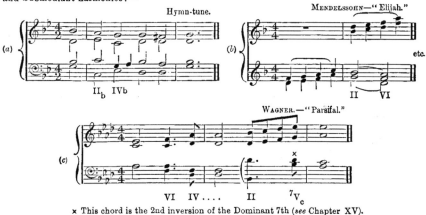

x This chord is the 2nd inversion of the Dominant 7th (*see* Chapter XV).

----

* *Note.* This Chapter may, at the discretion of the teacher, be deferred until Chapter XV (on the chord of the Dominant 7th) has been studied.

† The force of this remark will be realized more fully if the passage be played a second time with the following chords—

substituted for the two chords of the cadence; by this means it will be felt that the chords within the ⌐——⌐ might just as well belong to A minor as to C major. At times, of course, this very vagueness of tonality might be a distinct merit (*see* Chapter XIX on "Modulation ") ; everything would depend upon the context.

3. In connexion with the previous remarks, the following hints may be of service to the student :—

(i) A triad in direct position rarely proceeds well to another *direct* triad whose root is a 3rd higher :—

(ii) When roots ascend or descend by the interval of a 4th or 5th, or where they *descend* by the interval of a 3rd, the progressions are invariably effective and strong. (*See particularly* Exs. (*b*) and (*c*) in Sec. 2.)

THE TRIADS UPON THE MEDIANT AND LEADING-NOTE.

4. The remaining triads of either major or minor key (viz. III and VII) are of less frequent occurrence. The latter, being a diminished triad, is of little practical value in its direct position— but is decidedly useful in its first inversion, when it can often be employed effectively in places where *Dominant* harmony would be good (chiefly in harmonizing either the 2nd or 7th of the scale in the course of a melody) * *e.g.*—

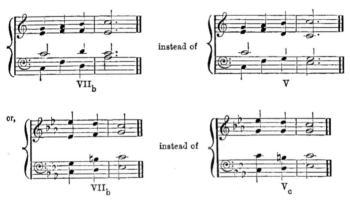

_____

* The ending with which the student is already familiar in his early two-part studies, is

of course an incomplete form of and provides a perfect cadence of an almost equally

emphatic nature as the more usual

The following is a familiar instance of its use :—

N.B.—In the majority of cases, it is best to double the bass-note of VII$_b$ (*see* Chap. XIII, Sec. 6 (*c*)).

and the two notes forming the diminished 5th (or its inversion, the augmented 4th) should usually *move by step.*

5. The chord of the Mediant (III) differs materially in effect in the two forms of a key. In the major mode it is a concordant (minor) triad, *e.g.*—(In C major.) but its introduction requires a good deal of care, and the student whose ear is not keenly alive to the niceties of musical effect will be in danger of many crudities if he uses it indiscriminately. It is generally safer for the beginner to avoid it *after* any chord containing the 4th degree of the scale :—

(All crude)

6. If it can be followed by a chord whose root is a 4th above (or 5th below) its own root, that is, by *Submediant* harmony, its effect is quite good :—

and it is useful in certain cases to harmonize the Leading-note in a melody descending scale-wise from the key-note, thus :—

7. In the minor mode of the key, the Mediant chord contains an augmented 5th from the

root, *e.g.*—(In C minor.) 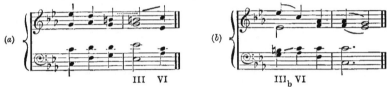 and as a consequence is a *dissonant* (augmented)

triad, requiring to be followed in a certain definite way. Its most frequent progression is (as in the case of III in the major key) to a chord whose root is a 4th above its own, *i.e.*, the Sub-mediant chord (VI), the augmented 5th *rising a semitone* to the 3rd of that chord, *e.g.*—

         III VI   III$_b$ VI

N.B.—The fixed progression of a discord is termed its *resolution*. In many cases the Mediant triad of a minor key can be introduced more effectively if the augmented 5th of the chord is *prepared* (*i.e.*, sounded as a concord in the preceding harmony, in the same "voice" or part. This is not actually necessary, but it often tends to produce a smoother and more musical result. The first example (*a*) above illustrates this "preparation" of the dissonance.*

8. With regard to the first inversion of the Secondary triads, it is useful to remember that

(i) In most cases the best effect is produced when the bass-note is quitted by step, *e.g.*—

    VI$_b$ II$_b$ III$_b$ III$_b$ VI$_b$

(ii) The first inversion of these triads usually sounds best with the 6th from the bass-note as the highest note of the chord :—

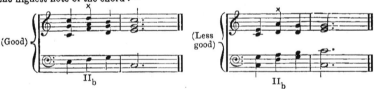

              II$_b$ II$_b$

* It will be remembered that the Supertonic chord in a minor key is a diminished triad, and as a consequence, *dissonant* in its root-position. It is hardly ever met with in this form, but if it is so used, it resolves (like the Mediant triad) upon a chord whose root is a 4th above its own (*i.e.*, upon the Dominant), *e.g.*—

         II V

the diminished 5th *falling* a semitone to the root of that chord. It is usually better to "prepare" the dissonant 5th, as above. In the first inversion this chord may be treated practically with the freedom of a concord, (*see* Chap. XIII, Sec. 5).

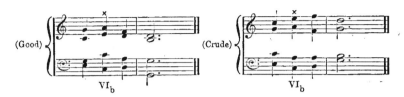

9. Although Secondary triads in the *second* inversion may occasionally be introduced with good results, the chances of their use *as chords within the key* are extremely rare. In this inversion they usually suggest very strongly the idea of a modulation, and the $\overset{6}{_4}$ chord gives the impression of I_c in the new key, *e.g.*—

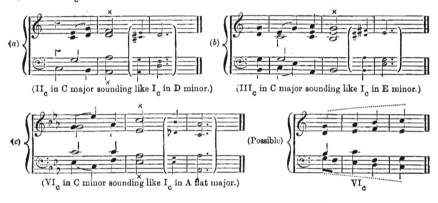

(II$_c$ in C major sounding like I$_c$ in D minor.)   (III$_c$ in C major sounding like I$_c$ in E minor.)

(VI$_c$ in C minor sounding like I$_c$ in A flat major.)   (Possible) VI$_c$

EXERCISES UPON THE FURTHER USE OF THE SECONDARY TRIADS OF THE MAJOR OR MINOR KEY.

A. Play, as isolated chords (both in 3 parts and 4 parts), the Secondary triads specially considered in this Chapter (viz., III, III$_b$ and VII$_b$), in both major and minor keys.

B. Play the following passages, inserting a suitable chord at each asterisk :—

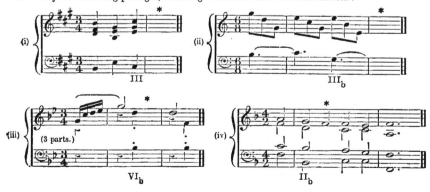

(Follow this chord in three different ways.)

N.B.—Continue the following passage in a descending Sequence, as suggested. Indicate the harmonies by Roman numerals ;—

C. Play (and write from memory) the following progressions, in various keys. Make the treble part melodious.

(a) Major keys only. $\overline{\text{I V III VI}}$; $\overline{\text{VI}_b \text{ II V}_b \text{ I}}$; $\overline{\text{III}_b \text{ VI II}_b \text{ V I}_b}$; .

$\overline{\text{I IV VII}_b \text{ VI}}$; $\overline{\text{I VII}_b \text{ I}_b}$; $\overline{\text{IV VII}_b \text{ I}}$.

(b) Minor keys only. $\overline{\text{I V III VI}}$; $\overline{\text{III}_b \text{ VI II}_b \text{ V I}}$; $\overline{\text{VI}_b \text{ V}_b \text{ I}}$;

$\overline{\text{I}_b \text{ IV II V I}}$.

---

* Remember that this is a dissonant (augmented) triad.

†   ,,   ,,   ,,   ,,   (diminished) triad.

D. Harmonize the following melodies, introducing Secondary triads where suitable. In the first two exercises these are indicated by the Roman numerals.

N.B.—Notes or rests underneath the staff are directions as to the length of the accompanying chords.

N.B.—(Except in the passage in three parts, do not harmonize more quickly than the crotchet pulse in the following exercise.)

x Passing-note.

† Accented passing-note; the chord taken against it should be one that harmonizes the *following* note.

E. Harmonize the following basses (figured and unfigured) :—

F. Improvisation at the keyboard to illustrate the resources of this chapter.

× Passing-note.

Concluding Note.

By the light of the harmonic knowledge now in his possession, the student should have no difficulty in fully realizing the chord-basis of the intervals he has been using in his two-part melodic studies. He should carefully analyse many of those he has already worked; the analysis of the examples given below will shew the method to be adopted.

(Chapter IV., Sec. 2.)

(Chapter III., Sec. 8.)

N.B.—The following hints are useful :—

    (a) The Mediant *bass* almost invariably implies Tonic harmony, I_b not III ;

    (b) The Leading-note *bass* always implies Dominant harmony, V_b not VII ;

    (c) The Supertonic *bass* (in a *minor key*) implies Leading-note harmony, VII_b not II.

The reasons for the above should be clear if the contents of this chapter have been mastered.

· Direction to Teacher and Student.

Although, in future chapters, Improvisation to illustrate the various subjects that are being studied is **not always specifically** indicated, such practice at the keyboard should invariably accompany all other **forms of exercise.**

CHAPTER XV.

THE CHORD OF THE *DOMINANT* SEVENTH.

1. The chord of the *Dominant* 7th consists of the common chord of the *Dominant* of either major or minor key, with the 7th from the root added, the chord being identical in both forms of the key, *e.g.*—

2. If the chord be analysed, it will be found to contain two dissonant intervals, each of which adds considerably to the expectant and inconclusive feeling of the *Dominant* triad, to which allusion was made on page 65. These dissonant intervals are :—

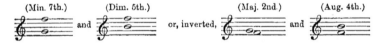

3. The *Dominant* 7th chord most frequently resolves upon Tonic or Submediant harmony, and its two most characteristic notes (the 3rd and the 7th of the chord) then always move *by step*, the 3rd rising a semitone to the key-note, and the 7th falling a semitone in the major form of the key, and a tone in the minor form ;—

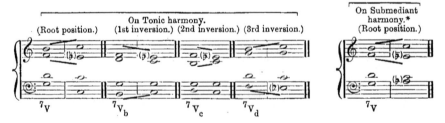

N.B.—The flats in brackets shew the resolution in the Minor form of the key. Notice that the 3rd of the *Submediant* harmony is always doubled—not the root (*see* page 106).

---

* The inversions rarely resolve on Submediant harmony; the following, however, are possible :—

4. The root position of the Dominant 7th chord, resolving upon *Tonic* harmony, is not often used save at a Perfect cadence, for the reason that its effect is so conclusive and final, *e.g.*—

BEETHOVEN.—Sonata (Op. 26).

It is, however, very effective—even in non-cadential positions—when resolved upon *Submediant* harmony, *e.g.*—

BEETHOVEN.—Sonata (Op. 53).

Key E major.   C♯ minor.   etc.

Interrupted Cadence.

** This resolution, in the form of an Interrupted Cadence, will also be found in the example from Beethoven on page 106.

5. The inversions may be freely introduced in the course of a phrase, and are often very useful in giving a certain grace and elasticity to the music, *e.g.*—

BEETHOVEN.—Sonata (Op. 14, No. 2).

Key F major.   D minor.   etc.

(*x*) Observe that a perfect 5th may always be followed by a Diminished 5th.

6. From the examples in Sections 3 and 5 it will be seen that the 3rd and 7th of the chord usually move in the same manner in the inversions as in the root-position ; but when (as often

happens) the 2nd inversion of the Dominant 7th proceeds to the first inversion of the Tonic chord, the 7th—instead of falling one degree—*may rise a whole tone*, as in Ex. (*b*) below :—

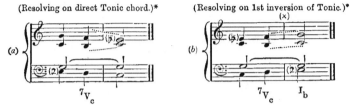

N.B.—The two 5ths at (×) are quite justifiable and of good effect; a diminished 5th may always be followed by a perfect 5th, provided that they do not occur between the *bass* and one of the other parts of the harmony.

The following extract illustrates the effective use of this form of progression :—

Mozart.—Sonata in A.

7. The inversions of the Dominant 7th chord are, further, of considerable value in the preservation of continuity in a musical passage, for by their means it is possible to avoid the too frequent occurrence of direct Perfect cadences. If either (or both) of the chords of a cadence be *inverted*, the effect of conclusion at the end of a phrase is minimized, and the flow of the music is not checked to any appreciable extent, *e.g.*—

* In each resolution, therefore, the best effect is produced when the 7th in the second inversion of the chord *follows the movement of the bass.* If this falls to the root of the Tonic chord, the 7th will also fall ; if it rise to the 3rd of the Tonic chord, the 7th will rise in like manner. The following is, however, possible :—

the doubling of the bass of the major chord of the 6th being justified by the movement to and from the doubled note by step, in contrary motion.

These so-called Inverted cadences are obviously of considerable value at the less emphatic rhythmic points in the course of a passage, and Beethoven in the following instance has most effectively postponed his final *direct* Perfect cadence by their use :—

DIRECTIONS AS TO PART-WRITING.

8.   If the chord of the *Dominant* 7th in its root-position resolves upon the Tonic chord in *its* root-position, the 5th of one or the other chord will—in *four-part* writing—have to be omitted and the root doubled, *e.g.*—

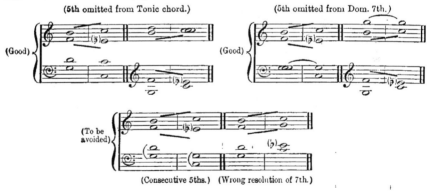

N.B.—In fuller harmony, such as is often found in Pianoforte music, this restriction does not apply, *e.g.*—

(5th in both chords.)

In the resolution upon Submediant harmony, *both* chords should be complete, *e.g.*—

VI

9. In the inversions, it is rarely desirable to omit any note of either the *Dominant 7th* chord or its resolution ;* the root of the *Dominant* 7th acts as a " binding-tone " between the two ;—

10. The notes requiring resolution (viz., the 3rd and 7th), may be transferred from part to part, provided that they resolve regularly in the parts in which they last appear, *e.g.*—

BEETHOVEN.—Sonata (Op. 10, No. 2).

etc.

$^{7}V_d$ $^{7}V_b$ $^{7}V_c$ ^{7}V

11. At times, also, the 3rd or the 7th temporarily disappears from the chord while the Dominant harmony lasts; but whichever note is thus for the moment omitted *must still resolve,* as soon as the harmony changes :—

^{7}V

$^{7}V_b$
(7th temporarily omitted
from second chord.)

$^{7}V_c$
(3rd temporarily omitted
from second chord.)

⁎ The resolutions described in Sections 10 and 11 are often termed Ornamental resolutions.

---

* The older masters, however, usually preferred to write the 2nd inversion of the Dominant 7th *with-out the root,* when the chord became identical with the Diminished triad of the Leading-note, in its 1st inversion. (*See* example from Handel's " Messiah," on page 113.)

12. It is *very rarely* good for two notes standing a 2nd, 7th or 9th apart (*e.g.*, the root and 7th in the chord of the Dominant 7th), to move by similar motion to a unison or an 8ve :—

(Bad)   (Possible)

PRELIMINARY (KEYBOARD) EXERCISES UPON THE CHORD OF THE *DOMINANT* 7TH.

A. Play the chord of the Dominant 7th in various keys (major and minor), and in all positions. Play these chords first in close position (with one hand), thus :— etc.

and afterwards in extended position (with both hands), *e.g.*— etc.

B. Insert a chord at each ×, to resolve the chords of the Dominant 7th satisfactorily. The resolution should be upon some form of Tonic harmony, unless otherwise specified :—

C. Insert a suitable position of the chord of the *Dominant* 7th at each × in the following passage, maintaining the arpeggiated form of accompaniment :—

D. Harmonize the following fragments of melody in various major and minor keys, introducing some *inversion* of the *Dominant* 7th in each, (at the ×) :—

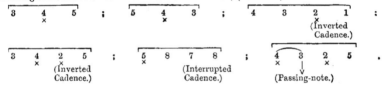

E. Play the following progressions in various major and minor keys:—

$$\text{I} \quad {}^{7}\text{V}_{d} \quad \text{I}_{b} \quad ; \quad \text{VI} \quad \text{II}_{b} \quad {}^{7}\text{V}_{d} \quad \text{I}_{b} \quad ; \quad \text{I} \quad {}^{7}\text{V}_{c} \quad \text{I}_{b} \quad ; \quad \text{I}_{b} \quad {}^{7}\text{V}_{b} \quad \text{I} \quad ;$$

$$\mathbf{^{7}V} \quad \text{VI} \quad \text{IV} \quad \text{I} \quad ; \quad \text{I} \quad \text{II}_{b} \quad {}^{7}\text{V} \quad \text{VI} \quad ; \quad \text{I} \quad {}^{7}\text{V}_{c} \quad {}^{7}\text{V}_{d} \quad \text{I}_{b} \quad .$$

RESOLUTION UPON SUBDOMINANT HARMONY.

13. A less usual diatonic resolution of the chord of the *Dominant* 7th remains yet to be noticed, viz., that upon *an inversion* of the *Subdominant* chord. It is comparatively rare, but can sometimes be introduced with extremely happy results. Generally speaking, it is effective when employed—

(i) To delay the resolution upon Tonic harmony, particularly at a "Feminine" cadence :—

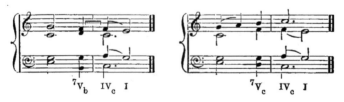

(ii) In passing by step (in the bass) from one to another position of Dominant harmony, *e.g.*—

^7V IV_b ^7V_b ^7V_b IV_c ^7V_c ^7V_c IV_c ^7V_b

N B.—In this form of resolution the 7th *remains* to form part of the Subdominant chord.*

DIRECTION AS TO PART-WRITING.

14. It is not as a rule good for two notes standing a 2nd, 7th, or 9th apart (*e.g.*, the root and 7th in the chord of the Dominant 7th) to proceed by oblique motion to a unison or an 8ve :—

(Undesirable)

⁎⁎ This fault may, unless a certain amount of care is taken, occur in resolving the Dominant 7th upon Subdominant harmony, as in the above examples.

THE *DOMINANT* 7TH IN A FIGURED BASS.

15. In a "figured" bass the Dominant 7th and its inversions appear as follows :—

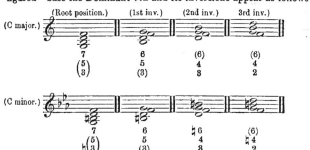

N.B.—The figures in brackets are usually *implied*, and not written out.

---

* The 3rd inversion does not resolve well upon Subdominant harmony :—

(Very crude)

^7V_d IV

PRELIMINARY (KEYBOARD) EXERCISES ON THE RESOLUTION OF THE DOMINANT 7TH UPON SUBDOMINANT HARMONY.

F. Insert a chord in each of the blank spaces, to resolve the Dominant 7th effectively. Introduce the Submediant resolution at (*a*) and the Subdominant resolution at (*b*). The absence of any special indication implies that the chord is to be resolved upon Tonic harmony.

G. Play the following progressions in various major and minor keys :—

$$I_b \quad {}^7V_c \quad IV_c \quad I \quad ; \quad {}^7V_b \quad IV_c \quad {}^7V_c \quad I \quad ; \quad {}^7V_b \quad IV_b \quad {}^7V \quad I \quad ; \quad {}^7V \quad IV_b \quad {}^7V_b \quad I .$$

(Fem. ending.)   (Major key only.)   (Major key only.)

H. Harmonize the following fragments of melody in various major and minor keys, illustrating the Subdominant resolution of the Dominant 7th. (The introduction of the Dominant 7th chord in each passage is indicated by a x).

$$\begin{array}{lll}
2 \quad 7_, \quad 1 \quad ; & 4 \quad 4 \quad 5 \quad 3 \quad ; & 2 \quad 1 \quad 7_, \quad 1 \quad ; & 1 \quad 2 \quad 4 \quad 4 \quad 3 \\
\text{x} & \text{x} & \text{x} \quad\quad \text{x} & \text{x}
\end{array}$$

(Fem.   (Fem.
ending.)   ending.)

MELODIES AND BASSES INCLUDING THE USE OF THE DOMINANT 7TH CHORD AND ITS VARIOUS RESOLUTIONS.

I. Harmonize the following melodies; the places where the Dominant 7th should be introduced are indicated by Roman numerals. (*N.B.*—Passing-notes are not always specified.)

(Tonic resolution only.)

(a) Leave this note unharmonized.

Begin the above exercise thus :—

N.B.—In the following exercise notes within the square brackets are to be left unharmonized. The use of a Dominant 7th is indicated by a ×.

(Including Submediant resolution.)

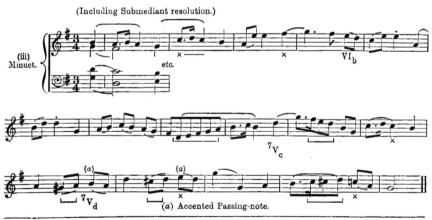

(*a*) Accented Passing-note.

* Passing-note.

(Notes within the square brackets to be left unharmonized.)

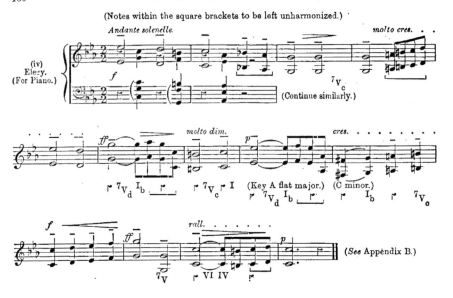

(Including Submediant and Subdominant resolutions.)

N.B.—The × denotes a Dominant 7th.

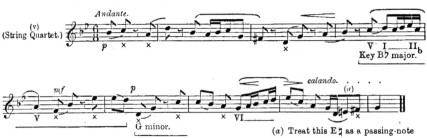

(*a*) Treat this E♮ as a passing-note

Note.—The following exercise is for the Pianoforte. The melody—somewhat in the manner of Haydn—is more or less florid in character, and harmonies should be filled in only where the bass-part is indicated. The desired "density" of the harmony is shewn by the directions "Three parts," "Four parts," etc.

(a) Treat this B as a passing-note.

J. Harmonize these Basses (figured and unfigured) in four parts :—

N.B.—In the next exercise the Dominant 7ths are indicated by a x.

(iv) *Gavotte.* (In this exercise the introduction of the *Dominant* 7th is rarely indicated ; the student must use his own discretion in the matter.   When rests occur in the bass-part, the inner parts of the harmony should be silent for a corresponding period.)

* Accented passing-note.

CHAPTER XVI.

THE HARMONIC ASPECT OF SUSPENSIONS.

1. THE exercises on the use of the tie (Chap. V.) will have shewn that a Suspension is a purely melodic "decoration," and that in no case does it form part of the harmony against which it is sounded. It is, however, customary (and convenient) to describe the relation of Suspensions to the harmony, by naming them according to the distance at which they stand from the *roots* of the various chords against which they are taken.

As it is possible for each of the notes of a triad to be delayed by the note next alphabetically above it, the Suspensions commonly available will clearly be as follows :—

(*a*) Above the root of the chord—the suspended 9th.*
(*b*)   ,,   3rd   ,,   ,,   —   ,,   ,,   4th.
(*c*)   ,,   5th   ,,   ,,   —   ,,   ,,   6th.

2. The following examples will illustrate the delaying of each of the notes of the Tonic common chord of C major (in each of its positions), by the note next above it. It will be seen that this note is sounded *as a concord* in the preceding chord ; this is termed its Preparation. The fourth part of the harmony is given in small notes, so that the examples may be considered from the standpoint of either 3-part or 4-part writing.

(*a*) Root delayed by note above (forming Suspended 9th), which resolves downwards by step :†—

Obviously, the above are merely melodic decorations of the following progressions :—

(*b*) Third delayed by note above (forming Suspended 4th), which resolves downwards by step:—

---

* Not the suspended 2nd. It will be remembered that the Suspension above the root is always taken at the distance of a 9th, thus :—

† Although all these examples are given with reference to the Tonic chord of C major, it should be remembered that Suspensions of the 9th, 4th and 6th may be added to any triad of the key (or an inversion of the same) that is concordant. A Suspension may occur in any part of the harmony ; when it is in the bass, it is usually called the "last inversion "—a not very accurate description.

(*c*) Fifth delayed by note above (forming Suspended 6th), which resolves downwards by step:—

$$I \qquad I_b \qquad I_c \qquad I_c$$

* Compare the examples given in this section with those in Chapter V, Section 5.

3.   Suspensions resolving *upwards* by step are occasionally met with, but they are not often of good effect.*   A notable exception is, however, to be found in the *delaying of the root of the Tonic triad* by the note below, forming what is usually known as the Suspended Leading-note, *e.g.*—

$$I \qquad I_b \qquad I_c \qquad I$$

* Compare the Suspension referred to on page 35 with the above.   The Suspended Leading-note, unlike the other Suspensions, is usually taken only against *Tonic* harmony, and it is best when it resolves upon the first inversion of that chord.   The following form of Suspended Leading-note is, however, occasionally met with:—

———————————————————————————————————

* One or two of these rarer Suspensions (or Retardations, as they are sometimes needlessly called) are given here.   It will be noticed that each is a *semitone* below its resolution;—

(*a*) Third of chord delayed by note *below*:—

(*b*) Fifth of chord delayed by note *below*—

(*c*) Root of chord delayed by note *below*:—

4. Although Suspensions are more frequently tied over from their preparation, it is quite possible for them to be *struck* against the harmony, as in the following example :—

when they have much of the feeling of Appoggiaturas (Chapter XVII). To bear out their special character, however, Suspensions must always be prepared *in the same part*, thus :—

In this last example the high F is, of course, an Appoggiatura and not a Suspension at all.

5. A Suspension, before resolving, may leap (i) to another note of the chord against which it is being sounded (as at (*a*) below), or (ii) to a passing-note (as at (*b*) and (*c*)) :—

N.B.—In the latter case, the passing-note should be at the distance of a 2nd from the resolution-note, upon the opposite side to that of the Suspension.

6. A Suspension, whether tied or not, should not appear at a less-strongly accented part of the bar than its resolution, *e.g.*—

7 When the 7th is added to the Dominant harmony, the Suspensions above the root, 3rd and 5th respectively produce combinations which—as in the case of the Appoggiaturas spoken of in Chap. XVII, Secs. 7 and 8,—are often considered as Dominant 9ths, 11ths and 13ths, *e.g.*—

The actual method of naming them is really immaterial, so long as their treatment and use are thoroughly understood.

PRELIMINARY EXERCISES ON SUSPENSIONS IN HARMONIC WRITING.

A. Analyse, in the light of the foregoing remarks, the following 3-part version of example (*a*) in Chapter V. Sec. 7, naming all the Suspensions in the manner indicated in Secs. 1 and 2 above :—

B. Re-write the following as passages of simple harmony, by removing all the Suspensions occurring in them :—

*** Describe fully all the Suspensions in the above exercises ; (*e.g.* in exercise (i) the combinations at (*x*) and (*y*) respectively would be analysed as VII$_b$ with suspended 9th in Treble, and I$_b$ with suspended 4th in Bass).

C. Introduce Suspensions in any of the parts of the following passages, where you think the effect would be satisfactory. Confine yourself to the Suspensions shewn in Sec. 2 above, and the Suspended Leading-note.

N.B.—The following direction with regard to the introduction and use of Suspensions should be carefully observed:—

A Suspension stands in place of the note upon which it is going to resolve, and it is desirable that this note of resolution should not be sounded at the same time as the Suspension, unless (i) *it appears in the Bass, as at* (c), (d), *and* (e), *or* (ii) *it is approached by step, in contrary motion to the direction of the Suspension, as at* (f) *—an exception to the general rule which is not often effective. In any case, the Suspension and its note of resolution must not appear in the same octave, as at* (g) *below.*

D. Play (and write from memory) the following progressions, adding Suspensions as indicated, at each ×. To be worked both in 3-part and 4-part harmony, and in major and minor keys, unless otherwise specified.

(a) **Suspended 9ths.**

     (i)   In Treble :—

$\text{II}_b \quad \overset{\times}{\text{I}}_c \quad {}^7\text{V} \quad \text{I}$; $\text{I}_b \quad \overset{\times}{\text{IV}} \quad \text{I}_c \quad {}^7\text{V} \quad \text{I}$; $\text{I} \quad \overset{\times}{\text{II}}_b \quad {}^7\text{V} \quad \text{I}$

     (ii)   In Alto :—

$\text{V}_b \quad \overset{\times}{\text{I}} \quad {}^7\text{V} \quad \text{VI}$; $\text{I}_b \quad \overset{\times}{\text{IV}} \quad \text{I}$; $\text{II}_b \quad \overset{\times}{\text{I}}_c \quad {}^7\text{V} \quad \text{I}$

     (iii)   In Tenor :—

$\text{VI} \quad \overset{\times}{\text{II}} \quad \text{V} \quad \text{I}$; $\text{II} \quad \overset{\times}{\text{V}}_b \quad \text{I}$; $\text{V} \quad \text{VI} \quad \text{II} \quad \overset{\times}{\text{V}}_b \quad \text{I}$

               (These three exercises in major keys only.)

     (iv)   In Bass :—

$\text{VII}_b \quad \overset{\times}{\text{I}} \quad \text{V}_b \quad \text{I}$; $\text{VI} \quad \text{III}_b \quad \overset{\times}{\text{IV}} \quad \text{I}_b$; $\text{I}_b \quad \overset{\times}{\text{II}} \quad {}^7\text{V} \quad \text{I}$

               (These two exercises in major keys only.)

(b) **Suspended 4ths.**

     (i)   In Treble :—

$\text{I}_b \quad \overset{\times}{\text{V}} \quad \text{I}$; ${}^7\text{V}_b \quad \overset{\times}{\text{I}} \quad {}^7\text{V} \quad \text{VI}$; $\text{IV} \quad \overset{\times}{\text{I}}_c \quad {}^7\text{V} \quad \text{I}$

     (ii)   In Alto :—

$\text{IV} \quad \overset{\times}{\text{I}} \quad \text{II} \quad \overset{\times}{\text{VI}} \quad \text{II}_b \quad {}^7\text{V} \quad \text{I}$; $\text{I} \quad \overset{\times}{\text{VII}}_b \quad \text{I}_b$

       (In major key only.)

     (iii)   In Tenor :—

$\text{I} \quad \overset{\times}{\text{II}}_b \quad \text{I}_c \quad {}^7\text{V} \quad \text{I}$; $\text{IV} \quad \overset{\times}{\text{I}} \quad \text{V} \quad \overset{\times}{\text{VI}} \quad \text{III} \quad \overset{\times}{\text{IV}} \quad \text{IV}_b \quad \text{I}$

               (In major key only.)

     (iv)   In Bass :—

$\text{IV} \quad \overset{\times}{\text{I}}_b \quad {}^7\text{V}_c \quad \text{I}$; $\text{I} \quad \overset{\times}{\text{V}}_b \quad {}^7\text{V} \quad \text{I}$; $\text{II} \quad \overset{\times}{\text{VI}}_b \quad \overset{\times}{\text{V}}_b \quad \text{I}$

               (In major key only.)

(c) **Suspended 6ths.**

(i) In Treble :—

IV $\overset{\times}{I}_b$ ^7V_c I   ;   I $\overset{\times}{V}_c$ I_b ;   IV $\overset{\times}{I}_c$ ^7V I

(ii) In Alto :—

IV $\overset{\times}{I}_c$ ^7V_d I_b ; V_b $\overset{\times}{IV}_b$ V   I

(In 8 parts, and in major key only.)

(iii) In Tenor :—

II $\overset{\times}{VI}$ V_b I   ; II_b $\overset{\times}{I}_c$ ^7V I

(In major key only.)

(iv) In Bass :—

IV_b $\underset{\times}{I_c}$ ^7V I I_b $\underset{\times}{V_c}$ I

Note.—When these two preceding exercises are worked in 4 parts, it is necessary to sound the resolution-note against the Suspension, under the second of the two conditions named on page 137, *e.g.*—

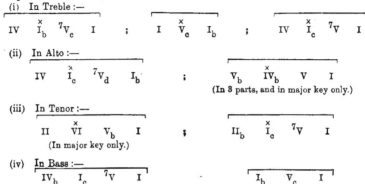

(Key C.)   (Key C.)

$\binom{I_c}{\times}$ $\binom{V_c}{\times}$

(d) **Suspended Leading-note.**

(i) In Treble :—

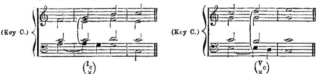

IV_b V $\overset{\times}{I}_b$;   IV I_c ^7V $\overset{\times}{VI}$

(ii) In Alto :—

^7V_d $\overset{\times}{I}_b$ ^7V_c I   ;   V $\overset{\times}{I}_c$ ^7V I

(iii) In Tenor :—

V $\overset{\times}{I}_b$ IV I_c ^7V I   ; ^7V_c $\overset{\times}{I}$ ^7V_b I

(iv) In Bass :—

^7V_b $\underset{\times}{I}$ ^7V_c I_b

E.   Harmonize the following fragments of melody, so as to illustrate the use of a Suspension in each case :—

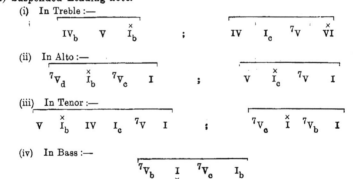

F. Harmonize these fragments of Bass, introducing a Suspension in each case :—

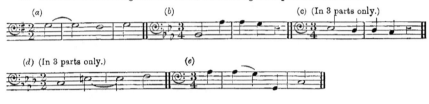

HINTS UPON THE USE OF SUSPENSIONS IN THE HARMONIZATION OF A MELODY OR A BASS.

8. The presence of Suspensions in a melody is usually indicated under the following conditions :—

(a) If a note is *tied* over to a stronger accent from one less strong, and then proceeds by step (usually downwards), thus :—

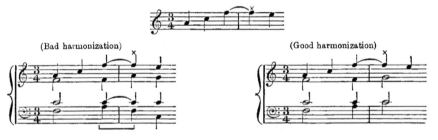

(b) If a note sounded on a weaker part of a bar is *struck again* on the next stronger accent, and then similarly moves by step, thus :—

---

* The C in this $\frac{6}{4}$ chord has much of the effect of a Suspension.

(c) If there is strongly-marked Syncopation, such as the following :—

It will readily be felt, by comparing the above two versions, that the "push" caused by the Syncopation can only be realized in the harmonization by some sort of dissonance, which the Suspension adequately supplies.

9. Although the foregoing directions are given in connexion with the harmonization of a melody, they apply in practically equal measure to the treatment of a bass part, *e.g.*—

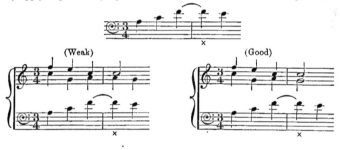

MELODIES AND BASSES CONTAINING SUSPENSIONS.

G. Harmonize the following melodies. The Suspensions in the first exercises are usually indicated by ties, but not invariably so ; where any reasonable doubt could exist in the matter, a Suspension is marked with a ×.

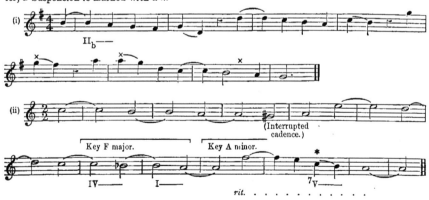

* Accented Passing-note.

N.B.—In the following exercise the Alto part is given: add parts for Treble, Tenor, and Bass.

(iii)

(iv) Tenor part given: add parts for Treble, Alto, and Bass.

(v) Fill up the harmony of the following: the parts may cross occasionally. Use occasional rests.

H. Harmonize these basses containing Suspensions, as indicated. Add occasional Suspensions in any of the upper parts, when there is no Suspension in the bass.

SUSPENSIONS AND THE FIGURED BASS.

10. The conventional means of indicating Suspensions in a Figured Bass involves a needless amount of complexity in the figuring, and—as will be seen later—not a little ambiguity. The following table shews the generally accepted method, and is included here merely for the sake of completeness:—

(i) Suspended 9ths.

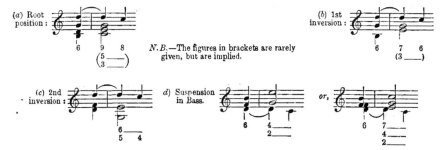

N.B.—The figures in brackets are rarely given, but are implied.

(ii) Suspended 4ths.

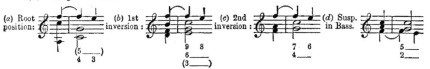

(iii) Suspended 6ths.

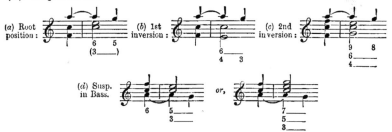

(iv) Suspended Leading-note.

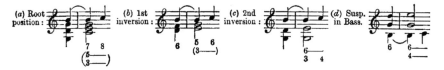

11. The ambiguity alluded to in Sec. 10 arises from the identity of the figuring of the Suspensions, in many cases, with that of other chords. The figuring of the inverted positions of the Suspended 9th, for example, is apparently the same as that for the root position, 1st and 3rd inversions, respectively, of a chord of the 7th.

In such instances, the fact of one of the notes moving *while the rest of the chord remains* should be sufficient to warn the student of the possibility of a Suspension. Wherever a double set of figures is found, such as $7\,6, \frac{6-}{5}\frac{}{4}, \frac{6}{3}\frac{5}{-}, \frac{6-}{4}\frac{}{3}$, it should be remembered that it is the *second* figure, or set of figures, which *indicates the real harmony*, the first merely shewing the suspension. The above therefore represent, respectively, a 6 (or 1st inversion), a $\frac{6}{4}$ (or 2nd inversion), a $\frac{5}{3}$ (or direct triad), and a $\frac{6}{(3)}$ (or 1st inversion). Moreover, $\frac{4-}{2-}$ (the Suspended 9th in the bass) should not be confused with $\frac{4}{2}$ (*without* the lines of continuation), signifying the 3rd inversion of a chord of the 7th.

EXERCISES.

I. Harmonize these Figured Basses containing Suspensions, in four parts :—

Note.—For further Figured Basses including Suspensions, the student is referred to the Author's "350 Exercises in Harmony, Counterpoint and Modulation." (Joseph Williams, Ltd.)

DOUBLE AND TRIPLE SUSPENSIONS.
SUSPENSION OF A WHOLE HARMONY.

12. Suspensions are often found occurring in two or more parts simultaneously ; of Double Suspensions the following is a beautiful example :—

BACH.—Prelude in F minor. ("Forty-eight." Bk. 2.)

(*a*) and (*d*) Double Suspensions of 4th and 6th from the *Dominant* (forming the familiar $\frac{6}{4}\frac{5}{3}$ progression);

(*b*) A Double Suspension of 9th and 4th from the Tonic ;

(*c*) ,, ,, ,, 9th and 4th from the Supertonic (the chord being taken in its first inversion).

13. Double Suspensions almost always move in parallel 3rds or 6ths, as in the above instances; two Suspensions a 4th or a 5th apart clearly cannot be successfully combined, *e.g.*—

14. The first inversion of the Tonic chord is often decorated with a Double Suspension of 9th and Leading-note, thus:—

Note.—Upward-resolving Suspensions are frequently more effective in combination than when taken alone, *e.g.*—

15. Triple Suspensions are possible, but rare, save in the form of the familiar Suspension of the *Dominant* 7th *harmony* over the Tonic or Submediant bass :—

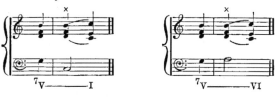

when all that is necessary to remember is that the notes of the Suspended chord *should move exactly as if they had not been suspended*, thus :—

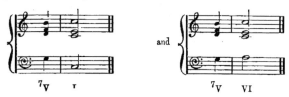

16. The Suspension of the *Dominant* harmony over the Tonic bass, forming a final cadence with a Feminine ending, is a very frequent and characteristic feature of the period of Haydn, Mozart and Beethoven, *e.g.*—

In such cases the notes of the *Dominant* harmony often change their positions when the chord is sounded against the Tonic bass :—

EXERCISES ON *DOUBLE* SUSPENSIONS AND THE SUSPENSION OF WHOLE CHORDS.

J. Play the following in various major and minor keys, adding suitable *Double Suspensions* at ×, and a Suspension of the whole harmony at ‡ :—

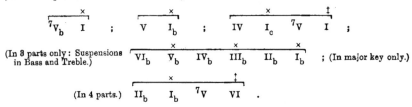

K. Harmonize the following fragments, treating the combinations marked with a × as Double Suspensions :—

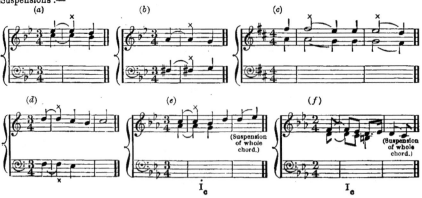

DOUBLE AND TRIPLE SUSPENSIONS IN A FIGURED BASS.

The generally-accepted method of figuring *Double* and *Triple* Suspensions is of necessity often obscure and involved ; but as the Figured Bass is still extensively used—particularly in examinations—it will be well for the student to work the following exercise, in order to familiarize himself with the matter.

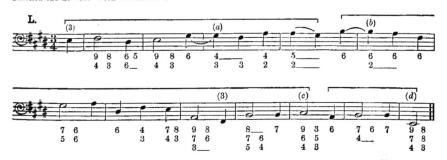

Notes on above Exercise.

(*a*) Double Suspension, with Suspended 9th in Bass.

(*b*)   „   „   „   „   4th „ „

(*c*) Suspension of Dominant 7th harmony over Submediant Bass.

(*d*)   „   „   „   „   „   Tonic   „

CHAPTER XVII.

THE USES OF THE ACCENTED PASSING-NOTE, OR "APPOGGIATURA."

1. THE importance of Accented Passing-notes in the development of the musical art can hardly be over-estimated, for until men found out how to take dissonances *upon the accent* the element of passion and of drama could be but feebly expressed. The intensity of effect produced by means of such accented dissonances will at once be felt in the two following examples :—

BEETHOVEN.—Sonata (Op. 81a).
Andante espressivo.

WAGNER.—"Tristan and Isolde."
Lento e languido.

2. The distinguishing mark of the "Appoggiatura"—as compared with the Suspension, to which it is in some senses akin—is just this feeling of *intensity* or stress, to which allusion has been made in Sec. 1. The Suspension, always entering "prepared," produces (at any rate, when tied) little more than a slight ruffling of the surface which gives interest and point to the music, without materially disturbing its serenity or tranquillity   Note the difference between the Suspensions in Example (*a*) below and the Appoggiaturas in Example (*b*), or those given in Sec. 1 :—

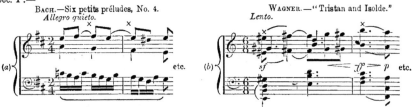

BACH.—Six petits préludes, No. 4.
Allegro quieto.

WAGNER.—"Tristan and Isolde."
Lento.

3. Technically, the difference between the unaccented and the accented passing-note* will be seen at once by a comparison of the two short phrases given below :—

(Unaccented passing-notes.)   (Accented passing-notes.)

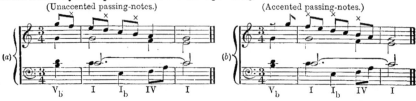

---

* Historically, the Accented Passing-note (or Appoggiatura) came later than the Unaccented. For centuries no dissonances were permitted in accented positions without being "prepared." When, at the beginning of the 17th century, experiments were made in the direction of a greater freedom in this matter, composers sought to give at least an *appearance* of conformity to the existing rule by writing the accented dissonance as a small note, to the left of the real note of the harmony, which

thus preserved its former place on the printed page! *e.g.* 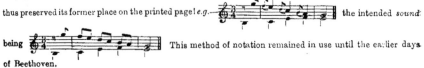 the intended *sound*

being [music] This method of notation remained in use until the earlier days of Beethoven.

4. Accented passing-notes, although often used to preserve the continuity of the scale-line, (*see* Chap. IV., Sec. 3 (*f*)), are frequently *approached* by leap :—

5. If they resolve downwards, they are usually diatonic, as in the foregoing examples ; but when they resolve upwards they sound better, in the majority of cases, at the distance of a semitone below their resolution. As a consequence of this, they are frequently chromatic, *e.g.*—

In such a case, one of these chromatic "Appoggiaturas" may even be sounded against the diatonic form of the same note without bad effect :—

6. When an accented passing-note is used, the result is often purer when the note upon which it is going to resolve is not sounded simultaneously with it, *e.g.*—

Even if the note of resolution *is* thus sounded in the chord, it should never be at so close a distance as a 2nd from the "appoggiatura" :—

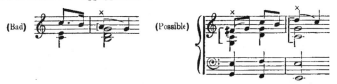

N.B.—It is only the student's growing aural perception that can really guide him in a matter such as this. He must carefully test the sound of each combination, and accept or reject it in accordance with its effect on the increased sensitiveness of his ear to varying tonal impressions.

7. When the chord of the *Dominant* 7th is "decorated" by accented passing-notes above the root, 3rd and 5th of the chord, the combinations produced are often spoken of as *Dominant* 9ths, 11ths and 13ths, respectively,* e.g.—

N.B.—The *upward*-resolving Appoggiatura 11th is usually too hard to be of much use (*see*, however, Sec. 8 below).

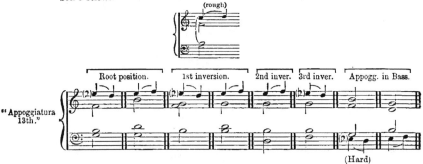

N.B.—All the above examples are equally available in the Minor form of the key, with the necessary modifications shewn in brackets. The "Appoggiatura 9th" resolving *upwards* to the 3rd of the chord is almost invariably the major 6th of the *melodic* minor scale, e.g.—

By this means the rough effect of the augmented 2nd (*e.g.*—A ♭—B ♮) is avoided.

---

* On the assumption that chords are usually formed by the process of adding a succession of 3rds above certain given roots, the notes A, C, and E in the above examples become, it will be seen, the 9th, 11th, and 13th respectively from G, the Dominant root, thus :—

The 11th and the 13th may be taken equally well as 4th and 6th from the root; the "appoggiatura" above the *root*, if resolving downwards, *must* be at the distance of a 9th (not a 2nd) from

it, *e.g.*—

Except in the case of the "Appoggiatura 9th" (in root-position), the recommendation in Sec. 6 applies with considerable force, and the note of resolution should *not* be sounded together with the "Appoggiatura" 9th, 11th or 13th.

This will also explain the absence of certain forms of the chords in the examples given in this Section.

8. Any of these "unessential" notes may be combined with the others, unless some faulty progression is produced, *e.g.*—

(9th and 11th.............................)   (9th and 13th) (11th and 13th.........)

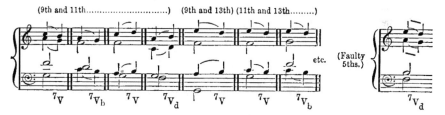

The following extract illustrates the effective use of "Appoggiaturas" over the 5th, 3rd and root of the Dominant 7th harmony, producing a so-called 13th, 11th and 9th respectively :—

and this passage from Schubert a Double Appoggiatura decoration of the Dominant 7th —;

EXERCISES ON THE USE OF THE "APPOGGIATURA."

A. Ornament the following passages by introducing Accented passing-notes (or Appoggiaturas), where possible, in the Treble part :—

(In the following begin as indicated, and use occasional *unaccented* passing-notes as well as Appoggiaturas) :—

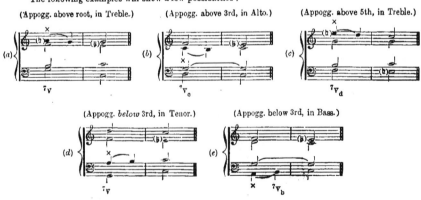

B. Play, in four parts, the chord of the Dominant 7th (in its various positions) in all keys— major and minor—and "decorate" its several notes with Appoggiaturas above and below them (as shewn on page 150). Place these Appoggiaturas in all the parts in turn. Resolve on Tonic harmony.

The following examples will shew a few possibilities :—

C. Harmonize the following fragments at the Pianoforte, using Dominant 7th harmony during the prevalence of the ⌐——¬ . Resolve on Tonic or Submediant harmony.

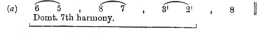

(a) 6   5 , 8   7 , 3¹   2¹ , 8 ‖
       Domt. 7th harmony.

*** The above might be treated as follows :—

(i) or, (ii) or, (iii)

⁷V————I   ⁷V_c ⁷V   ⁷V_d I_b   ⁷V_b ⁷V_c ⁷V VI

(b) 3¹ 2¹ , 8   7 , 6   5 , 5 ‖   (c) 8   7 , ♯4 5 , 3· 2¹ , 8 ‖

(d) 6   7 , 3¹   2¹ , 8   2¹ , 5¹ . ‖

N.B.—The line proceeding upwards from left to right of a figure indicates that the note represented by that figure is to be chromatically raised.

D. Harmonize the following fragments, containing double Appoggiaturas, with Dominant 7th harmony (in various positions), and resolve in each case upon I or VI :—

(a)   (b)   (c)   (d)

(e)   (f)

E. Harmonize the following melodies. In the first five exercises the indication of the harmonies by Roman numerals will shew which notes are to be treated as Appoggiaturas, or accented passing-notes.

(i)   I   IV   ⁷V   I

(ii)   I   I_b   IV   IV_b   I_c   ⁷V   I

(iii)   (a)
I_b——   I   IV——   IV_b   I_c——   ⁷V — I

(a) Leave these two notes unharmonized.

Allegretto delicato.

(iv)
(In three parts only.)
I   II_b   VII_b   V_b   I   IV_b   II_b   VII_b.   ⁷V   I————

Begin thus :   etc.

(v)
(In four parts.)

I_b II I_c ^7V

Begin thus :—   etc.

(b)

(b) The consecutive 7ths between the outer parts here are quite good; the rule against "consecutives" of this kind is often relaxed where unessential notes are concerned. It will be noticed that both the G♭ and the F are "unessential."

Note.—In the next three melodies the harmonies (save in a few instances) are not specified, but the Appoggiaturas are indicated by a ×.

(vi)

(vii)

(a)   (Minim chords.) IV_c I

(a) Harmonize with ^7V_d.

(viii)   *Mesto.*

p ^7V_d ^7V_c

I_c

In the remaining three melodies, the presence of Accented passing-notes is only rarely indicated. Although the determining of which notes of a melody should be treated as "unessential" is a matter concerning which the pupil's ear and growing musical sense must be the guide, the following hints may be useful :—

(a) In most cases the harmony should not be changed more frequently than the rate of movement of the pulse (or beat).* Compare these two passages :—

Allegretto.

(Good : harmony spaced well.)

Allegretto.

(Bad : harmony far too crowded.)

* In slow *tempo* there are, of course, exceptions to this; but in such cases, the *half*-pulse (as written) frequently becomes the actual pulse of the music.

(*b*) Notes upon the unaccented beats in quick *tempo* (or upon the unaccented portions of beats in slow *tempo*)—if they move by step—are most frequently " unessential."

(*c*) When an *unaccented* note is quitted by leap, but approached by step, *e.g.*—

it is usually advisable to treat the *accented* note that precedes it as an " Appoggiatura," *e.g.*—

. It will readily be realized that the feeling of stress, impulse and warmth given to the little groups of two slurred quavers is entirely due to this method of treatment. It should be remembered that this feeling can be produced only by some form of *dissonance* upon the accent, such as that which the " Appoggiatura " supplies.

F. More difficult melodies containing Accented Passing-notes.

* The 5ths on the first half of each beat here (between the two upper parts) are quite good ; the real harmony being :—

(*a*) This unusual resolution of the Dominant 7th is justifiable by reason of the movement of the melody.

(Four parts.)

G. Harmonize the following Bass, according to the indications supplied by the Roman numerals. Do not let the chords proceed more rapidly than the pulses. Where the bass moves in crotchets, "decorate" the melody of the top part in quavers, by the use of Appoggiaturas.

H. Add *one* part of a more or less florid nature (chiefly in quavers and semiquavers) to the following unfigured broken-chord accompaniment (for Pianoforte). Continue in a similar manner to the indicated commencement :—

THE FREER TREATMENT OF PASSING-NOTES.—ANTICIPATIONS.

9.   Although it is the most obvious and natural thing for a passing-note to be approached and quitted by the step of a 2nd, good effect is often obtained from certain relaxations of this strict treatment, which may be summarized as under :—

(*a*) An unaccented passing-note may (like the Appoggiatura) be *approached* by leap, *e.g.*—

N.B.—It will be seen that the passing-note in each case is *quitted* by step.

When a passing-note approached by leap resolves *upwards*, it is usually (again like the Appoggiatura) best at the distance of a semitone from its resolution :—

(Implied harmony.)

** Compare the effect of the above passage with the roughness caused by the whole-tone steps at (*x*), (*y*) and (*z*) :—

(*b*) A passing-note may sometimes leap to a note of the chord against which it is sounded, before resolving, *e.g.*— *Moderato.*   WAGNER.—" Die Meistersinger."

N.B.—It will be seen that this proceeding is in reality no exception to the general rule that a passing-note resolves by step ; the resolution of the passing-note (A) in the above example upon the G harmony-note is only *deferred* for the moment by the leap to another note of the chord (E). A similar deferring of the resolution of a passing-note takes place in the figure called " Changing-notes " (*see* page 30) where a passing note, instead of resolving at once, skips a 3rd to *another passing-note* and then resolves, *e.g.*—

(c) The only genuine exception to the quitting of a passing-note by step occurs when **two** successive harmony-notes stand at the distance of a 2nd from one another; in this case the passing-note a step above the first may effectively resolve downwards by the *leap of a 3rd, e.g.*—

Note.—Very occasionally a similar *upward* leap of the passing-note is met with, but the effect is rarely so good. The following, however, is possible :—

10. One other type of unessential discord remains to be noticed here, viz., the *Anticipation*, which occurs when a note of a chord is introduced, as it were, prematurely, and is thus made to sound against the preceding chord. Its most familiar use is seen in the *portamento*, or sliding of the voice on to the final note of a cadence, *e.g* —

A well-known instance of the Anticipation occurs in " Home, sweet home " :—

11. The two following extracts from Beethoven's " Waldstein " Sonata illustrate most effectively (i) a theme in chord form, (ii) the same theme decorated by a tracery of passing-notes—some accented, others unaccented; some taken by step, others by leap; some diatonic, others chromatic. The scheme of decoration deserves the closest analysis throughout.

(Bars 43–46.)

etc.

EXERCISE.

I. Comment fully upon all the unessential notes in the following passage, and re-write it as a piece of plain harmony (*i.e.*, omitting all passing-notes, etc.) :—

CHAPTER XVIII.

THE MELODIC MINOR SCALE IN CHORD-FORMATION.

1. THE Harmonic Minor Scale—as its name implies—provides the foundation for the principal harmonies of the Minor key. It is possible, however, (as has been seen in connexion with Two-part Melodic writing—Chapter VI), to use the Major 6th and the Minor 7th of the Melodic scale in the formation of chords which, although requiring some care in treatment, greatly enhance the possibilities of the minor key, and·are often the means of producing remarkably beautiful effects. The following are the additional triads formed in this way in the key of C minor:—

2. The usual condition under which the above chords may be successfully introduced is that the note of the Melodic scale should proceed along the scale-line, the major 6th *upwards* from Dominant to Leading-note, and the minor 7th *downwards* from Tonic to Submediant,† thus:—

---

* The diminished triad on the Major 6th degree can hardly ever be used in its root-position, although available in its 1st inversion. The triads ⁸V and VII, *in root-position*, are usually too suggestive of the Relative major key (*see*, however, Ex. (*g*)).

N.B.—The diagonal stroke drawn downwards from right to left through a figure, thus: ꝑ, VI, signifies the use of the *major 6th* of the Melodic minor scale; a similar stroke from left to right, thus: ꝑ, VII, the *minor 7th*, (*see* p. vi, Sec. 10).

† Of the *Harmonic* minor scale.

N.B.—The major 6th of the Melodic minor scale should not be doubled.

3. Any chord containing the minor 7th usually requires to be followed as soon as possible by a chord containing the Leading-note, *e.g.*—

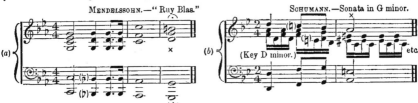

otherwise the tonality easily becomes vague and indeterminate, and the music may tend to hover somewhat aimlessly between the minor key and its so-called "relative" major *e.g.*,—

4. The use, cadentially, of the minor 7th—in the chord preceding the final Tonic—lends a "Modal" * flavour to the music, *e.g.*—

which has been very effectively exploited by modern composers; here is a notable instance :—

* *See* Appendix D.

EXERCISES UPON THE USE OF TRIADS AND THEIR INVERSIONS FORMED FROM THE MELODIC MINOR SCALE.

A. Introduce at (*a*) a chord containing the major 6th of the melodic minor scale, and at (*b*) one containing the minor 7th ;—

(*x*) The major third in the final Tonic chord here is very frequently found in older music. (*See* page 71, Note to Exercise 4.)

B. Harmonize, in 3 and 4 parts, the following fragments of melody, introducing in each example an instance of a chord including a note of the melodic minor scale. Harmonize each in two different ways :—

C. Harmonize the following fragments without leaving the key indicated. Introduce an example of a chord containing a note of the melodic minor scale in each case :—

D. Harmonize the following, introducing a chord containing a note of the melodic minor scale at each * :—

E. Harmonize the following Figured Bass. Mark with a × all the chords that are formed from the melodic minor scale.

CHAPTER XIX.

MODULATION.

1. MODULATION (or change of key), one of the most striking and valuable resources open to the musician, is caused by the shifting of the Tonic, or key-centre, from one pitch to another, *e.g.*—

At first used sparingly, and between nearly-related keys only, modulation has become in the course of time more frequent and complex, and to-day the remotest keys are brought into relation to one another with a boldness which would have been unthinkable a century ago.

2. The greater daring of later writers does not, however, imply that an indiscriminate use of extreme modulation is to be commended. The case is quite the reverse, and the student has to learn that considerable discretion is often needed in the matter. Hence his first experiments will be confined to modulation between keys which are described as *Nearly-related*, a term applied to those that have the greater number of notes and chords in common.*

3. The "nearly-related" keys to any given major or minor key-centre are ;—

> I. To a major key-centre.
> (*a*) The (so-called) Relative minor.
> (*b*) The Dominant major and *its* Relative minor.
> (*c*) The Subdominant major and *its* Relative minor.

> II. To a minor key-centre.
> (*a*) The (so-called) Relative major.
> (*b*) The Dominant minor and *its* Relative major.
> (*c*) The Subdominant minor and *its* Relative major.

The following diagrams shew the "nearly-related" keys of C major and C minor respectively :—

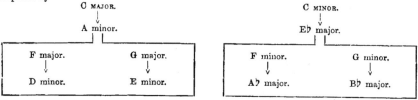

* The student will have observed that instances of modulation have already occurred in many of his previous exercises. These, however, have invariably been planned *for* him; henceforward his task will be to learn how to modulate for himself with ease and certainty. The pianist or organist should never be satisfied until he can do this readily, *at the key-board*, not merely on paper.

4. No single chord in the course of a musical passage can be said to define or establish a key.* Although the two examples given below end respectively upon the chord of G and the chord of A minor, they do not pass from the key of C major (in which they begin) to the *keys* of G major and A minor, for the reason that they contain no chords *outside the bounds of the key of C itself :—*

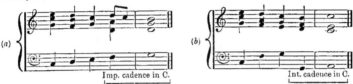

(a) Imp. cadence in C. (b) Int. cadence in C.

In order to make a modulation it is necessary (i) to introduce some chord not in the original key, (ii) to follow it by some other chord which, together with it, will define the new key. Compare the foregoing examples (a) and (b) with examples (c) and (d):—

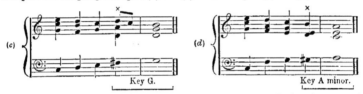

(c) Key G. (d) Key A minor.

N.B.—The chord of the Dominant 7th succeeded by that of the Tonic, will usually determine a key.

5. In order to modulate successfully between any two keys, it is clearly necessary to set up some sort of connexion between them ; a "plunge" such as the following is simply absurd :—

The requisite connexion may consist (i) of a *chord common to the two keys,* approached as belonging to the first and quitted as part of the second, *e.g.*—

HANDEL.—"Messiah."

(x) (y)

Key D. Key A. Key D.

(x) "Pivot-chord" between keys of D and A.
(y) "Pivot-chord" between keys of A and D.

* A moment's thought will be enough to reveal the fact that the chord of C major (to take a simple instance) can belong diatonically to five keys, viz.—C, G and F major ; and E and F minor.

or it may be set up (ii) by one or more *notes* in common, as in the following extract from Beethoven, where the B forms a " pivot-note " between the two keys :—

BEETHOVEN.—Sonata (Op. 10, 3).

Key E minor. Key G major.

In modulating between nearly-related keys the connexion can invariably be made by one or other of these means.

6. As the *Dominant* chord of the new key (most frequently its *Dominant* 7th) is in the majority of cases the transitional harmony, *i.e.*, the harmony which heralds that new key, it is well, in making a modulation, for the preceding harmonies to lead towards it without unnecessary delay. Supposing that it were to be desired to pass from the key of C (at (*x*)) to the key of G, the following method would be a foolish one, for the simple reason that all the harmonies after the * tend, not in the direction of G, but *away from it*, thereby causing an abrupt and unpleasant transition from one key to the other at (*y*) :—

* Useless harmonies.

It would obviously have been far better for the Submediant chord of C major (the third chord of the passage) to be used as the " pivot-chord " (*i.e.*, as II in key G), and at once followed by a close in that key, thus :—

Key G.

Or, the Tonic chord of C major itself could even have been regarded as the " pivot " (*i.e.*, as IV in key G), and the modulation successfully brought about as follows :—

Key G.

⁎ Observe the strong tendency of the $\frac{6}{4}$ chord on D bass to sound as I_c in the *new* key. (*See* Chapter XIV, Sec. 9.) The $\frac{6}{4}$ chord upon the Dominant of the new key $\left(I_c\right)$ is, as a consequence, a most useful objective in making a modulation.

7. In transient modulations the principle of the "pivot-note" is particularly useful, and in the case of nearly-related keys, the common note can in most cases be found in the Tonic chord of one key and the *Dominant* 7th of the next,* *e.g.*—

The "pivot-note" need not appear in the same part in the two chords :—

If a series of transient modulations is carried out in this way, great care must be taken to avoid a mechanical and poverty-stricken result like the following :—

in which each key is introduced by the root-position of the *Dominant* 7th chord, followed by the Tonic chord, also in root-position, with irritating persistency.

---

* This principle is also seen where—as not infrequently happens—the Dominant 7th of one key resolves upon the Dominant 7th of another; thus :—

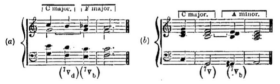

Passages like the following are often found, constituting a series of "transitional" Dominant 7ths :—

Obviously the only keys that are at all clearly established are the first and the last (in the above instance, C major and D♭ major), the tonality between these two points being rendered intentionally vague by the absence of any chords defining the keys of F, B♭, E♭ and A♭ major, *suggested* in turn by the Dominant 7ths of those keys.

N.B.—It will be observed that in example (*c*) the "pivot-note" is not actually *sounded* every time, owing to the omission of the 5th in each alternate chord.

The following version is clearly much better, owing to the far more melodious nature of the bass :—

But even here the modulations are perhaps too crowded, and the need is for a better spacing of the harmonies, *e.g.*—

*** The foregoing examples illustrate a point of some importance, viz. that when a note of one chord is inflected by an accidental in the next, the inflection should usually be made in the same part ;—

The neglect of this precaution often causes the fault known as *False Relation*, which may even occur between two chords separated by an intervening one, *e.g.*—

A progression like the following is, however, quite satisfactory :—

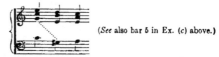

(*See* also bar 5 in Ex. (*c*) above.)

and many other exceptions occur in Chromatic harmony. A chromatic passing-note, or Appoggiatura, does not cause False Relation. (*See* Chapter XVII, Sec. 5.)

EXERCISES IN MODULATION TO NEARLY-RELATED KEYS.

A. Supply the chords necessary to bring each of the following passages to a conclusion in the required key :—

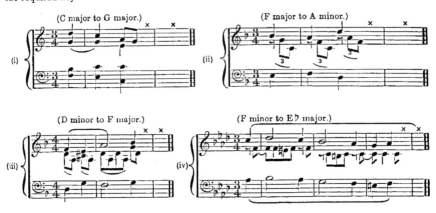

B. Insert at the asterisk a chord (or chords, as the case may be) common to the two keys between which each example modulates, in order to lead naturally from one key to the other :—

C. Supply the necessary modulating chord at each asterisk (using the principle of the "pivot-note"), in order to pass through the keys indicated. (Be careful to make the bass move melodiously.)

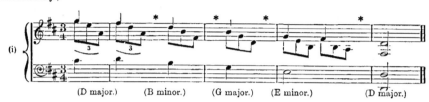

(i)

(D major.)   (B minor.)   (G major.)   (E minor.)   (D major.)

(ii)

(C major.) (A min.) (D min.) (C maj.) (F maj.) (D min.) (C major.)

D. Harmonize the following melodic fragments containing simple modulations to related keys :—

(i)

₊ Pass quickly—by means of the "pivot-*note*"—from C major, through A minor, F major and D minor, in a sequential manner, and then conclude in C major.

(ii)

₊ Pass similarly from A major through F♯ minor, E major and D major, concluding in A major.

N.B.—In the following passages the modulation is to be made by means of a "pivot-*chord*."

(F major to C major.)   (C minor to B♭ major.)

(iii)   (iv)

$\left(^{7}V_{d}\right)$

(D major to F♯ minor.)   (A♭ major to F minor.)

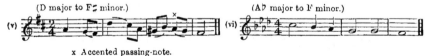

(v)   (vi)

x Accented passing-note.

(E minor to G major.)   (C♯ minor to G♯ minor.)

(vii)   (viii)

E. Complete the following Pianoforte pieces, as indicated.

. In the above exercise pass (in order) from G minor through the keys of E♭ major, C minor, G minor, D major, G minor and C minor, concluding in G minor.

The exercise illustrates the "pivot-note" principle almost exclusively, and the inversions of the Dominant 7th chord are freely used in this connexion. Observe that in a Pianoforte accompaniment such as the one suggested the 3rd and 7th of the chord of the Dominant 7th may be doubled in the upper and middle parts of the harmony, *e.g.*—

and the consecutive 8ves produced thereby are quite permissible.

The 3rd and 7th, however, should never be doubled if either of them is in the *bass, e.g.*—

The effect of the consecutives here is, moreover, distinctly bad. (*See* Appendix B.)

⁎ In the above begin and end in G major, passing (in order) through the keys of D major, G major, E minor, G major, A minor, B minor, G major, and C major in the course of the exercise.

F Play and write short melodious and rhythmical phrases (two to four bars),* to exemplify these modulations :—

(i) E♭ major to B♭ major. (ii) D major to G major. (iii) F major to D minor.

(iv) D major to E minor. (v) A major to C♯ minor. (vi) B♭ minor to D♭ major.

(vii) C minor to G minor. (viii) F♯ minor to E major. (ix) G♯ minor to C♯ minor.

(x) E♭ minor to C♭ major.

G. (i) Modulate (in a transient manner) from D major through B minor, E minor, A major and G· major, and then return to the original key, in which a Perfect cadence is to be made.

(ii) Modulate similarly from C minor through A♭ major, F minor and E♭ major, and then return to C minor, closing in that key.

⁎ Each of these exercises should consist of from four to eight bars.*

THE "PIVOT-NOTE" PRINCIPLE AND MODULATION TO MORE DISTANT KEYS.

8. The principle of the "pivot-note" may be extended so as to provide a means of modulation to keys beyond the range of those commonly classed as nearly-related. Its most usual application is then for a note of some chord in the first key (most frequently a triad) to be retained to form part either of (i) the Dominant 7th, or (ii) another triad (especially the 2nd inversion of the Tonic chord) in the *new* key.†

The following are a few of the possibilities in this direction; to save space they are given in simple chord-form; the student should endeavour to "decorate" them with passing-notes, etc. at the key-board. They should also be transposed in every instance.

I. From a major centre (C major) :—

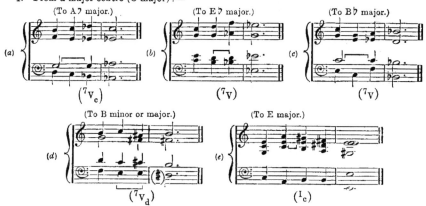

---

* If any difficulty is at first experienced in making these modulatory phrases *rhythmical*, the student may begin by using the schemes on page 6, either complete or in portions as indicated by the square brackets.

† In this connexion it is useful to remember that any note of a triad in one key can be regarded as the root, 3rd, or 5th of a triad in some other key, or as the root, 3rd, 5th, or 7th of its Dominant 7th chord.

II.   From a minor centre (C minor) :—

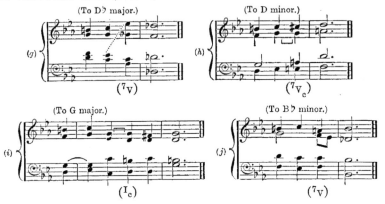

N.B.—The use of one of the notes of a triad to form a " pivot " with the new *Dominant 7th chord* is not usually good between a major key and another whose opposite " mode " is a nearly-related key. The crude effect of the following modulations will readily be recognized :—

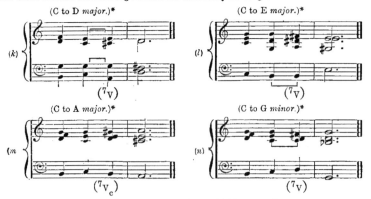

N.B.—Compare the bad effect of Exs. (*l*) and (*m*) with Exs. (*e*) and (*f*) above, and (*n*) with (*b*) in *Sec.* 9 below, where the same modulations are carried out successfully.

---

* C major and D *minor* are nearly-related keys.⎱   The above examples would be perfectly **good**
C major and A *minor* are nearly-related keys.⎰   if the " mode " of the second key were **changed**
C major and E *minor* are nearly-related keys.⎱   from major to minor (or *vice versâ*) in **each**
C major and G *major* are nearly-related keys.⎰   instance.

9. The 3rd of a major chord may be lowered a semitone, and the chord cnanged from major to minor, if by so doing a more successful approach to the new key can be made, *e.g.*—

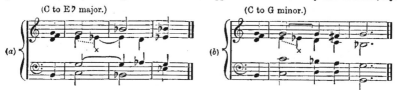

(C to E♭ major.)   (C to G minor.)

(a)   *(b)*

⁂ This is specially useful in leading into a minor key; the introduction of its *minor 6th* degree is always effective in approaching either I_c or ^7V, and the above plan of flattening the 3rd of a chord is very often the means by which this can be carried out. (*See* Ex. (*b*) above.)

EXERCISES IN MODULATION TO NON-RELATED KEYS.
THE "PIVOT-NOTE" CONNEXION.

H. Supply the chords necessary to bring each of the following examples to a conclusion in the required key :—

(F major to D♭ major.)   (G major to B♭ major.)   (B♭ major to G major.)

(i)   **(ii)**   **(iii)**

(D major to F♯ major.)
Vivace.

(iv)

(E minor to F major.)

(v)   *Scherzando.*

N.B.—In the following exercise pass quickly (sequentially) through B major, A major and A♭ major, and conclude in C major.

(vi)

I.   Begin in the keys indicated, and lead naturally to the given chords.

⁎⁎⁎ Exemplify the "pivot-note" connexion in every case.

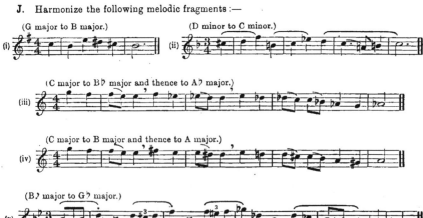

(*a*) *See* remarks in Sec. 9 above.

J.   Harmonize the following melodic fragments :—

10. The principle of the "pivot-note" is at times used by modern composers to link together a succession of chords belonging to different keys in such a way as to create an intentional vagueness of tonality, *e.g.*—

GRIEG.—Violin Sonata (Op. 8).

₊ In the above extract no single key is established or defined, but each triad hints at, or suggests, the key of which it is the Tonic.

₊ Further remarks upon Modulation will be found in Chapter XXIX.

HINTS ON HARMONIZING A MELODY.
EXPRESSED AND IMPLIED MODULATION.

11. A modulation may be clearly indicated by the notes of a melody, or it may be merely implied. The two examples given below illustrate both cases :—

(Expressed mod.)   (Implied mod.)

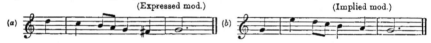

The most natural and obvious harmonization would involve a modulation from C to G major in each passage :—

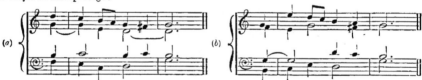

It would, of course, be *possible* to consider (*b*) as entirely in the key of C; but the long note at the end clearly suggests the termination of a rhythmic period, and a harmonization such as the following would be very far-fetched and strained * :—

* It is useful to note that movement downwards along the scale-line at the end of a phrase frequently implies a modulation into the key of which the last note.is the Tonic, *e.g.*—

(C to A minor.)   (C to F major.)   (C to G major.)

The following might suggest either a modulation to D minor, or an Imperfect cadence in C major :—

N.B.—In the *midst* of a phrase, however, the following version would be quite acceptable :—

12. In the harmonization of a melody it is impossible (one almost says, *fortunately*) for definite rules to be laid down as to when accidentals should be regarded as suggesting changes of key, and when they should be treated merely as chromatic passing-notes or "appoggiaturas." A melody like the following, for instance—

would be utterly ruined by adopting the former plan :—

Clearly the passage should remain in the key of *D* major throughout, thus :—

In every case the character of the particular melody to be harmonized must obviously be the deciding factor, and it is here that the musicality of the student will be put to the test, and his aural perception taxed to the full. It is quite fatal to imagine—as inexperienced harmonists often do—that the presence of an accidental is of necessity the signal for the key to be changed. It *may* be ; but at least the possibility of its being merely a "decorative" unessential note (as in the foregoing example) must always be present in the student's mind in his endeavour to arrive at a suitable harmonization.*

---

* The exercises in succeeding Chapters will give him many opportunities of practice in this important matter.

CHAPTER XX.

SECONDARY CHORDS OF THE SEVENTH.

1. THE name Secondary 7ths is given to those chords of the 7th—mainly diatonic, but occasionally chromatically " altered "—which are not formed like the Dominant 7th, and therefore do not contain a major 3rd, perfect 5th and minor 7th from the root.

⁎ The chord of the Dominant 7th will already have been recognized by the student as a dissonance readily acceptable by the ear. A possible reason for this is that its several sounds correspond to those of a fundamental tone and its earlier and most noticeable harmonics (or " upper partials "), *e.g.*—

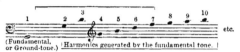

Nature thus familiarizing the ear with this particular combination. Chords of the 7th formed upon this principle (such as the Dominant 7th and certain chromatic chords to be spoken of in later chapters) are for this reason sometimes called Fundamental (or *Primary*) *7ths* ; the others, owing to their more artificial construction, *Secondary 7ths.*

2. The importance of Secondary chords of the 7th is considerable, modern composers using them with increasing frequency and with striking effect. They can be formed diatonically upon every degree of the major or minor scale except the Dominant, *e.g.*—

N.B.—The above chords should be carefully played, their special character and their varying degrees of harshness being noted and memorized. It will be observed that, after the Dominant 7th, those chords having a minor 3rd and minor 7th from the root possess a milder and less biting dissonance than the others.

NORMAL RESOLUTION OF SECONDARY 7THS.

3. Formerly, a Secondary chord of the 7th was invariably resolved upon a triad, or chord of the 7th, whose root was a 4th above (or 5th below) its own root, the 7th itself falling one degree to the 3rd of the resolution-chord :—

This resolution may still be regarded as the normal one, and its effect is invariably vigorous and strong.

N.B.—The 3rd is free in its progression ; in the chord of the Dominant 7th the 3rd rises a semitone, as it is the Leading-note of the key.

4. In the music of the older writers (*see* example from Corelli in the foot-note below) the 7th—the dissonant note—was always *prepared*, *i.e.*, sounded as a concord in the preceding chord, and in the same part. Later composers freely dispense with this preparation which, however, often tends towards smoothness of effect.*

5. Secondary chords of the 7th, having four notes, obviously possess three inversions :—

$$(^7\text{II})\qquad (^7\text{II}_b)\qquad (^7\text{II}_c)\qquad (^7\text{II}_d)$$

---

* It is probable that the Secondary 7th arose in the first instance from a device dating from the 17th century, by which a suspension of 7-6, such as the following :—

was embellished by making the bass move a 4th up or a 5th down, at the same moment that the suspension resolved, thus :—

when the 7th from the bass ceased to be a mere suspension, and became an essential part of a *chord* of the 7th resolving upon a new harmony whose root was a 4th higher. Sequences of such chords are frequently to be found in the works of the earlier masters, *e.g.*—

CORELLI.—Sonate da Camera (No. XI).

The above passage is clearly a development from a series of 7-6 Suspensions :—

6. The chords of the 7th upon the Supertonic and Mediant of the Harmonic minor scale, it should be remembered, contain respectively a diminished and an augmented 5th, each of which requires to be resolved—the former *downwards* by step of a semitone, the latter *upwards* by a similar step, *e.g.*—

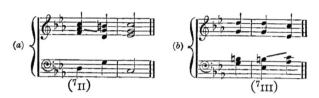

7.   Certain Secondary 7ths (particularly in the minor form of the. key), by proceeding to a chord whose root is a 4th above, would necessarily resolve upon *dissonant triads*, *e.g.*—

producing a very crude result.   The "normal" resolution is therefore unavailable in these cases,* except sometimes in the course of a Sequence.

8. The chord of the 7th upon the Tonic of the Harmonic minor scale is practically useless, owing to its very awkward resolution, *e.g.*—

*** As will be seen later, the major 6th and minor 7th of the Melodic minor scale are frequently used in the construction of Secondary 7ths with excellent effect.

---

* Save occasionally when the Secondary 7th is in its 3rd inversion : —

BACH.—Christmas Oratorio.

etc.

9. Sequences of Secondary 7ths, especially in the major key, are often to be found. One such example has already been given (foot-note to Sec. 4); two others from different authors are now added, the first, from Chopin, shewing a Sequence of 7ths in root-position, dispersed in "arpeggio" figures:—

CHOPIN.—Etude in C (Op. 10).

The second example, from Bach, affords an instance of the strong effect of the **3rd** inversion:—

BACH.—Eight little Preludes and Fugues for the Organ.

N.B.—In a Sequence of chords of the 7th *in root-position throughout*, the 5th of each alternate chord will always have to be omitted, and the root doubled, if the passage is written in four-part harmony, *e.g.*—

10. The addition of a 7th to the "pre-cadential" Supertonic triad (especially in its first inversion) is very usual, the mild form of dissonance providing a pleasant degree of impulse to the harmony :—

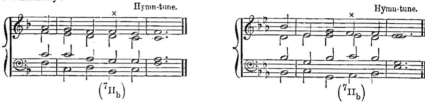

⁎ In this inversion the chord is often spoken of as the "chord of the Added sixth." (*See* page 188, foot-note.)

11. The chord of the 7th upon the Supertonic was the first in which the strict rule of "preparation" became relaxed; moreover, composers soon found out that, when it resolved upon the Dominant 7th harmony, its own 7th could *rise* a second quite satisfactorily, instead of falling :—

Mozart has a typical instance of this in one of his best-known overtures:—

EXERCISES UPON THE FIRST (OR "NORMAL") RESOLUTION OF SECONDARY CHORDS OF THE SEVENTH.

A. Play Secondary chords of the 7th on the several degrees of the major and minor scales, in various keys and in all positions. Play the chords first in "close position" (with one hand), thus :—

and afterwards in "extended position" (with both hands), thus :—

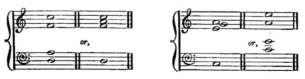

B. Play, in various major and minor keys, the following progressions. Give two versions of each, varying the top part, and arranging the examples in different times and rhythms :—

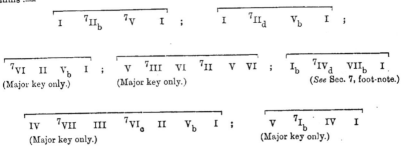

I ^{7}II$_b$ ^{7}V   I ;   I ^{7}II$_d$ V$_b$ I ;

^{7}VI II V$_b$ I ;   V ^{7}III VI ^{7}II V VI ;   I$_b$ ^{7}IV$_d$ VII$_b$ I .

(Major key only.)   (Major key only.)   (*See* Sec. 7, foot-note.)

IV ^{7}VII III ^{7}VI$_o$ II V$_b$ I ;   V ^{7}I$_b$ IV I

(Major key only.)   (Major key only.)

C. Continue the following in Sequence, bringing each passage to a suitable conclusion :—

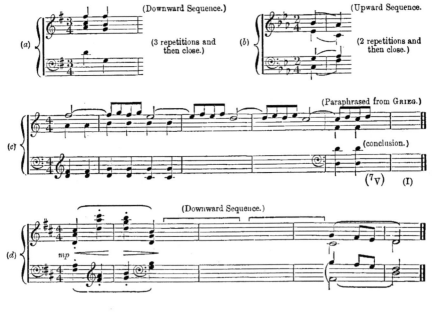

(a)   (Downward Sequence.)   (3 repetitions and then close.)

(b)   (Upward Sequence.   (2 repetitions and then close.)

(c)   (Paraphrased from GRIEG.)   (conclusion.)   (^{7}V)   (I)

(d)   (Downward Sequence.)   *mp*

D. Harmonize the following melodies.

N.B.—In the first two exercises the special Secondary 7th required from time to time is indicated by a Roman numeral.

(i)   (^{7}II$_d$)   (^{7}II)   (^{7}I)   (^{7}II$_b$)

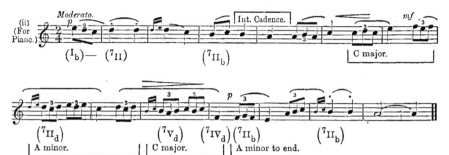

N.B.—Begin the above exercise thus:—

Note.—In the following exercises a cross denotes the use of a Secondary 7th.

(Add two inner parts.)

(Bass part.)

N.B.—In the remaining exercises, the introduction of a Secondary 7th is indicated only very occasionally. The student is, for the most part, left to his own judgment in the matter.

(v) Choral.

(In three parts: the harmony to run in minims and crotchets only.)

(vi) *Moderato.*

(^7II_d) (^7II) (^7I)

cres.

poco rit.

Four parts to end.

(vii)
(For Piano.
The number
of parts may
vary.) *Allegro.* (One chord in each bar.)

p delicato. *etc.*

f (^7IV_d)

$(^7III_d)$ *calando.*

   * Accented Passing-note.   ‡ Two chords in this bar.

E. Harmonize the following Basses (figured and unfigured).

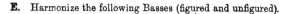

(A Secondary 7th, either in root-position or in one of its inversions, is indicated by each ×)

---

* These exercises are taken from the author's " 350 Exercises." (Joseph Williams, Ltd.)

CHAPTER XXI.

SECONDARY CHORDS OF THE SEVENTH—(Cont^d.).

1. In Sec. 11 of the preceding chapter it was shewn that composers soon began to modify the original strict treatment of Secondary chords of the 7th. This modification was at first specially noticeable in the case of that upon the Supertonic, but it was not long before others followed suit, particularly in the direction of a greater freedom of resolution.

2. The chords of the 7th most frequently to be found resolving in other ways than the "normal" one described in Chapter XX are those upon the Supertonic, Subdominant and Submediant * (^{7}II, ^{7}IV and ^{7}VI), which often proceed either to Tonic or to Dominant harmony, as will be seen by the following examples:—

I. *Supertonic Secondary 7th resolving upon* Tonic *harmony.*

In this form of resolution, it will be seen, the 7th of the Supertonic usually *remains* to be the root of the Tonic chord.

N.B.—The above examples (and also those given below under heading II), are equally available in the minor form of the key, with the necessary modifications.

---

* The chord of the 7th upon the Leading-note (^{7}VII) often resolves upon Tonic harmony, thus:—

but it is then usually regarded as an inverted form of the Dominant major or minor 9th, and its consideration is for this reason deferred until Chapter XXIII.

It is worth while here to note that the combination of the 4th and 7th degrees of the scale in any chord almost invariably implies its derivation from the Dominant root, *e.g.*—

† As was stated in Chapter XX, Sec. 10, the first inversion of the Secondary 7th upon the Supertonic is frequently spoken of as the "Chord of the Added 6th." The expression in all probability owes its origin to the fact of the 6th from the bass-note having first been used merely as a passing-note "decorating" the Subdominant chord in a Plagal Cadence, thus:—

the striking of this note *against* the chord instead of after it, thus:—

being a later development. Compare this example with Exs. (*b*) and (*c*) above.

II. *Subdominant Secondary 7th resolving upon either* DOMINANT *or* TONIC *harmony.*

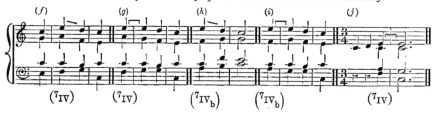

III. *Submediant Secondary 7th resolving upon* DOMINANT *harmony.**

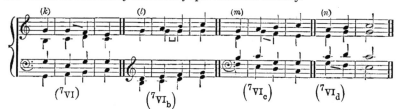

3. The extracts that follow are typical of the above-named resolutions of the Supertonic, Subdominant and Submediant 7ths:—

I. *Supertonic 7th.*

---

* When the Submediant 7th resolves thus in the minor key, it is usually taken upon the *major 6th* of the Melodic minor scale, thus:— (*See* Sec. 4, Ex. (c), and Sec. 5, Ex. (b).)

II. *Subdominant 7th.*

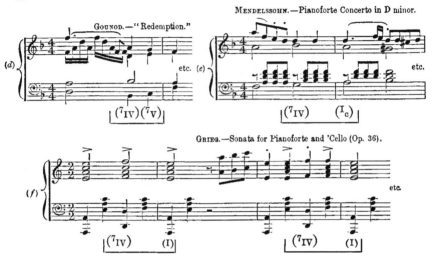

III. *Submediant 7th.*

EXERCISES UPON SECONDARY 7TH (FREER RESOLUTION).

A. Play, in various major and minor keys, the following progressions, arranging the examples in different times and rhythms :—

$$^7\text{II} \quad \text{I}_c \quad ^7\text{V} \quad \text{I} \quad ; \qquad \text{VI} \quad ^7\text{II}_b \quad \text{I}_c \quad ^7\text{V} \quad \text{I} \quad ; \qquad \text{I}_b \quad \text{IV} \quad ^7\text{II}_b \quad \text{I} \quad ;$$

$$\text{VI} \quad ^7\text{IV} \quad ^7\text{V} \quad \text{I} \quad ; \qquad \text{I}_b \quad ^7\text{IV} \quad \text{I}_c \quad ^7\text{V} \quad \text{I} \quad ;$$

(The following in major keys only.)

$$\text{I}_c \quad ^7\text{IV}_b \quad ^7\text{V}_b \quad \text{I} \quad ; \qquad \text{V} \quad ^7\text{VI} \quad ^7\text{V}_b \quad \text{I} \quad ; \qquad ^7\text{V}_d \quad ^7\text{VI}_c \quad ^7\text{V}_c \quad \text{I} \quad ;$$

$$\text{V} \quad ^7\text{VI}_d \quad ^7\text{V}_d \quad \text{I}_b$$

B. Harmonize the following melodies :—

₊ In the next exercise, harmonize only where indicated by the ⌐_⌐ . A cross denotes the use of a Secondary 7th.

C. Play and write short rhythmical phrases, introducing the following chords, **and** exemplifying the resolutions dealt with in the present chapter :—

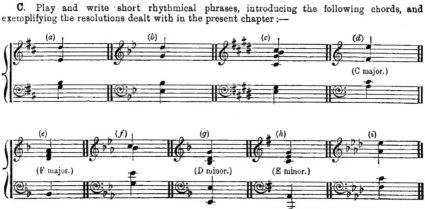

D. Harmonize the succeeding Figured Bass, in 4 vocal parts :—

SECONDARY 7ths INVOLVING USE OF MELODIC MINOR SCALE.

4. Reference to Chapter XVIII will remind the student that the variable upper tetrachord of the Melodic minor scale enables us largely to increase the range of triads in the minor key, the main condition in this connexion being that whenever the inflected note (*i.e.*, the major 6th or the minor 7th) occurs, it should usually form part of an ascending or descending scale-line between Dominant and Tonic. The same principle may be applied successfully in the case of Secondary 7ths, *e.g.*—

I. *Secondary 7ths containing Major 6th.**

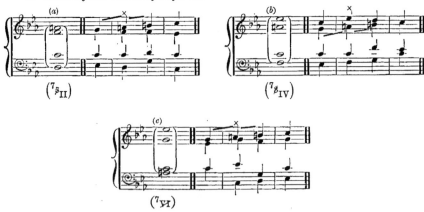

___

* These chords are, it will be found, more effective in certain positions than in others.

II. *Secondary 7ths containing Minor 7th.**

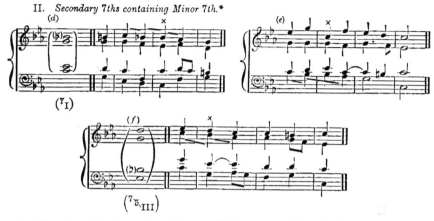

5. The extracts that are given below provide instances of the effective use of some of the above chords :—

I. *Subdominant 7th containing major 6th of Melodic minor scale :—*

II. *Secondary 7th upon major 6th of Melodic minor scale :—*

III. *Tonic 7th containing minor 7th of Melodic minor scale :—*

N.B.—Exs. (b) and (c) provide instances of Secondary 7ths used as " Passing " chords.

* These chords are, it will be found, more effective in certain positions than in others.

EXERCISES UPON SECONDARY 7THS INVOLVING USE OF
MELODIC MINOR SCALE.

E.　Play, in various minor keys, the following progressions (in different times and rhythms.)
N.B.—Take special care that the note of the Melodic minor scale moves in every case by step
(as indicated in Chapter XVIII, Sec. 2).

F.　Harmonize the following fragments of melody and bass.　Introduce a Secondary 7th
including a note of the Melodic minor scale in each example :—

(*a*)　(Major 6th.)　　(*b*)　(Major 6th.)　　(*c*)　(Major 6th.)

(*d*)　(Minor 7th.)　　(*e*)　(Major 6th.)　　(*f*)　(Major 6th.)

(*g*)　(Major 6th.)　　(*h*)　(Minor 7th.)

G.　Play and write short rhythmical phrases introducing the following chords :—

(*a*) (B minor.)　(*b*) (A minor.)　(*c*) (G minor.)　(E minor.)　(*d*) (A minor.)　(*f*) (B♭ minor.)

CHAPTER XXII.

CHROMATICALLY-ALTERED CHORDS.

1. THE principle of the "chromatic alteration" of one or more of the notes of certain diatonic chords is the logical outcome of the use of chromatic passing-notes and Appoggiaturas, and it has proved to be the means whereby composers have, in the course of time, been able largely to increase the possibilities of harmonic colour.

2. Like so many other notable harmonic effects, the chromatically-altered chord has resulted from the substitution of an *unessential* note for the harmony-note it was intended in the first place to decorate.* For example, if such a progression as the following were to be taken :—

(a)

it would, of course, be possible to "decorate" the treble part by means of a chromatic passing-note between the G and the A, thus :—

(b)

From this it would be a natural step to *substitute* the chromatic note, G♯, for the original diatonic one :—

(c)

⁎ It will perhaps be noticed that the "colour" imparted by the use of the chromatic note is obtained in example (c) without the somewhat weak and sentimental effect of the chromatic semitone in passing from G and G♯ in example (b). The result of the chromatic alteration—which, be it observed, *causes no change of key*—is to form a triad with a sharpened (or raised) 5th upon the Tonic of the scale.

---

* The simplest example of this is to be found in the chord of the Dominant 7th, where the 7th itself was undoubtedly first treated as a mere passing-note, thus :—

afterwards being taken (*circa* A.D. 1600) as *part of the chord*, in the manner familiar to everyone to-day :—

(*See* also Chapter XXI, Sec. 2 (foot-note), on the "Added sixth.")

3. Chromatically-altered chords are far more often met with in the major form of a key than in the minor form, and it should be observed ·that the original diatonic note may not only be chromatically raised (as in Sec. 2), but *lowered* semitonically in a similar manner.* The following are the most commonly used Chromatic alterations :—

I. Tonic or Dominant triad with *raised* 5th, forming an augmented triad in each case, *e.g.*—

II. Dominant 7th with *raised* 5th, *e.g.*—

N.B.—These are available in the major key only; the chromatically-raised note, forming a dissonance in each case, resolves by semitone *upwards*. It causes no False Relation by occurring in a different part from that in which the original diatonic note appears. (*See* ex. (*a*).) The raised 5th should always be placed *above* the 7th in the chord of the Dominant 7th.

---

* A familiar instance of this is the "dying fall" so often affected by certain church-organists at special moments in the course of the service. The reader will probably recognize an old friend in the following progression :—

where, between the 3rd of the Subdominant chord and the 5th of the succeeding Tonic harmony, a chromatic passing-note, A♭, is inserted. As in the example in Sec. 2, the somewhat mawkish effect of the semitonic movement from A to A♭ and G could be removed by the *substitution* of the chromatic note for the original diatonic one, thus :—

a new colouring being given to the key of C major by the use of the chromatic note A♭ instead of the usual diatonic A♮.

III   Subdominant triad of major key with *lowered* 3rd, *e.g.*—

$$\left(\,^{3}_{\,}IV\right)$$

IV.   Supertonic triad * (or Secondary 7th) of major key with *lowered* 5th, *e.g.* :—

$$\left(\,^{5}II_{b}\right) \qquad \left(\,^{7}_{5}II\right) \qquad \left(\,^{7}_{5}II_{b}\right)$$

N.B.—The lowered note generally falls a semitone, but *not invariably.* The chromatically-altered harmonies of IV and II (identical with the triads upon the corresponding degrees of the Tonic minor key) may usually be employed under the same conditions as the original diatonic chords.

V.   Supertonic triad of *minor* key, with *lowered* root, *e.g.*—

$$\left(\,^{N}_{b}\right) \qquad \left(\,^{N}_{b}\right)$$

N.B.—This chord, through being a chromatically-altered form of Supertonic harmony, is most frequently followed by either a Dominant or an inverted Tonic chord, and often precedes a Cadence (as shewn above). It is, in the majority of instances, taken in the first inversion, when it is known as the chord of the "Neapolitan Sixth." † Although a major chord, the bass-note of this first inversion can be doubled with good effect.

---

* This chord becoming, when "altered," a Diminished triad, is of course taken in the first inversion only.

† It is possible to use this chord in the *major* key also, but this involves the chromatic alteration of *two* notes of the original diatonic harmony, viz., the root and the 5th, *e.g.*—

(C major.)

A similar double chromatic alteration of the Submediant triad of the major key, is sometimes found, *e.g.*—

In this case also, both root and 5th are lowered a semitone, producing a chord identical with the Submediant triad of the Tonic minor key.

4. The extracts given below are typical of some of the chromatic alterations already spoken of :—

(a) *Tonic triad with raised 5th :—*

(b) *Dominant 7th with raised 5th :—*

(c) *Subdominant triad with lowered 3rd :—*

(d) *Supertonic triad with lowered 5th :—*

(*e*) *Supertonic Secondary 7th with lowered 5th :—*

(*f*) *Supertonic triad of minor key, with lowered root (Neapolitan Sixth) :—*

5. Further examples of chromatically-altered chords will be found in succeeding chapters.

EXERCISES ON CHROMATICALLY-ALTERED CHORDS.

A. Alter chromatically any of the chords in the following passage that you deem suitable, according to the principles set forth in the foregoing sections of this chapter.

B. Play, and write from memory, the following progressions in the usual way:—

(*a*) Major keys only.

I I_b ♯V I ; I ♮IV_b I_c 7V I ; I ♯II_b 7V I ; 7♭V_b I ♭I_b IV IV_b I ;

I I_b 7♯II 7V I ; I 7♯II_b I_c 7V I ; I_b IV 7♯II_b I .

(*b*) Minor keys only.

I ♮_b 7V I ; I_b ♮_b I_c 7V I ; IV ♮ I_c 7V I .

(*c*) Major keys only.

I ♯♭I ♮IV I ; I ♯♮_b 7V I ; I_b ♯♮_b I_c 7V I .

C. Harmonize the following fragments of melody, introducing a chromatically-altered chord at the × :—

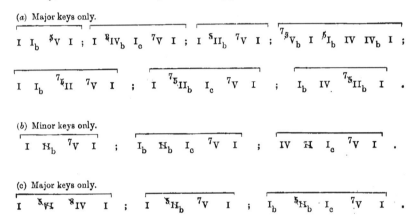

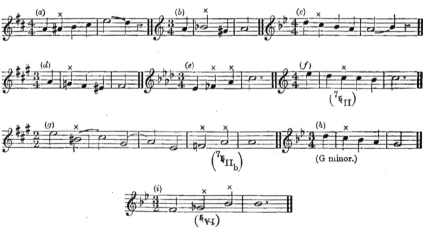

D. Harmonize the following melody for the Pianoforte, maintaining the form of accompaniment indicated in the opening bars. The × denotes a point at which a chromatically-altered chord should be used.

E. Write (in four parts, for voices) eight bars of music introducing the following chords, in the order given. Begin and end in E minor.

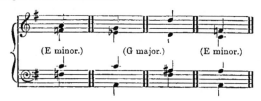

(E minor.)　　　(G major.)　　　(E minor.)

CHAPTER XXIII.

CHORDS OF THE NINTH.

I.—THE CHORD OF THE DOMINANT 9TH.

1. THE exercises in Chapter XVII upon the use of the Appoggiatura have already shewn that accented passing-notes above the root, 3rd or 5th of the Dominant 7th chord produce combinations which are frequently described as Dominant 9ths, 11ths and 13ths, *e.g.*—

(Dominant 9ths.)   (Dominant 11ths.)   (Dominant 13ths.)

2. It was also seen that the unessential note above the root of the Dominant 7th chord (forming the 9th from the Dominant root) might resolve in either of the following ways :—

   (i) Downwards to the root of the chord ;

   (ii) Upwards to the 3rd of the chord :—

*** The ♭ in brackets in the above examples indicates that the 9th in the major form of a key may be either a major or minor 9th, the latter being a "chromatically altered" note ; in the minor form of a key, the 9th is always *minor*, save when it rises by step to the 3rd of its own chord—that is, along the line of the Melodic minor scale :—

(See Chapter XVII, Sec. 7.)

The A♮ here clearly produces a smoother melodic progression than would result from A♭ proceeding upwards to B♮ and thereby causing the somewhat unvocal interval of an augmented 2nd. This interval might, however, in certain cases have a distinct beauty of its own, particularly in instrumental music, (*see* example from Beethoven in Sec. 3).

3. The "Appoggiatura" treatment of the 9th is illustrated by the following extracts :—

   (i) Ninth resolving to root :—

MOZART.—Fantasia in C minor.

(*a*)   etc.

(ii) Ninth resolving to 3rd :—

BEETHOVEN.—Sonata (Op. 53).

BEETHOVEN.—Pianoforte Concerto in C minor.

⁎ Ex. (*c*) shews the "Appoggiatura 9th" resolving by the *descent* of a 7th (minor or diminished), instead of by the ascent of a 2nd (major or augmented). This is often a very effective resolution.

4. Occasionally, the "Appoggiatura 9th" resolves by leaping in arpeggio to the 5th or the 7th of the *Dominant* harmony : *

SCHUMANN.—Pianoforte Concerto.

(9th leaping to 5th.)

* It may be objected that, if the 9th leaps in this manner (or as in **Ex.** (*c*) in Sec. 3), it cannot be regarded as an "Appoggiatura"; but it must be remembered that unessential notes (either unaccented or accented) do sometimes resolve otherwise than by step, even in the music of comparatively early instrumental writers :—

MOZART.—Sonata in A (No. 12).   BEETHOVEN.—Sonata (Op. 31, No. 1).

(*a*)   etc.   (*b*)   etc

(9th leaping to 7th.)

etc.

$\left(^9V_c\right)$

THE 9TH AS AN "ESSENTIAL" NOTE.

5. Instead of appearing as an Appoggiatura, the 9th frequently assumes the character of an "essential" note, and becomes an integral part of the Dominant harmony, resolving together with the rest of the chord upon a *new* harmony (usually the Tonic, to the 5th of which the 9th falls by step), *e.g.*—

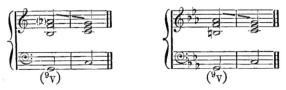

$\left(^9V\right)$ $\left(^9V\right)$

6. It is obvious that, as the *complete* chord of the Dominant 9th contains five notes, one of these must be omitted in four-part harmony. In the root-position this note is the 5th; in the inversions, the *root itself* (save occasionally in the 3rd inversion) :—

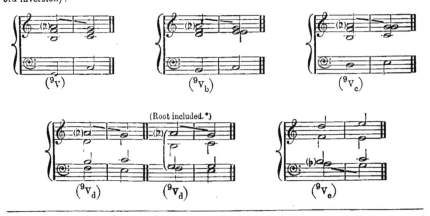

$\left(^9V\right)$ $\left(^9V_b\right)$ $\left(^9V_c\right)$

(Root included. *)

$\left(^9V_d\right)$ $\left(^9V_d\right)$ $\left(^9V_e\right)$

---

* When the root is included, as here, the 9th must be at the distance of a *ninth* (not a *second*) from it.

N.B.—The *major* 9th usually (but not *invariably*—*see* example from Beethoven in Sec. 8) sounds better *above* the 3rd of the chord; as a consequence, the 4th inversion of the Dominant major 9th is rarely met with. All the progressions given above are available in the minor form of the key, with the proviso that the 9th is always *minor*. César Franck has an effective instance of the Dominant minor 9th in root-position;—

CÉSAR FRANCK.—Symphony in *D* minor.

7. The inversions of the chord of the Dominant *minor* 9th (when the root is omitted) produce the harmony which is often conveniently described as the " chord of the *Diminished* Seventh " :—

(Root G omitted. . . . .)

Two well-known examples are given below :—

BEETHOVEN.—Sonata (Op. 57).

CHOPIN.—Etude in C♯ minor (Op. 10).

8. The inversions of the Dominant *major* 9th (with the root omitted) produce a chord identical with the Secondary 7th upon the Leading-note of the major key, and it is for that reason sometimes termed the " chord of the Leading 7th " :—

(Root G omitted. . . . .)

It is of course *possible* to regard it as a Secondary 7th with a freer resolution, *e.g.*—

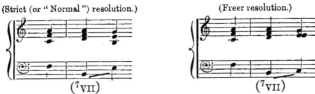

(Strict (or " Normal ") resolution.)   (Freer resolution.)

(^{7}VII)   (^{7}VII)

but for all practical purposes it is simpler and clearer to think of the chord as derived from the Dominant root, that is, as $\left(^{9}V_{b}\right)$

N.B.—It is of comparatively small importance how a chord is *named*, so long as its effect has been aurally recognized, and its treatment mastered.

A most effective instance of the use of the inversions of the Dominant major 9th (the "Leading 7th") is to be found in the slow movement of Beethoven's 5th Symphony :—

BEETHOVEN.—Symphony (No. 5.) in C minor.

(Key E flat major.)   etc.

$\left(^{9}V_{d}\right)$ $\left(^{9}V_{b}\right)$ $\left(^{9}V_{d}\right)$ $\left(^{9}V_{b}\right)$ $\left(^{9}V_{d}\right)$ $\left(^{9}V_{b}\right)$ $\left(^{9}V\right)$ (I)

PART-WRITING.

9. In resolving the inversions of the chord of the Dominant *major* 9th upon the Tonic triad (or one of its inversions), care should be taken to avoid clumsy consecutive 5ths, by making the 5th and major 9th move in contrary motion to one another (if the 5th is placed below the 9th) :—

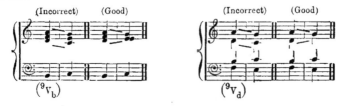

(Incorrect)   (Good)   (Incorrect)   (Good)

$\left(^{9}V_{b}\right)$ $\left(^{9}V_{d}\right)$

N.B.—Such 5ths are sometimes possible in the case of the *minor* 9th :—

one of the 5ths being diminished, but even then their avoidance is usually to be recommended.

A progression such as the following (with the consecutive 5ths between the *bass* and another part) should not be tolerated :—

but should be modified thus :—

10. Ordinarily the 3rd and 7th in the chord of Dominant 9th move as in the case of the Dominant 7th chord, but a not uncommon treatment of the 7th in the inversions of the Dominant *minor* 9th (chord of Diminished 7th) is represented by the following, where the 7th *leaps* a 4th down to the root of the Tonic triad :—

MENDELSSOHN.—"Lauda Sion."

The 7th is then not infrequently doubled, as in the above example.

EXERCISES UPON THE DOMINANT 9TH.

A. Play and write examples of the following (in various major and minor keys) :—

(*a*) The Appoggiatura 9th resolving upon the root of the Dominant 7th chord ;

(*b*) The Appoggiatura 9th resolving upon the 3rd of the Dominant 7th chord ;

(Illustrate this by making the 9th sometimes rise a 2nd, and sometimes fall a 7th.)

(*c*) The 9th as an "essential" note of the Dominant harmony.

*** In every instance resolve the Dominant harmony upon that of the Tonic.

B. Play, and write from memory, the following progressions, in various major and minor keys. When working the examples in the major form of a key, the 9th should be sometimes major, and sometimes minor ; in the *minor* form of a key, it should always be minor.

$$\overline{\text{I } \ ^9\text{V } \text{I}} \ ; \ \overline{\text{I } \ ^9\text{V}_b \ \text{I}} \ ; \ \overline{\text{I}_b \ \text{I } \ ^9\text{V}_d \ \text{I}_b} \ ; \ \overline{\text{I } \text{IV } \ ^9\text{V}_c \ \text{I}_b} \ \overline{^9\text{V}_e \ \text{I}_c \ ^9\text{V}_d \ \text{I}_b}$$

(Be careful of the part writing here.)

C. Add Alto and Tenor parts to the following, according to the figuring.

N.B.—Analyse the harmony throughout.

D. Harmonize the following melodies, introducing a chord of the 9th (direct or inverted) where indicated. An "Appoggiatura" 9th resolving on the root of the *Dominant* harmony is indicated by the letter (*a*); a similar "Appoggiatura" 9th resolving on the 3rd, by (*b*); while an "essential" 9th is implied by the letter (*c*). The student is left to decide whether a major 9th or a minor 9th is preferable on each occasion:

| C major. | F minor. | A♭ major. |

N.B.—Consider the following as written for the Pianoforte. Maintain an accompaniment similar to that suggested in the opening bars.* The *rhythm* of this is indicated throughout, underneath the melody itself:—

E. Harmonize the following Unfigured basses. The various forms of 9th are indicated as in the foregoing section :—

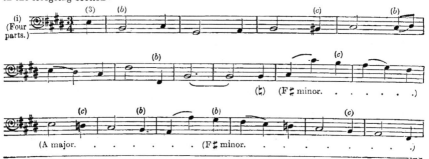

* See Appendix B.

x The 6th added to the Tonic triad in a final cadence is a not unusual modern idiom, which, however, easily becomes a somewhat trying mannerism.

F. Play or write, several phrases of your own, including one or more of the succeeding chords in each. Vary your key each time (transposing the given chords), and use both major and minor forms of the key (making the necessary modifications of the 9th).

11. The " essential " chord of the 9th (particularly in the form known as the *D*iminished 7th) is frequently decorated by " appoggiaturas " above or below its various notes, *e.g.*—

(Above 3rd.*) (Above 5th.†) (Above 7th.) (Above 9th.) (Below 3rd.) (Below 5th.) (Below 7th.)

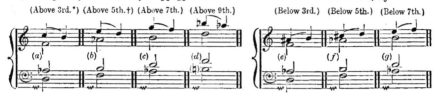

(Double Appoggiaturas.)

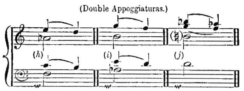

Examples (*c*), (*i*) and (*j*) shew that the root itself is sometimes sounded as an " unessential " note against the 9th, when it loses its fundamental character altogether, and needs resolution. Examples (*d*) and (*j*) are illustrations of the fact that the " unessential " note a tone above the minor 9th makes no false relation with the 3rd of the chord. A beautiful instance of this is to be found in the " Intermezzo " of Schumann's Pianoforte Conerto :—

SCHUMANN.—Pianoforte Concerto.

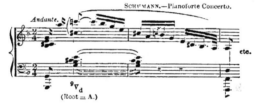

EXERCISES (*Cont*ᵈ·).

G. Play, in four parts (or amplified for the Pianoforte), the chord of the *D*iminished 7th (in its various positions) in all keys—major and minor—and " decorate " its several notes with appoggiaturas above and below them. Do not confine the appoggiaturas to the Treble part. Resolve on Tonic harmony.

H. Harmonize the following fragments, using *D*iminished 7th harmony during the prevalence of the | ⌐ ⌐|. Resolve on Tonic harmony.

(*a*)

₊ The above might be treated as follows :—

---

* " Appoggiatura " 11th. ⎫
† " Appoggiatura " 13th. ⎬ Compare with examples in Chapter XVII, Sec. 7.
⎭

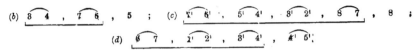

I. Harmonize the following double appoggiaturas with *D*iminished 7th harmony (in various positions), and resolve in each case upon Tonic harmony :—

J. Harmonize the succeeding melody in full harmony for the Pianoforte. Wherever a × is found, the note so indicated should be harmonized with a *D*ominant 9th chord :—

II.—SECONDARY CHORDS OF THE 9TH.

12. Chords of the 9th formed diatonically upon other degrees of the scale than that of the Dominant are much rarer and more difficult of introduction than chords of the 7th upon the same degrees. The following passage illustrates a series of secondary 9ths.* It will be seen that the 9th falls a 2nd in each case, and that the 7th (which should always be included) resolves similarly :—

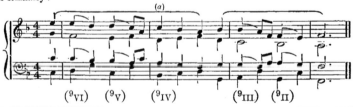

(^9VI) (^9V) (^9IV) (^9III) (^9II)

---

* As a secondary 9th contains *five* notes, it is of course necessary to omit one of the notes of the complete chord ; this is almost invariably the 5th. In five-part harmony this necessity would not arise.

13. As will be seen by the preceding example, a secondary chord of the 9th most frequently resolves upon a chord whose root is a 4th above its own; but that on the Supertonic often resolves more freely, upon *Tonic* harmony (the 9th *remaining*), thus :—

$$\left(^9_{\text{II}}\right) \left(\text{I}_c\right)$$

and that on the Subdominant (as at (*a*) in Sec. 12) upon *Dominant* harmony. In each of these cases the chords of the 9th follow the same procedure as the Secondary 7ths on the corresponding degrees of the scale. (*See* Chapter XXI, Sec. 2). Sterndale Bennett has a very happy instance of the Subdominant 9th resolving on Dominant harmony :—

STERNDALE BENNETT.—"Woman of Samaria."

etc.

$$\left(^9_{8_{\text{IV}}}\right)$$

14. Debussy introduces an interesting sequence of Secondary 9ths in his "Doctor Gradus ad Parnassum" :—

DEBUSSY.—"Children's Corner" Suite.

(Key G major.) etc.

$$\left(^9_{\text{II}}\right) \qquad \left(^9_{\text{III}}\right)$$

and a striking example of alternate diatonic 9ths and 7ths is afforded by the 12th Prelude of Book 2 of Bach's "48" :—

BACH.—"48" (Book 2, Prelude No. 12).

Harmonic scheme :—

Key A♭ major.   Key F minor.

$$\left(^7_{\text{V}}\right) \ \left(^9_{\text{I}}\right) \left(^7_{\text{IV}}\right) \left(^9_{\text{II}}\right) \left(^7_{\text{V}}\right)$$

15. The inversions are impracticable with the root included; with this note omitted, they become identical with Secondary 7ths, *e.g.*—

Clearly, the above chord is nothing more than the Secondary 7th upon the Subdominant, resolving upon *D*ominant harmony.

EXERCISES UPON SECONDARY 9THS.

A. Resolve the following chords, bringing each exercise to a full close.

(*f*) Play and write the following (in five parts), in various *major* keys.

$$V \ {}^9VI \ {}^7II \ {}^9V \ I \ {}^9IV \ {}^7V \ I$$

B. Harmonize the following Figured Bass in four parts:—

* Let the melody here run thus:—

CHAPTER XXIV.

CHORD OF THE DOMINANT 11TH.

1. THEORETICALLY (as was seen in Chapter XVII), the addition of thirds above the chord of the *Dominant* 7th produces in succession the chords known as *Dominant* 9ths, 11ths and 13ths respectively :—

The 11th and 13th (like the 9th) are frequently nothing more than accented passing-notes or Appoggiaturas sounded against the *Dominant* 7th harmony, and little need be said as to their treatment beyond what has already been set forth in preceding chapters. Sometimes, however, the 11th and 13th assume the character of "essential" notes, and it is to their use under such conditions that the following remarks will mainly apply.

2. The true "chord of the *Dominant* 11th" exists only in the root-position, and is of very rare occurrence; in four parts the notes present are the root, 7th, 9th and 11th, thus :—

In the resolution upon Tonic harmony—its most frequent progression—the 11th *remains*, while the 7th and 9th fall in the usual way. Grieg has a delightful example of this chord in his "Vöglein" :—

GRIEG.—Lyrische Stückchen (Op. 43).

pp

*** Not being limited to four parts, Grieg includes the 5th of the chord; the 3rd is *always omitted.*

Another very striking instance of the true Dominant 11th is to be found in the 2nd Act of "Madam Butterfly" :—

PUCCINI.—"Madam Butterfly."

(D minor.)

where the 11th is accompanied by the *major* 9th—an unusual proceeding in a minor key.

3. In all the inversions the root is omitted, as well as the 3rd, and the chord then consists of the *four upper notes only* of the entire series :—

becoming identical with the Secondary 7th upon the Supertonic treated of in Chapters XX and XXI—with or without the chromatic alteration of its 5th.   Beyond the examples and remarks that follow, further comment is unnecessary.

INVERSIONS (SO-CALLED) OF THE DOMINANT 11TH (= SECONDARY 7TH UPON THE SUPERTONIC).

Theoretically it would be possible to analyse the chord marked × as the fourth inversion of a chord of the Dominant minor 9th and 11th in A minor (with root and 3rd omitted); but it is far simpler to think of it as the Secondary 7th of the Supertonic, in its second inversion.

The above extract shews various positions of the Supertonic Secondary 7th—with its 5th chromatically lowered—resolving upon the second inversion of the Tonic triad. The following is the simple harmonic scheme, omitting passing-notes, etc. : —

Again, it would be possible (theoretically) to regard the chord of the 7th as being derived from an absent Dominant root, and to explain it as a chord of the Dominant minor 9th and 11th (with root and 3rd omitted). But there is little object in doing so.

EXERCISES UPON THE *DOMINANT* 11TH.

Note.—From the remarks in the present chapter, it will be clear that few exercises will be needed upon the Dominant 11th, as most of the combinations sometimes described as forming different aspects of that chord have already been treated of in the exercises upon the Accented Passing-note, or Appoggiatura, and upon Secondary 7ths.

A. Play and write the true "chord of the 11th" (Sec. 2, p. 215), in various major and minor keys, resolving it upon Tonic harmony. Place the parts above the bass-note in different positions from time to time, *e.g.*—

B. Play and write (for the Pianoforte) rhythmical phrases and sentences, introducing the following harmonies, which should also be transposed into other keys.

CHAPTER XXV.

CHORD OF THE DOMINANT 13TH.

1. As in the case of the Dominant 11th, many of the combinations frequently classified as 13ths merely result from the sounding of Appoggiaturas against the chord of the Dominant 7th or the Dominant 9th; others, again, are nothing more than Secondary 7ths (with, occasionally, one or more of their notes chromatically altered). As a consequence, the number of genuine chords of the 13th is comparatively small, as will be seen from what follows in the present chapter.

2. The complete chord of the Dominant 13th, as built up from the Dominant root by the addition of 3rds, will be found on page 150, but it need hardly be said that it is rarely, if ever, found with all its notes present.* Certain selections from the whole series are made, and—as with the 11th—it is when the four upper notes of that series are so drawn upon that the combinations become identical with Secondary chords of the 7th.

3. Like the 9th and 11th, the 13th from the Dominant may—

    (i) Move as an Appoggiatura, up or down to a note of the chord of the Dominant 7th or 9th;

    (ii) Resolve (as an "essential" note) upon a new chord.

4. The Appoggiatura combinations are many and varied; several of these have already been given in Chapter XVII, Secs. 7 and 8; others will be found in Chapter XXIII, Sec. 11; it is therefore hardly necessary to say more about them here. The following extracts, however, are interesting:—

BEETHOVEN.—Sonata (Op. 10. No. 3).

(a)

(Appoggiatura 13th against Dominant 9th harmony.)

GRIEG.—Pianoforte Stücke (Op. 1).

(b)   Key G.   Key C.   etc.

(Appoggiatura 13th against chord of Dominant minor 9th in G major, and Dominant 7th in C major.)

---

* The celebrated example from Beethoven's Choral Symphony, made so much of by many theorists as an instance of a *complete* chord of the Dominant 13th :—

Root = A. (?)

even if—as is not improbable—it did not arise from an error in the original horn-parts, is far more ration-ally considered merely as the first inversion of a chord of D minor, with four accented passing-notes. This is clearly the effect upon the musical ear.

WAGNER.—"Die Meistersinger."

(c)

etc.

(Leaping Appoggiatura 13th against Dominant major 9th harmony.)

THE 13TH AS AN "ESSENTIAL" NOTE.

5. When the 13th is taken as an essential note it displaces the 5th of the chord, and resolves—usually upon Tonic or Submediant harmony—by (i) falling a 3rd,* *e.g.*—

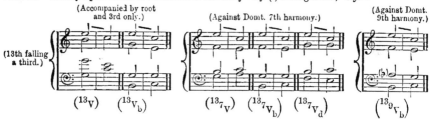

(13th falling a third.)

(Accompanied by root and 3rd only.)   (Against Domt. 7th harmony.)   (Against Domt. 9th harmony.)

$\left(^{13}_{}V\right)$ $\left(^{13}_{}V_b\right)$ $\left(^{13}_{7}V\right)$ $\left(^{13}_{7}V_b\right)$ $\left(^{13}_{7}V_d\right)$ $\left(^{13}_{9}V_b\right)$

or (ii) remaining stationary, *e.g.*—

(13th remaining.)

(Without 7th.)   (With 7th.)

(*See* Sec. 11 (*b*).)

$\left(^{13}_{}V\right)$ $\left(^{13}_{}V_b\right)$ $\left(^{13}_{7}V\right)$

N.B.—All the above may be taken equally well in the minor form of the key, in which case, however, the 13th should always be *minor.* It will be observed that *the 5th and 13th never appear together.*

6. The following extracts contain typical examples of the "essential" chord of the 13th :—

DVOŘÁK.—"Stabat Mater."

(a)

(Minor 13th accompanied by root and 3rd only— 13th falling a minor third.)

---

* Exceptionally the 13th *rises* a 3rd thus :—

$\left(^{13}_{7}V_d\right)$

$\left(^{13}_{7}V_d\right)$

Cɪopɪɴ.—Ballade in F (Op. 38).

(b)   etc.

(Major 13th accompanied by root, 3rd and 7th—
13th falling a major third.)

Césaʀ Fʀᴀɴᴄᴋ.—Symphony in D minor.

(c)

(Major 13th accompanied by root, 3rd and 7th—
13th remaining stationary.)

7. The "sharpened 5th" of the *Dominant* chord in a major key is sometimes spoken of as a Minor 13th in disguise, the $D\sharp$ in the following examples, for instance, being regarded as "Expedient False Notation" for E♭, the minor 13th from the *Dominant* root (G):—

It is, however, simpler, and in accordance with the actual musical impression produced, to consider the $D\sharp$ as a "chromatic alteration" of the 5th of the *Dominant* chord $(D\natural)$.—(*See* Chapter XXII).*

8. When the 11th is included in the chord of the 13th, the harmony usually consists of the four upper notes only of the complete series :—

] omitted.

It then becomes identical with the *Secondary* chord of the 7th upon the *Subdominant*, and it is quite needless to refer the combination to a supposed *Dominant* root. (For examples *see* Chapter XXI, Secs. 3 and 5.)

---

* It is significant that no composer would dream of writing E♭ in such cases as the above, however he might regard the origin of the chord, for the simple reason that he would be making the passage more difficult to read, the E♭ needing, in the majority of cases, to be contradicted by a ♮ in the following chord.

9 The occasional lowering of the 3rd and 7th by " chromatic alteration " produces many new and interesting varieties of this chord, *e.g.*—

I.—With 3rd chromatically lowered.

II.—With 7th chromatically lowered.*

III.—With both 3rd and 7th chromatically lowered.*

N.B.—All the above chords *could*, of course, be regarded as having a Dominant origin, thus:—

(Root G (?)).

and then the F, A, C, and E would be considered as the 7th, 9th, 11th, and 13th respectively, from G root. This method of analysis is, however, somewhat cumbersome, and pre-supposes an "absentee" root whose existence is at the least doubtful.

---

* It is possible that these chords are actually instances of the " chord of the Added 6th " $\left(^{7}II_{b}\right)$, with the 6th chromatically raised, on the principle referred to in Sec. 7 above, *e.g.*—

(*See* also Chapter XXVIII, Sec. 9.)

The classification is unimportant, when once the musical effect has been aurally discerned and memorized.

10. The following example from Grieg is interesting as affording a very beautiful use of 7_{IV} and the chromatic alteration of the same into $7_{\sharp IV}$.

GRIEG.—Pianoforte Concerto.

(Appoggiatura.)

The progressions at (*a*) and (*b*) give the undoubted impression of a Plagal Cadence in each case, *i.e.*, of Subdominant (not Dominant) harmony proceeding to Tonic.

PART-WRITING.

11. In addition to the important rule that the note upon which the 13th resolves should not be sounded against it, the following hints are useful :—

(*a*) The 13th, in by far the greater number of instances, sounds better *above the 7th, e.g.*—

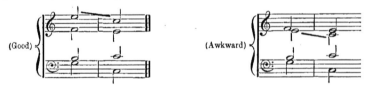

N.B.—The *Appoggiatura 13th*—particularly if it is melodically prominent—is, however, quite frequently of good effect below the 7th, *e.g.*—

Dominant harmony.

(*b*) If the 7th is included in the chord, it is better—as a rule—that the 13th should not resolve by *remaining*, but that it should leap a 3rd down, *e.g.*—

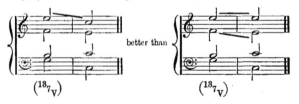

(*See*, however, example from César Franck in Sec. 6.)

EXERCISES UPON THE DOMINANT 13TH.

Note.—As many of the combinations frequently classified as chords of the 13th have already been dealt with in the exercises upon the Appoggiatura and upon Secondary 7ths, the following exercises merely supply further practice in those directions, and include examples of the few cases where the 13th comes into neither of these categories.

A. Play the progressions in Sec. 5 in various major and minor keys.

B. Play the following chord-successions in various major and minor keys :—

$$^{13}_{7}\text{V} \quad \text{VI} \quad \text{II}_b \quad ^{13}_{7}\text{V} \quad \text{I} \quad ; \quad \text{VI} \quad ^{7}\text{II}_b \quad ^{13}_{9}\text{V}_d \quad \text{I}_b \quad ; \quad ^{13}\text{V}_b \quad \text{I} \quad ^{13}\text{V} \quad \text{VI}$$

(No 7th in chord of 13th.)

C. Harmonize the following melody, including "essential" chords of the 13th (direct or inverted, and with or without the major or minor 9th—as shewn in Sec. 5)— at the x.

D. Play and write phrases and sentences introducing the following harmonies. Transpose into various major or minor keys.

CHAPTER XXVI.

CHROMATIC HARMONY.

I.—THE SUPERTONIC CHROMATIC TRIAD AND CHORD OF THE SEVENTH.
II.—THE TONIC CHROMATIC CHORD OF THE SEVENTH.

1. As the art of music developed, particularly on its instrumental side, the boundaries of the key began in course of time to be enlarged, not only by means of the "chromatic alterations" already spoken of in Chapter XXII, but by the use of certain diatonic chords belonging to adjacent keys in such a transient manner as to cause no actual modulation from the original Tonic centre. The chords that obviously lend themselves most readily to this procedure are the *Dominant harmonies* of the Dominant and Subdominant keys.

2. In example (*a*) below, the Dominant chord of the key of G clearly produces a modulation from key C to key G :—

but in example (*b*)—for the reason that no single chord defines or establishes a key—no modulation takes place at all, the key of C major both preceding and following the chord in question, which therefore becomes a *chromatic triad* on the Supertonic of that key. The tendency of the F♯ to suggest G major is clearly checked by the succeeding F♮ :—

3. A chromatic chord, therefore, is a chord which contains one or more notes foreign to the diatonic scale, but which, although *suggesting* or threatening a modulation, does not actually disturb the original key-centre.

N.B.—The major 6th and minor 7th of the Melodic Minor scale are not chromatic, but diatonic— even although the former has of necessity to be indicated by an accidental.

THE SUPERTONIC CHROMATIC TRIAD.

4. The chromatic triad on the Supertonic is a major triad, its 3rd being the chromatic note,* *e.g.*—

* *See* note in Sec. 3 above with reference to the 5th of this chord in the minor form of the key.

5. If followed by a Dominant common chord, this triad induces a modulation to the Dominant key (*see* example (*a*) in Sec. 2) ; it is therefore chromatic only if it is succeeded by—

(i) A chord containing a note that contradicts the sharpened 3rd (usually a Dominant *discord*—7th, 9th, etc.) :—

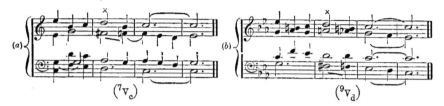

or (ii) some form (usually an inversion) of Tonic harmony :—

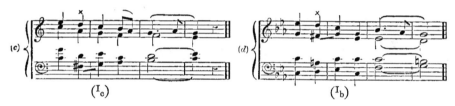

⁎ Compare the more usual progressions of the *diatonic* triad of the Supertonic given in Chapter XIII, Secs. 3 and 4, with the above examples.

6. The chromatically raised 3rd is as sensitive as a Leading-note, and *should not be doubled.*⁎ In whatever part of the harmony it appears it should—in proceeding to the next chord—either rise or fall a semitone (*see* above examples).

N.B.—The chromatic 3rd, however, in many cases does *not* stand in False Relation to the 7th of the Dominant harmony, sounded in another part in the following chord, *e.g.*—

WAGNER.—"Tannhäuser."

⁎ It is, of course, the Leading-note of the Dominant key. The prohibition as to doubling is relaxed at times in amplifying four-part harmony for the Pianoforte, but even then, only under certain well-defined conditions (*see* Appendix B).

THE SUPERTONIC CHROMATIC CHORD OF THE 7TH.

7. A 7th is frequently added to the Supertonic chromatic triad, when the chord produced is obviously identical with the *Dominant 7th* of the *D*ominant key :—

This chord is treated in practically the same manner as the chromatic triad already considered, the only additional point to be noticed being that of the movement of the 7th itself which, in the majority of cases—

(i) Falls (or, at times, *rises*) one degree, if followed by a *D*ominant discord :—

or (ii) *remains*, if followed by Tonic harmony :—

*** Compare the resolutions of the diatonic (Secondary) chord of the 7th upon the Supertonic (Chapters XX and XXI) with the above examples.

8. As the inversions follow the same principles of progression as the root-position, further remarks under this head are unnecessary. The succeeding extract from Schumann provides a beautiful example of the 2nd inversion of the Supertonic chromatic chord of the 7th, in key F, resolving upon the 1st inversion of the *D*ominant 7th :—

N.B.—The 7th rises, to avoid the doubling of the Leading-note (compare Chapter XV, Sec. 6).

9. Although the treatment of the 7th as detailed in Secs. 7 and 8 is that which is most frequently adhered to, it is not uncommon to find the 7th *leaping* to a note of the Tonic chord :—

10. As in the case of the chord of the Dominant 7th, the root is sometimes omitted (usually when the chord is in its second inversion), when the 7th may be freely doubled, *e.g.*—

(G omitted.)

EXERCISES UPON THE SUPERTONIC CHROMATIC TRIAD AND CHORD OF THE 7TH.

A. Insert a suitable chord in each blank space, in order to follow the Supertonic chromatic triad (or chord of the 7th) without changing the key :—

B. Play (and write from memory) the following progressions, arranging them in various times, and endeavouring to decorate them with passing-notes (accented and unaccented), and chord-figures. Transpose them into all keys, major and minor.

$$I \quad I_b \quad {}^{\sharp}II \quad {}^{7}V_b \quad I \quad ; \quad I \quad V \quad VI \cdot {}^{\sharp}II_b \quad I_c \quad {}^{7}V \quad I \quad ; \quad I_c \quad {}^{7\sharp}II_b \quad {}^{7}V_d \quad I_b \quad ;$$

$$I \quad {}^{\sharp}II \quad I \quad I_b \quad {}^{7}II_b \quad V \quad ; \quad I \quad {}^{7}_{\sharp}II_c \quad I_c \quad {}^{\sharp}V_d \quad I_b \quad ; \quad I \quad {}^{\sharp}II \quad {}^{\sharp}IV \quad I_c \quad {}^{7}V \quad I \quad ;$$
(In minor key only.)   (In major key only.)

$$I_c \quad {}^{7\sharp}II_c \quad {}^{7}V_b \quad I \quad ; \quad I \quad {}^{7}_{\sharp}II_d \quad {}^{7}V_b \quad I \quad .$$

C. Harmonize the following melody for the Pianoforte, introducing a Supertonic chromatic triad (or chord of the 7th)—direct or inverted—at each ×.

D. Beginning as under, write a Long-metre Hymn-tune, in the key of A minor, modulating to the key of C major in the second line, touching the keys of E minor and *D* minor in the third line, and concluding with the fourth line in A minor. Introduce four examples of the Supertonic chromatic triad (or chord of the 7th), each to be treated differently from the others, during the course of the piece.

E. Work the following Figured-bass in four parts. Make the highest part as melodious as possible, introducing occasional passing-notes (in *any* of the parts), where suitable :—

THE TONIC CHROMATIC CHORD OF THE 7TH.

11. Just as the *Dominant* harmony of the *Dominant* key in Ex. (*a*) in Section 2 caused a modulation from C major to G major, so the *Dominant* 7th chord of the *Subdominant key* in the following passage produces an equally emphatic modulation to *F major :*—

12. This chord can, however, be also used in such a transient manner as not to affect the key-centre; it then becomes a chromatic chord of the 7th upon the *Tonic :*—

13. The various positions of the chord, in C major and C minor respectively, appear as follows :—

** It will be observed that the 7th is chromatic in the major form of the key, the 3rd chromatic in the minor form.

14. The Chromatic chord of the 7th upon the Tonic is far less frequently used than that on the Supertonic, and the opportunities for its effective introduction (unless accompanied by a minor 9th) * are somewhat rare, particularly in the minor key. It resolves upon—

(i) A *Dominant* discord (7th, 9th, etc.) as in Sec. 12 or in the following example :—

$$(^7V_c)$$

. In this resolution the 3rd moves a 2nd up or down, and the 7th rises a chromatic semitone.

(ii) Supertonic chromatic harmony :—

$$(^7g_{II_c})$$

. Here the 3rd rises a *whole tone*, and the 7th falls a 2nd. This example would be equally effective in the minor form of the key, thus :—

(iii) A Subdominant triad, provided that some form of Dominant harmony immediately follows, to check the tendency towards the Subdominant key, *e.g.*—

$$(IV_c)$$

. In the above passage the Subdominant triad is succeeded by a Dominant minor 9th; the B♭ is thus counteracted by a B♮, and the original tonality is undisturbed. A familiar and charming instance of this resolution is to be found at the conclusion of the slow movement of Mendelssohn's Pianoforte Concerto in G minor :—

MENDELSSOHN.—Concerto (Op. 25).

$$(^7I) \qquad (^{IV}c) \qquad (^7v) \ (I)$$

. The Bass E in bars 2–4 of the above extract is a Tonic Pedal (*see* Appendix A).

---

* *See* Chapter XXVII.

EXERCISES ON THE TONIC CHROMATIC CHORD OF THE 7TH.

F. Insert a suitable chord at each ×, in order to follow the Tonic chromatic chord of the 7th without changing the key :—

G. Play (and write from memory) the following progressions, arranging them in various times, and endeavouring to decorate them with passing-notes (accented and unaccented), and chord-figures. Transpose them into all keys.

$$I \quad {}^{7}I \quad {}^{7}V_c \quad I_b \quad ; \quad I \quad {}^{7}I_d \quad {}^{7}\sharp II_c \quad I_c \quad {}^{7}V \quad I \quad ;$$

$$I_b \quad {}^{7}I_b \quad IV \quad {}^{9}V_d \quad I \quad ; \quad I_b \quad {}^{7}I_b \quad {}^{7}\sharp II_b \quad I_c \quad {}^{7}V \quad I \quad .$$

H. Harmonize the following Unfigured Bass : a Tonic chromatic chord of the 7th is implied at each ×. Do not leave the key of F major.

I. Write an exercise of your own (in four parts), introducing each of these progressions (in any key and in any order) :—

$$^{7}I_d \quad {}^{7}\sharp II_c \quad ; \quad {}^{7}I_b \quad {}^{7}V_c \quad ; \quad {}^{7}I \quad {}^{7}V_c \quad .$$

Begin and end in a major key, but modulate to the Relative minor in the course of the exercise.

CHAPTER XXVII.

CHROMATIC CHORDS OF THE NINTH, ELEVENTH AND THIRTEENTH.

I.—SUPERTONIC AND TONIC NINTHS.

1. A MAJOR or minor 9th from the root may obviously be added to the Supertonic and Tonic chromatic chords of the 7th, under similar conditions as obtain in the case of *Dominant* harmony, *e.g.—*

the 9th being either major *or* minor in the major key, and almost invariably minor in the minor key.

2. The 9th in these chords may, like the 9th of the *Dominant,* be (i) merely an Appoggiatura, when its treatment needs no further comment, or (ii) an " essential " note of the chord. In the latter case, the 9th will usually (*a*) move up or down a 2nd, or (*b*) remain, *e.g.—*

(i) Supertonic 9ths.

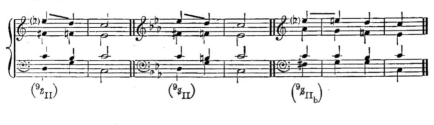

(ii) Tonic 9ths.

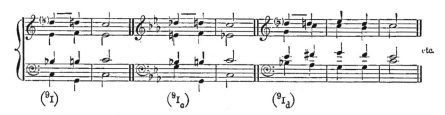

3. The inversions of these chords—in which the root does not appear—are much more often met with than the direct position, and in the case of the *minor* 9th they provide further instances of the familiar *Diminished* 7th chord :—

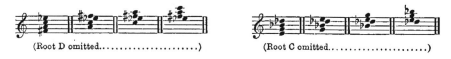

(Root D omitted......................)   (Root C omitted......................)

The following extracts illustrate some effective uses of the inversions of the "essential" Supertonic and Tonic 9ths :—

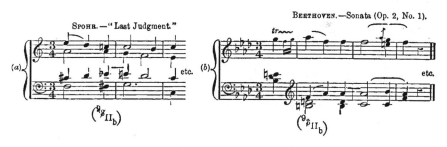

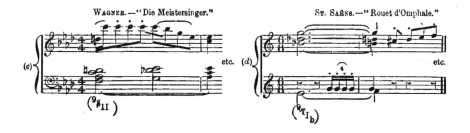

In the next example, some interesting " Appoggiatura " uses of the direct *Dominant* and Supertonic 9ths are shewn :—

ZDENKO FIBICH.—" Stimmungen " (Op. 41, No. 11).

$$(^9\text{V})\qquad(^9\text{V})\qquad(^9_3\text{II})\qquad\qquad(^9\text{V})$$

" EXPEDIENT FALSE NOTATION."

4. The well-known passage in Beethoven's Sonata (*Op.* 31, No. 3)—

$$^7\text{II}_b \text{————————————} ^9_3\text{II}_b\text{——} \quad \text{I}_c \quad ^9_{\sharp}\text{II}_b\,\text{I}_c \quad ^9_{\sharp}\text{II}_b\,\text{I}_c$$

is an illustration of the case of a chord being written in two different ways. The Supertonic minor 9th (G♭) in the key of E flat major is, in bars 6 and 7, changed to F♯, for the apparent purpose of avoiding the contradiction of the G♭ by G♮—as is necessary in the first instance. The minor 9th (either from the Supertonic or the Tonic root) is frequently written as an augmented 8th from that root (as here), in order to avoid the use of needless accidentals, and the change so made in the method of writing the chord is usually known as *Expedient False Notation.**

The passage from St. Saëns' " Rouet d'Omphale " also, quoted in Sec. 3 is, as a matter of fact, written as follows in the score :—

etc.

that is, with a two-fold example of Expedient False Notation, which clearly saves the use of two accidentals (B♮ and D♮) in the following bar.

** ** The author of the present volume, in his *Practical Harmony*† (page 82) refers to the matter of Expedient False Notation in these terms :—" Such false notation, however convenient to the *reader* of music, is certainly puzzling at first to those who may be trying to analyse any particular chord. The student must, therefore, carefully ascertain by the context in what key the chord in question is, and then compare the notation of the chord with the notation of the Harmonic Chromatic scale‡ of that key. Any note that differs from this constitutes a case of Expedient False Notation. When

---

* Why Beethoven did not adopt this in bars 4 and 5 of the above extract is difficult to see.
  † Joseph Williams, Ltd.   ‡ *See* Appendix C.

once the true notation has thus been arrived at, no difficulty will be experienced if, in dealing with *inverted* chords of the minor 9th when the root is absent, it is borne in mind that

(i) The presence of the augmented 4th *from the key-note* indicates *Supertonic* root.

(ii) The presence of the Leading-note indicates *Dominant* root.

(iii) The presence of the minor 7th *from the key-note* indicates *Tonic* root."

Applying these hints to the foregoing examples, it will be seen that the A♮ in the passage from Beethoven (the augmented 4th from E♭, the key-note) implies Supertonic (F) root, the chord consequently being the first inversion of the Supertonic minor 9th, and the F♯ "false notation" for G♭. Similarly, in the case of the St. Saëns extract, as the Harmonic chromatic scale of C major (in which key the music is) contains a B♭ and a D♭, and not an A♯ and a C♯ (*see* Appendix C), these latter are again instances of "false notation." The B♭ is the minor 7th from the key-note; therefore the chord, correctly notated in Sec. 8, is the first inversion of the Tonic minor 9th, resolving upon Dominant 7th harmony.*

EXERCISES UPON CHROMATIC CHORDS OF THE NINTH.

A. Supply suitable resolutions (at each ×) for the chords of the 9th in the following example. Describe each of these chords fully. Do not leave the key of F major, save where a change of key is specially indicated.

B. Harmonize the following melody, for the Pianoforte. Harmonize only those notes within the ⌞____⌟ . A chord of the 9th (usually without its root) is indicated by a ×.

* In a case such as—

the F♯, D♯ and A in the combination marked × are so clearly felt as merely "Appoggiaturas" over the chord of C major, that it is quite unnecessary (though, of course, *possible*) to regard the chord as the 3rd inversion of the Supertonic minor 9th, with D♯ as false notation for E♭.

(a) Suspension of Dominant harmony over Tonic bass.

₊ Begin the above exercise thus :—

C. Harmonize the following Figured Bass in four parts.*   Analyse the harmony throughout.

D. Play and write phrases including each of the following chords :—

* The melody of the top part will be found to proceed mainly along the Chromatic scale line (ascending and descending).

E. (i) Analyse the harmony of the following passage, pointing out any examples of chords of the 9th with Expedient False Notation. Re-write these according to the notation of the Harmonic Chromatic scale of the key in which they are found.

SPOHR.—"Last Judgment."

(ii) Re-write similarly the following extract, with notation in accordance with the derivation of the various chords (in the key of C♯ major). Analyse the harmonies fully.

CHOPIN.—Nocturne (No. 6), in G minor.

(iii) *Deal* similarly with the following (key D♭ major):—

CHOPIN.—Nocturne (No. 8), in D♭ major.

N.B.—The D♭ in the bass throughout this passage is a Tonic pedal in the key of D♭ major, and may be disregarded in the analysis, unless it definitely forms part of the harmony.

II.—SUPERTONIC AND TONIC ELEVENTHS AND THIRTEENTHS.

5. By adding thirds above the Chromatic chords of Supertonic and Tonic 9th, it is, of course, possible to form Supertonic and Tonic 11ths and 13ths, in the same manner as in the case of Dominant harmony. Very few words are necessary upon these rarely-used chords ; the 11th and 13th are most frequently met with in the form of Appoggiaturas, and, as such, merely embellish the Supertonic or Tonic chords of the 7th or 9th, *e.g.*—

(× Supertonic minor 9th (in key C) in second inversion, with "appoggiatura" 11th (or 4th) resolving on 3rd.)

(× Tonic minor 9th (in key F)—F♯ = G♭—with "appoggiatura" 13th (or 6th) resolving by leap upon 3rd of same chord. The C in the bass is a Dominant "pedal.")

6. As an "essential" harmony the *Supertonic 11th* is only found in certain inverted forms (the root and 3rd being omitted), *e.g.*—

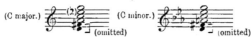

when it is obviously nothing more than a Secondary 7th upon the major 6th of the scale (with its 5th sometimes chromatically lowered). Examples of this chord will be found in Ex. (*g*) in Chapter XXI, Sec. 3 ; also in Ex. (*b*) in Sec. 5 of the same chapter.

7. The *Tonic 11th* is possible under similar conditions (*i.e.*, without root or 3rd), but—save in the form given below—

it is practically useless. Even then it is extremely doubtful if it is an essential harmony at all, the musical effect being much more that of Dominant 7th harmony preceded by a "double Appoggiatura" (A♯ and C♯), thus :—

than of the 3rd inversion of a Tonic minor 9th and 11th (root C), resolving upon the 1st inversion of the chord of the Dominant 7th. The combination would certainly in the great majority of cases be written with A♯ and C♯, in preference to B♭ and D♭.

8. The very rare " essential " *13ths upon the Supertonic and Tonic* are mainly found in the form of augmented triads, which are often far more simply and naturally thought of as being the result of " chromatic alterations " of existing major triads, *e.g.*—

(*a*) Tonic triad with "raised 5th" (or Tonic minor 13th—G♯=A♭—with root and 3rd only).

(*b*) Supertonic chromatic triad with "raised" 5th (or Supertonic minor 13th—A♯=B♭—with root and 3rd only).

9. These augmented triads are very useful for the purpose of modulation, as will be seen in Chapter XXIX. Moreover, they have been considerably exploited by modern composers, particularly by Debussy and others of the modern French school, as in the following instance :—

CLAUDE DEBUSSY.—Prélude, from Suite for Pianoforte.

etc.

Harmonic scheme of the above passage—

10. A case like this—

has clearly the effect of a Tonic chromatic chord of the 7th (in key C), with its 5th chromatically raised, and it is quite needless (though, of course, possible) to imagine the G♯ to be Expedient False Notation for A♭, and to consider that particular note as a Tonic minor 13th in disguise.

EXERCISES ON SUPERTONIC AND TONIC ELEVENTHS AND THIRTEENTHS.

I. Harmonize the following Figured Bass, analysing the harmony throughout.

N.B.—In Figured Basses the 11th and 13th are almost invariably indicated as a 4th and a 6th from the root, in the direct position of the chord. The 13th, in *any* position of the chord, usually sounds best when it is placed in the highest part (or at any rate, above the 7th). In this connexion, therefore, it should be remembered that, whenever a 7 and a 6 occur in the same set of figures (as in bars 1 and 2 of the above exercise), the note represented by the 6 should be placed *above* the 7th.

II. Write phrases for the Pianoforte, introducing the following chords :—

CHAPTER XXVIII.

CHROMATICALLY-ALTERED CHORDS (*Cont^d.*).

THE CHORD OF THE AUGMENTED SIXTH.

1. THE chord of the Augmented Sixth provides another instance of a chord produced by "chromatic alteration." In example (*a*) below—

the 5th of the chord of the Dominant 7th, occurring on the second beat of bar 1, is "decorated" on the third beat by a chromatic passing-note (D♭), on its way down to the root of the Tonic chord in the next bar. Similarly, in example (*b*)—

the 5th of the chord of the Supertonic minor 9th is "decorated" by a chromatic passing-note (A♭), inserted between the A and the G in the bass.

2. On the plan described in Chapter XXII, the D♭ and the A♭, instead of being taken as passing-notes, may be *substituted* for the diatonic notes from which they spring, thus:—

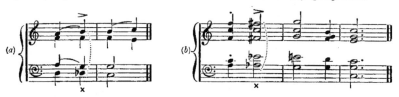

by this means forming in each case a chord in which there appears the striking interval of Augmented 6th (as shewn by the dotted lines).

3. These harmonies are described as chords of the Augmented Sixth upon the minor 2nd and minor 6th degrees of the major or minor scale respectively, and are found in the following forms :—

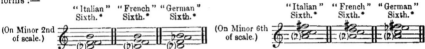

N.B.—In each instance the ♭ in brackets indicates the chromatically-altered note in the above examples, which are obviously merely variants of Dominant or Supertonic harmony :—

4. The chord of the Augmented Sixth upon the minor 6th of the scale is far more often met with than that upon the minor 2nd. Its most usual resolutions are those common to the Supertonic discord of which it is a varied form (as shewn above), viz., upon—

(i) *Dominant harmony.*

(ii) *Tonic harmony.*

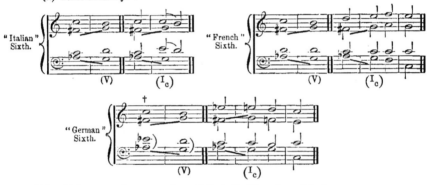

N.B.—All these examples are equally available in the Minor form of the key.

The following is a beautiful illustration of the "German" 6th (probably the most common form of the chord), resolving upon Tonic harmony :—

BEETHOVEN.—Sonata (Op. 10, No. 3).

N.B.—All the above examples shew that the natural tendency of the two notes forming the actual interval of Augmented 6th is *to move in contrary motion to one another,* by step of a semitone.

---

* The three most usual forms of the chord are frequently described by these special names. They have little or no meaning, but are perhaps a convenient means of description and of memorization.

† The consecutive 5ths here, by step of a semitone, are *possible,* if not always desirable.

5. The Augmented Sixth chord upon the minor 2nd of the scale, being an " altered " form of *D*ominant harmony, resolves (as is the case with a *D*ominant discord) upon—

   (i) Tonic harmony.

   (ii) Subdominant harmony.

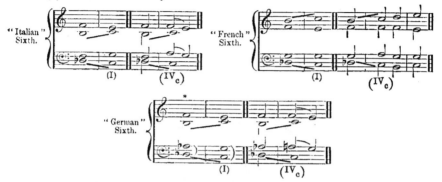

Beethoven again supplies us with a familiar instance—this time the " French " Sixth :—

BEETHOVEN.—Sonata (Op. 31, No. 3).

(Key C major.)   etc.

N.B.—Although the examples given above are all possible in the minor form of the key, the Augmented Sixth on the minor 2nd does not then resolve so happily upon the Tonic chord, as in the major form ; the following is, however, an instance of this somewhat rare resolution :—

BRAHMS.—Variations in B♭ for Orchestra.

etc.

6. The Augmented Sixth chord resolves at times upon the harmony of which it is the chromatically-altered form, when the " altered " note has largely the character of an Appoggiatura, *e.g.*—

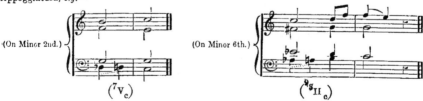

(On Minor 2nd.)   (On Minor 6th.)

The D ♭ and A ♭ would then be frequently written as C ♯ and G ♯ respectively.

---

* *See* Footnote to Sec. 4.

7. The inversions of the chord are possible :—

—and so on. Also similarly with the Augmented Sixth upon the minor 2nd. It is, however, only the "German" Sixth which is at all frequently found in an inverted form.

8. Two less used forms of the chord of the Augmented 6th upon the minor 6th of the scale are illustrated by the following examples :—

Upon the minor 6th of key C the above chords would appear thus :—

(Compare these with the examples in Sec. 3.)

9. A combination similar in construction to the "German" chords of Augmented 6th spoken of above can be formed upon the Subdominant of the major key, as follows :—

× Chromatic passing-note, forming interval of augmented 6th from the root of the Subdominant chord.

This combination may be used as an independent chord resolving upon Tonic harmony :—

and is virtually a chromatically-altered version of the chord marked (a) below :—

N.B.—Some theorists regard the D ♯ as Expedient False Notation for E♭, and describe the chord as the 3rd inversion of the Dominant 9th, 11th and 13th, but this is a cumbersome explanation. (*See* Chapter XXV, Sec. 9, Ex. II.)

EXERCISES UPON THE CHORDS OF THE AUGMENTED 6TH.

A. Play (and write from memory) the following progressions in the usual way, transposing them into all keys.

N.B.—The chord of the Augmented 6th upon the minor 6th of the major scale is indicated thus, ${}^{6}\text{VI}$; that upon the minor 2nd, thus, ${}^{6}\text{II}$. The abbreviations It., Fr., Ger. imply respectively the Italian, French and German forms of these chords.[*]

B. Precede and follow each chord of the Augmented 6th by a suitable harmony :—

C. Harmonize the following melody in full harmony for the Pianoforte. Harmonize only where indicated by the small notes beneath the melody, and introduce a chord of the Augmented 6th (direct or inverted) wherever the letters I, F and G (signifying an Italian, French and German 6th respectively) occur :—

---

[*] The stroke from left to right through the VI is actually not necessary in the minor key, as the sixth degree of the scale is already a *minor sixth* from the Tonic. As, however, the exercises in Sec. A are intended to be worked in both major and minor keys, it is convenient to let the one indication, ${}^{6}\text{VI}$, represent this particular chord of Augmented 6th in all cases.

D. Play and write phrases and sentences introducing the following harmonies. Transpose them into various keys, major and minor.

CHAPTER XXIX.

MODULATION (*Cont^d.*).

I.—CHROMATIC PIVOT-CHORDS.   II.—ENHARMONIC MODULATION.

1. THE triads formed by the process of "chromatic alteration" * are often particularly useful for the purpose of modulation. It will be remembered that the more familiar and frequently-used of these chords are :—

.(i) *Major key.* (*a*) The major triad on the lowered 2nd, (*b*) the diminished triad on the Supertonic (taken only in the first inversion), (*c*) the major triad on the Supertonic,† (*d*) the minor triad on the Subdominant, and (*e*) the major triad on the lowered 6th, *e.g.*—

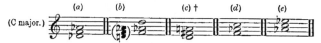

(ii) *Minor key.* (*f*) The major triad on the lowered 2nd, and (*g*) the major triad on the Supertonic, *e.g.*—

(C minor.)

2. Further, certain Secondary chords of the 7th are often found with similar chromatic alterations, of which the most common instance is that of the Secondary 7th on the Supertonic of the major key, with a lowered 5th, *e.g.*—

(C major.)

3. The use of chromatic chords such as the foregoing enables the principle of the "pivot-chord" in modulation to be considerably extended, for it is then possible (i) to approach a chord as a diatonic harmony in the first key, and to quit it as a *chromatic* harmony in the second, *e.g.*—

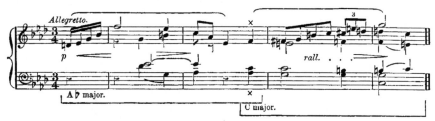

•.• Here the (diatonic) Submediant triad of A♭ major becomes the (chromatic) minor triad on the Subdominant of C major, and is quitted as such in that key.

---

* *See* Chapter XXII.   † Discussed in Chapter XXVI as a chord borrowed from the Dominant key.

(ii) To approach a chord as a chromatic harmony in the first key, and to quit it as a *diatonic* harmony in the second, *e.g.*—

• Here, conversely, the (chromatic) triad on the "lowered" 2nd of the scale of C major becomes the (diatonic) Subdominant triad of A♭ major, and is quitted as such.

• In this instance the 2nd inversion of the Secondary 7th on the Supertonic of C major (with flattened 5th) is quitted as the 3rd inversion of the Dominant major 9th of the key of E♭ major.

(iii) To regard the "pivot-chord" as chromatic in *both* keys, *e.g.*—

• In this case the chromatic triad on the "lowered" 6th of C major becomes the chromatic triad on the "lowered" 2nd of G major.

4. Further, the plan of making a single-note the bond of union between one key and another, may be adopted where the "common note" is found in (say) the Tonic chord of the first key and a *chromatic chord of the 7th or 9th* in the second key, *e.g.*—

• Here two pivot-notes, C and E, are found in (i) the Tonic chord of A minor, and (ii) the Supertonic chromatic chord of the 7th in B♭ major.

. In this case the pivot-notes A and C are found in (i) the Tonic chord of A minor, and (ii) the Tonic minor 9th of B major.

ENHARMONIC MODULATION.

5. Modulation by enharmonic* means is most readily accomplished by the chords of Diminished 7th and Augmented 6th. The chord of the Diminished 7th is by its nature an ambiguous chord, and—unlike the Dominant 7th—is not in itself characteristic of any particular tonality, as will be seen from the following examples :—

CHOPIN.—Etude in E (Op. 10).

? Key E . . . .

Ibid. (with changed notation).

? Key E? . . . .

The fact is that there are actually only three Diminished 7th chords on the Pianoforte or Organ keyboard, *e.g.*—

but that each of these may in practice belong to every one of the twelve major and twelve minor keys by change of notation, and consequent *change of root*. Even without such change of root any Diminished 7th chord will be found in three major keys and three minor keys. For

---

* *See* Glossary.

example, chord (*a*) the first inversion of a minor 9th with root G, could clearly occur in the keys of C, F and G as *Dominant, Supertonic* and *Tonic* minor 9th respectively, *e.g.* —

Key C major or minor. 　　'Key F major or minor. 　　Key G major or minor.

a modulation between any of the above-named keys being, as a consequence, rendered possible. The following passage shews a modulation from C major to B♭ major by means of the chord marked (*x*), which is approached as the 1st inversion of the Tonic minor 9th in the key of C, and quitted as the 1st inversion of the *Supertonic* minor 9th in the key of B♭.

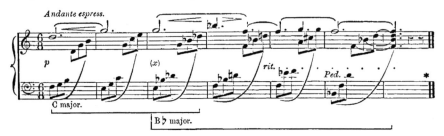

6. But chord (*a*) in Sec. 5 may—by enharmonic change of one or more of its notes—be thought of as being derived from E, C♯ and A♯ (=B♭) roots respectively :—

Roots = G 　　　　E 　　　　C♯ 　　　　A♯ (=B♭)

each note therefore in turn appearing as the 3rd, 5th, 7th and minor 9th. Moreover, as each of the above roots could be regarded as a *Dominant*, a *Supertonic* or a *Tonic*, and could therefore belong to three major or three minor keys, it will be seen that it would be possible to use this (or any other) chord of the *Diminished* 7th as a means of modulation between any two major or minor keys. A few enharmonic modulations from standard works are given below :—

BEETHOVEN.—Sonata in C minor (Op. 13).

** In the foregoing extract the chords (*a*) and (*b*)—identical upon the Pianoforte keyboard—are approached each time in the same manner, viz., as the 3rd inversion of the Dominant minor 9th in the key of G minor (root D). At (*b*), however, an enharmonic change of E♭ to D♯ is made, by which the chord becomes the 4th inversion of the Dominant minor 9th in the key of E minor (root B♮). The unexpected and strikingly beautiful resolution of the bass-note (*c*) upon the root (B♮) will hardly escape observation.

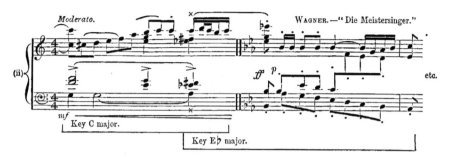

*** Here the chord marked x is approached as the 2nd inversion of the Supertonic minor 9th in the key of C (root D), and—by an implied enharmonic change of the F ♯ to G ♭—is quitted as the 1st inversion of the Supertonic minor 9th in the key of E ♭ major (root F), resolving upon the Tonic triad in its 2nd inversion.

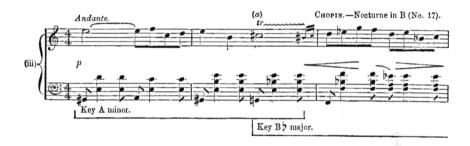

*** Two instances of modulation by means of the Diminished 7th harmony are exemplified by the above extract from Chopin. The chord marked (*a*), approached from A minor as the 3rd inversion of the Tonic minor 9th (root A) is quitted enharmonically as the 2nd inversion of the Supertonic minor 9th (C ♯ = D ♭) in the key of B ♭ major. Further, the chord marked (*b*), approached as the 2nd inversion of the Tonic minor 9th in B ♭ major (root B ♭) is resolved (as Supertonic minor 9th) into the key of A ♭, no enharmonic change here taking place, the root remaining the same.

7. Although, as the preceding examples will have shewn, it is possible to effect an enharmonic modulation by means of a Diminished 7th chord derived from the Dominant, Supertonic or Tonic root of either key, the student will do well to remember (until he is to some extent experienced in the matter) that the safest and most successful modulation of the kind will be made by means of the Supertonic 9th of the *new* key, *e.g.*—

.˙. The chord marked × is, in the key of B♭ major—the *new* key—the 1st inversion of the Supertonic minor 9th (root C). The 9th (D♭) is written C♯ to avoid the necessity of contradicting the D♭ by D♮ in the following bar, and is an example of Expedient False Notation.

8. The chord of the Augmented 6th (German form) is another means by which modulation may be carried out. By use of the "pivot-note" connexion the Augmented 6th upon the minor 6th of the *new* key may often be introduced in such a way as to connect two fairly distant keys very happily, *e.g.*—

Great importance attaches, in such modulations, to the smooth and musical movement of the bass at the point of approach to the Augmented 6th chord.

9. Moreover, by enharmonic change of the Augmented 6th itself, the chord of the "German 6th" becomes a fundamental chord of the 7th, and it is obvious that a modulation can be effected by approaching the chord in one way and quitting it in the other, *e.g.*—

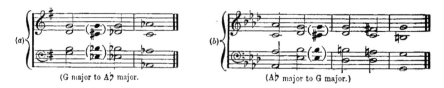

In example (*a*) the German 6th upon the minor 6th degree of G major becomes, by enharmonic change of C♯ to D♭, the Dominant 7th of A♭ major. The reverse process is seen in example (*b*). It should be clear that modulations to other keys could be made equally well by regarding the fundamental 7th as a Supertonic or Tonic chromatic chord of the 7th, instead of as a Dominant 7th.

Chopin has a remarkable instance of an enharmonic modulation by means of the "German 6th":—

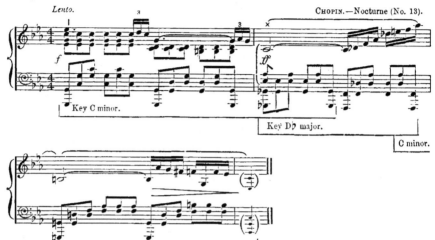

*** Here the chord marked x is led up to as the last inversion of the German 6th in C minor $\begin{cases} C \\ A\flat \\ E\natural \\ F\sharp \end{cases}$ and—by enharmonic change of F♯ to G♭—is quitted as the 3rd inversion of the Dominant 7th in the key of D♭. It will be noticed that the chord of D♭ itself is then used as the "pivot-chord" between the keys of D♭ and C minor, in which latter key it forms the "Neapolitan 6th."

10. Yet another means of modulating enharmonically is to be found in the Augmented triads which are usually classified as chords of the 13th (with only root, 3rd, and minor 13th present).* Grieg has a charming instance of this :—

*** In the above extract the modulation from the key of D to the key of F is brought about by means of the chord marked x, which is approached as a Dominant minor 13th in D major :—

---

* *See* Chapter XXVII.

and quitted (by enharmonic change of C ♯ to D ♭) as a Tonic minor 13th in F major :—

(13th in bass.)

11.   The ambiguous nature of these Augmented triads makes them peculiarly adaptable for the purposes of modulation, for it is clear that any position of one of them may be treated as the enharmonic equivalent of another, and quitted accordingly, *e.g.*—

Roots ⁎ :   F   A   C♯

N.B.—It is obviously possible to consider chord (*a*) as being derived from a Dominant, a Super-tonic, or a Tonic root, belonging as a consequence to the keys of B♭, E♭, or F (major or minor). As each of the chords (*b*) and (*c*) could, on a similar principle, be found in an equal number of keys, it will be seen that (*a*) or its enharmonic equivalent could actually be found in nine major and nine minor keys, a modulation between any two of which could be effected by its means.

.12.   It will be well here to warn the student against the too frequent use of modulation by enharmonic means.   The ease with which changes of key can thereby be made, when once the trick has been learnt, tempts many an inexperienced writer to fly to this particular resource at the least suggestion of a difficulty.   Let it be said that such a proceeding will usually prove to be inartistic and mechanical to a degree.   An *occasional* enharmonic modulation may be of the greatest possible beauty ;   the frequent introduction of this special form of effect, however, creates a feeling of restlessness and of artificiality which is peculiarly irritating to the really· musical mind.

13.   In connexion with the subject of this present chapter, viz., modulation between keys *not* in the first degree of relationship to one another, the following hint is specially useful and appropriate:—"If the new key contains any particular note which jars on the old key, then this note should be carefully withheld as long as possible, *e.g.*—the note A ♮ is so foreign to the key of E flat (in the succeeding example) that the third chord will sound harsh and unpleasant " :—

(E flat to F.)

" By playing a semibreve G in the tenor of bar 2 (thus avoiding the sudden introduction of the A ♮) the progression becomes quite smooth and musical." (Percy C. Buck—" Unfigured Harmony.")

⁎ On the assumption that these chords are derived from the complete chord of the minor 13th.

EXERCISES.

A. (i) Modulate (first in plain four-part harmony, and afterwards in some more decorated scheme) by means of the following chord *

(a) From F major to D major.
(b) „ B♭ „ „ D „
(c) „ D „ „ F „
(d) „ D „ „ E♭ „

(ii) Modulate similarly by means of the following chord *

(a) From A major to D minor.
(b) „ D minor „ A „
(c) „ D „ „ G♯ „
(d) „ E major „ D „

(iii) Modulate similarly by means of the following chord *

(a) From D major to F♯ major.
(b) „ A „ „ F♯ „
(c) „ D „ „ C minor.
(d) „ C♯ „ „ G major.

(iv) Modulate similarly by means of the following chord (Neapolitan 6th)

(a) From C minor to D♭ major.
(b) „ D♭ major „ C „
(c) „ C „ „ A♭ „
(d) „ A♭ „ „ C minor.

(v) Modulate similarly by means of the following chord

(a) From D major to F major.
(b) , F „ „ D „

(vi) Modulate similarly by means of the following chord (or one of its inversions)

(a) From B♭ major to D♭ major.
(b) „ D♭ „ „ B♭ minor.

B. Modulate between C major and F♯ major by means of a triad chromatic in both keys.

C. Lead up to the chord marked with a cross (the German 6th in the *new* key), in such a way as to modulate naturally and effectively between the two specified keys in each case:—

(i) (From D major to F♯ major.) ✕

(*Moderato.*)

✕

---

* The " pivot-chord " may, in these instances, be placed in whatever position may be the most suitable.

(From C major to G minor.)

(ii)

(*Andante.*)

D. Modulate, by means of the enharmonic change (where necessary) of the notes of the following chord  (which may be placed in any convenient position), from the key of E (major or minor) to each of the remaining eleven keys (major or minor).

E. Write sixteen bars for the Pianoforte, commencing thus :—

Allegretto.

(Piano.) *p* etc.

Modulate through E minor to B minor, in which key the music should come to a close at the eighth bar; then continue through C major and A♭ major, returning to G major by means of an enharmonic change of the chord of the Diminished 7th (*see* recommendation in Sec. 7 on page 252).

F. By means of the enharmonic change of the "German 6th" on the minor 6th degree of E major, modulate into F major, returning to E major by the Neapolitan 6th of that key.

G. Complete this passage in four bars, modulating (i) to A♭ major, (ii) to G♭ major, (iii) E major, (iv) C major, by means of the enharmonic change of the chord marked × (four examples in all) :—

Andante.

(Piano.) *p* (Two more bars to close.)

APPENDIX A.

CONCERNING SEQUENCES AND PEDALS.
I.—SEQUENCES.

1. THE reproduction of a melodic figure or phrase, at a higher or lower pitch (generally known as a Sequence) is, as a reference to almost any example of vocal or instrumental music will shew, an important factor in the development of a musical idea or thought. The quotation from Bach's 1st *Two-part Invention* on page 11 affords proof of this assertion, which is further strengthened by the following passages :—

The first of the above examples would be described as a *Melodic* Sequence, as it is confined to a single part ; the second as a *Harmonic* Sequence, for the reason that the repetition of the original passage is carried out exactly in every part of the harmony (compare bars 1 and 2 in ex. (*b*)).

2. Sequences are usually classified under the headings of Tonal, Real, and Mixed (or Modulating). A *Tonal Sequence* is one in which, as in (*a*) and (*b*) above, the *number* of each original interval (2nd, 3rd, 4th, etc.) is preserved in the repetitions, but not always its *quality* (major, minor, etc.). A *Real Sequence*, on the other hand, is one in which both number and quality are reproduced, *e.g.*—

In a Real Sequence the key obviously has to be changed at each repetition, and—especially in the case of rising Sequences in major keys—it is at times difficult to produce a wholly satisfactory result, *e.g.*—

The type of Sequence sometimes described as "Mixed," or "Modulating," is one in which there is an interchange of major and minor keys in the repetitions, and in which the effect is often far better than in the case of a *Real* Sequence. For example, the above passage could be rendered much more musical in the following manner :—

C major.   D *minor*.   E *minor*.   F major.

3. In the music of the Handelian period the use of the Sequence becomes at times a somewhat trying convention, and hundreds of instances of this can be found, of which the extract that follows is a typical specimen :—

HANDEL.—"Messiah."

4. A more artistic result is in very many cases produced by a form of Sequential progression in which room is left for differences of detail, and in which the original idea is carried out with a certain degree of freedom in outline, *e.g.*—

BEETHOVEN.—Sonata in C sharp minor (Op. 27. No. 2).

In such cases the general effect of the music is sequential, although—for the reason that the reproduction of the intervals of the first idea is not exact—an actual *Sequence* does not occur. Beethoven and the more modern composers have made conspicuous use of this freely sequential type of writing in the development of their themes, realizing that it provides with marked success the elements both of unity and variety.

5. In the carrying-out of a Tonal sequence (*i.e.*, one not leaving the key), certain licences are permitted :—

(*a*) Augmented intervals may occur melodically without restriction, *e.g.*—

(*See* also bars 1–2 in Ex. (ii) below.)

(*b*) The Leading-note ceases to be a note with a special tendency, and may also be doubled (*see* (*x*) and (*y*) in Ex. (i) below :—

(c) Diminished and Augmented triads may be treated with the freedom of concordant triads, the 5th in such chords being absolved from the usual rules of resolution (*see* (*y*) in Ex. (i) and (*z*) in Ex. (ii)) :—

The above-named licences should occur, however, only in the *repetitions*—not in the original progression—and it is important that the junction between that original progression and the first repetition shall be correct, and not involve any fault of melodic or harmonic movement, *e.g.*—

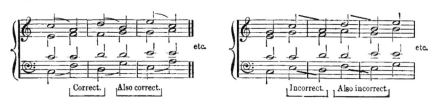

6. The examples of Sequence in this Appendix will have shewn that the length of the actual passage to be reproduced sequentially may vary considerably. As the majority of those given have been short, it will be well to conclude with one in which the original progression is of con-

siderable size ; Beethoven has provided a superb instance of what the late Sir Hubert Parry called a " long-limbed " Sequence, in the opening of his *Op.* 57 :—

BEETHOVEN.—Sonata, Op. 57.

II.—PEDALS.*

7. A pedal (or pedal-note) is a note, generally in the bass part, sustained through a suc. cession of harmonies of which it may or may not form a part.

8. The pedal-note will almost invariably be either the Dominant or the Tonic,† the mental effect of the former being that of incompletion, or unrest ; the effect of the latter being generally one of tranquillity or conclusiveness. The following example will demonstrate this :—

* The greater part of the following matter concerning Pedals is reproduced from the Author's *Practical Harmony.* (Joseph Williams, Ltd.)

† Modern composers occasionally use other degrees of the scale as pedal-notes, *e.g.*—

BRAHMS.—Symphony in D.

TSCHAÏKOWSKY.—Symphony in E minor.

9. The above passage illustrates several points in connexion with the treatment of pedals ;—

(i) That, where the pedal *forms no part* of the harmony, as at (*a*), the part next above the pedal should be regarded as the *bass*, and proceed according to the rules of progression applicable to a bass part.

(ii) That modulations may occur on a pedal, the most usual from a major key being to the keys of the Supertonic minor (as in bars 3 and 4), and the Mediant minor (as in bars 5 and 6) upon a Dominant pedal, and to the Subdominant key (bars 9 and 10) upon a Tonic pedal.*

(iii) That, where a Dominant pedal and a Tonic pedal occur in succession, the Dominant pedal usually precedes that on the Tonic.

(iv) That a pedal should, in most cases, be quitted only when it forms part of the harmony. (*Vide* bar 8 of example in Sec. 8.)

10. Occasionally the Dominant and Tonic pedals are used at one and the same time. They then form what is known as a "double pedal." The Tonic pedal is then almost invariably placed *below* that of the Dominant, *e.g.*†—

Double Pedals are frequently to be found in music of a pastoral nature.

* When a modulation occurs on a pedal in a minor key, it is generally a transient one to the Subdominant minor key, *e.g.*—

† A notable instance of the disregard of this generally observed rule is to be found towards the end of the Scherzo in Beethoven's C minor Symphony, where there occurs a Double Pedal, lasting through many bars, with the Dominant *below* the Tonic.

11. When the pedal-note occurs in one of the ·upper parts, instead of in the bass, it is termed an "inverted pedal," *e.g.*—

12. Sometimes the pedal-note is taken in the bass and in an upper part at the same time, as in the following passage :—

13. A pedal is occasionally found in a "decorated" form, as in the following instance, where the pedal G is in every bar preceded by an accented passing-note, A♭ :—

BEETHOVEN.—Sonata, Op. 2, No. 3.

etc.

or as in this well-known passage from Chopin, where the inverted pedal G♯ is taken in a "broken" form over a range of two octaves :—

CHOPIN.—Ballade in A flat.

etc.

APPENDIX B.

SPECIAL PIANOFORTE IDIOMS.

EXPERIMENTING AT THE PIANOFORTE.

1. IT is important that the student should, at a comparatively early stage of his work, become familiar with the method of laying-out his chords and progressions in a manner specially suitable for the Pianoforte.* Although the main principles of four-part harmony will be the foundation of his work in this direction, it almost goes without saying that the chords need not be restricted to that number of actual parts, but that the notes may (where necessary) be doubled more freely, and the form of the chords themselves regulated by the special effects of "colour" from time to time desired, as in the following example :—

CHOPIN.—Etude in E (Op. 10).

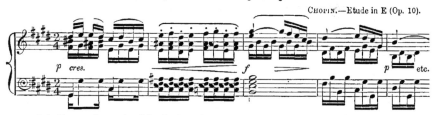

₊ Observe the varying "density" of the harmony.

I.—THE SINGLE CHORD.

2. In his first experiments at the keyboard he should endeavour to arrange *single chords* in as many different ways as possible, carefully discriminating between their varying degrees of effectiveness.

He will be helped in this task by the following considerations :—

(*a*) The massiveness, brilliancy, or delicacy of a chord largely depends upon the spacing of its notes (together with its actual pitch), *e.g.*—

(Massive and weighty.) (Light and graceful.) (Vigorous.) (Brilliant.)

* In the present volume this end has from the first been kept in view, and certain directions in the matter have, it will be remembered, been given from time to time for the student's guidance. This Appendix deals, however, with a wider application of the subject, and may profitably be studied con. currently with the earlier portions of the book.

(b) The lower their pitch, the less closely (as a rule) should the notes of a chord be placed to one another.   Roughly speaking, it is better to separate sounds lying between

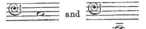

by an interval larger than a 3rd, *e.g.*—

Below  it is advisable, usually, to place the sounds an 8ve apart.

N.B.—In this connexion, the 3rd of a chord requires particular care in doubling, and should not be duplicated too low down, *e.g.*—

(c) The Pedal is the means by which a wide range of sounds (impossible to be sustained by the fingers alone) may be included within the chord :—

L. H.

Ped....   Ped. ...   Ped....   Ped.... Ped....

EXERCISES.*

A.   Arrange the Tonic triad † (in various major and minor keys) in as many different ways as possible, varying the *density* of the harmony in the manner indicated above.

N.B.—The amount of tone should range from *pp* to *ff*.

B.   Treat similarly (a) the Subdominant,† (b) the Dominant † triad in various major and minor keys.

C.   Proceed in the same way with the Secondary triads † of major and minor keys.

II.—CHORD-PROGRESSION.

3.   The next stage in the consideration of Pianoforte-writing is that of the *progression* from chord to chord when the harmony is amplified in the manner already alluded to.

4.   As it is the effect of the chord *in the mass*, rather than the movement of single parts, that is the chief concern, the actual progression will largely depend upon (a) convenience of

---

* To be both played and written.   † In root-position.

playing, (*b*) effects of " colour." Passages such as the following are frequently to be met with in Pianoforte music :—

BEETHOVEN.—Sonata (Op. 2, No. 3).

containing examples of consecutive 5ths and 8ves which in vocal writing would be not only objectionable but silly. It is obvious that the chords are here arranged so as to lie easily under the hands, and it is no less clear that the ear does not recognize any actual movement of separate parts (except the " extreme " parts), but only that of the chords as *tone-masses*.

5. The principles set forth below may be taken as affording some guide in the matter which, however, is clearly one for the exercise of the most careful aural judgment.

(*a*) The strict rules of four-part harmony as to " consecutives " do not apply to the same extent, particularly between chords whose roots lie more than a 2nd apart, *e.g.*—

(Vocal writing.)   (Amplified for the Pianoforte.)

(Good)

But no upper or middle part of the harmony should proceed in consecutive 8ves with the bass,* *e.g.*—

(Bad)

(*b*) The number of notes in successive chords may vary considerably ; this is largely due to the need for laying-out the harmonies in the most convenient manner for the hands of the player, as well as for the actual musical effect required :—

---

* As already mentioned (page 84, Sec. 11 (*b*) and foot-note thereon), any *melodic* part may be freely doubled in 8ves, for the purpose of making it prominent, *e.g.*—

BEETHOVEN.—Sonata (Op. 26).

&c.

and the bass-part itself is frequently strengthened in 8ves, as shewn on page 68.

(*c*) Notes that are in any degree " sensitive " as regards doubling or progression (*e.g.*, the major 3rd of a triad, the Leading-note, or any note requiring special resolution) should **not** be doubled *if they appear in the bass :—*

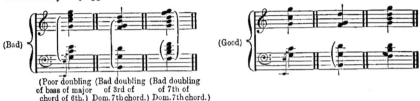

(Bad)   (Good)

(Poor doubling   (Bad doubling   (Bad doubling
of bass of major   of 3rd of   of 7th of
chord of 6th.)   Dom.7th chord.)   Dom.7th chord.)

but such " sensitive " notes may be doubled freely when they occur only in the parts *above* the bass, *e.g.*—

(Good)

· (*d*) The actual movement of notes requiring resolution is often freer in the upper parts of massive harmony for the Pianoforte, than in four-part vocal writing, and such notes may, if the instrumental effect justifies it, be resolved in a different octave from that in which they themselves appear :— .

(Possible)   (Possible)

N.B.—Such freedoms are, however, unallowable in the *bass* :—

(Bad)   (Good)

EXERCISES.*

D. Arrange the various positions of both Primary and Secondary triads (in major and minor keys), in as many different ways as possible, for the Pianoforte, taking a chord-succession such as the following as the basis of these experiments :—

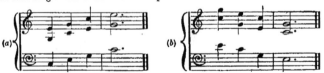

(*a*)   (*b*)

---

* To be both played and written.

E. Take any of the chord-successions given in Roman numerals in the chapters on Triads and their inversions (Chapters IX–XIV), and similarly arrange them for the Pianoforte.

F. Arrange the various positions of the chord of the *Dominant* 7th (in all keys) in several ways, resolving each on Tonic harmony. (Chapter XV.)

G. Take the chord-successions given in Roman numerals in Chapter XV and succeeding chapters, and arrange them for the Pianoforte.

III.—DECORATION AND FIGURATION.

6. Chords (as has already been seen on pages 90, 95, 100, etc.), are often taken in succession in "broken" or arpeggiated forms, and in many cases the strict four-part writing is distinctly traceable :* *e.g.* —

(Plain chords.) etc.

The same in simple arpeggio-forms :—

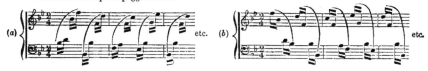

(a) etc. (b) etc.

7. But much more can be done, by the amplification of the chords in the manner already described ; their treatment will then be regulated by the principles set forth in Sec. 5.

(c) *mf* etc.

(d) *p* etc.

* In most instances, the success of the figurated harmony may be tested by playing the chords in an unbroken form :—

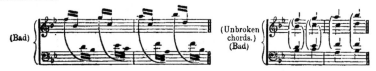

(Bad) (Unbroken chords.) (Bad)

8. The addition of unessential notes widens the possibilities considerably :—

9. In the case of a melody for a voice, or any solo instrument (such as the Violin), the Pianoforte accompaniment may double the melody in the unison or the 8ve, but this should be done sparingly, as it is likely to interfere with the spontaneity of the soloist's rendering *:—

but—as has already been seen—(i) the *bass* and the melody, (ii) the bass and the upper parts of the accompaniment, must proceed in pure harmony :—

N.B.—In the following example, the L.H. part marked |____| is not the *actual bass*, but merely a strengthening of the melody. The low C is virtually implied as bass :—

---

* A melody played by a bowed instrument should rarely, if ever, be doubled *in the same octave* on the Pianoforte ; the effect is usually bad.

10. A dissonant note in the melody, particularly if reproduced somewhere in the accompaniment, is free to move to other notes of the chord, provided that the resolution takes place in that accompaniment:—

11. Any figure chosen for the accompaniment of a melody should be carried out with a certain degree of consistency; rapid changes of style such as the following are clearly absurd :—

EXERCISES.

H. Take any of the Exercises in chord-progressions, given in Roman numerals in earlier chapters of this volume, and invent "decorated" versions similar to those in Secs. 6, 7, and 8.

I. Take any of the songs in "The National Song Book "* (edition without harmonization) and write Pianoforte accompaniments to them.

---

* *Boosey & Co.* Many melodies suitable for the purpose will also be found in "Additional Exercises to Counterpoint," by the late Dr. E. Prout (*Augener & Co.*).

APPENDIX C.

CONCERNING THE NOTATION OF THE CHROMATIC SCALE.

1. Two methods of writing the chromatic scale have, up to the present time, been fairly generally recognized ; these are known as the Harmonic and the Melodic respectively. The former, as its name implies, is based upon the idea that the formation of certain frequently-used chromatic chords necessitates its special manner of notation. For example, taking the key of C major for illustration, the chromatic triad upon the Supertonic manifestly demands an F♯ (the augmented 4th from the key-note), and not a G♭, thus :— *(musical example)* not *(Impossible)* *(musical example)*

Again, such familiar chords as the minor triad upon the Subdominant, *(musical example)* and the so-called "Neapolitan sixth," *(musical example)* obviously compel the use of the minor 6th and minor 2nd from the key-note respectively ; the following would be absurd :— *(musical example)*

Further, the chord of the *Dominant* minor 9th *(musical example)* (Chapter XXIII) demands an A♭, and not a G♯, and the chord of the Supertonic minor 9th, *(musical example)* (Chapter XXVII) calls for an E♭, and not a D♯. Finally, the chromatic chord of the 7th found upon the Tonic *(musical example)* (Chapter XXVI) needs a B♭, and not an A♯.

2. As a consequence of such considerations as these, and the regarding of certain chords as being written with *Expedient False Notation*, a more or less logical method of writing the Chromatic scale has been rendered possible, sufficient for most ordinary purposes.

3. Each key therefore has its own *Harmonic* chromatic scale, formed according to the following plan. The notes of the major diatonic scale are taken as the foundation, to which are added the notes that differ from these in both forms (Harmonic and Melodic) of the Tonic minor scale :—

(Key C.)

In order to fill up the gaps existing between the 1st and 2nd, and the 4th and 5th diatonic degrees, the *minor 2nd* and the *augmented 4th* from the key-note (as explained in Sec. 1) are added to the above :—

4. For the purpose of passing-notes, and melodic writing generally, this notation of the chromatic scale has never been consistently adhered to, and the name given to any *passing-note*—when foreign to the key-signature of any particular passage—has usually varied according to the direction of its subsequent movement. The chief point to be remembered is that, in order to avoid the use of unnecessary accidentals, it should be so written as to stand at the distance of a *diatonic semitone from the note to which it progresses*, whether up or down, e.g.—

(a) Upward progression of passing-note.

(b) Downward progression of passing-note.

N.B.—Composers, however, usually prefer to write, even in downward progressions, the augmented 4th from the key-note, rather than the diminished 5th, *e.g.*—

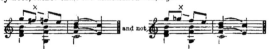

5. The outcome of these variations in notation is the form of scale called the *Melodic* (or *Arbitrary*) Chromatic scale, which differs in detail according to the particular mode of the key that is being used at the time :—

(Key C Major.)   (or G♭)

(or G♭)

6. In the case of chromatically-altered chords, it is clear that, as they are produced by the substitution of a chromatic passing-note for the original diatonic note of the harmony, the directions given in Sec. 4 for the notation of passing-notes will apply with equal reason and force, *e.g.*—

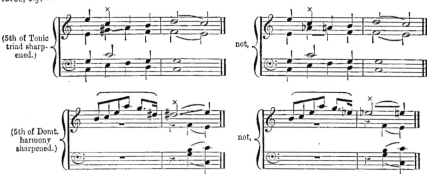

(5th of Tonic triad sharpened.)

not,

(5th of Domt. harmony sharpened.)

not,

7. As a basis for the notation of chromatic *chords* (as distinct from the chromatic alterations spoken of above), the Melodic chromatic scale has usually been rejected by later theorists, and the so-called Harmonic form exclusively used. In the case of most of the more usual and obvious chromatic harmonies its adoption is undoubtedly reasonable, practical and convenient; but it is necessary to qualify this statement by saying (i) that in the light of many modern harmonic developments it cannot be regarded as entirely adequate : (ii) that its exclusive use involves us in many far-fetched attempts to prove the existence of Expedient False Notation, even in the explanation of chords by no means confined to the experiments of Modernists.

8. In a passage such as the following :—

(*a*)

(I) (I)

which is virtually a progression from one position of the Tonic chord of G major to another, by a series of "passing-chords," the use throughout of the Harmonic chromatic scale would, it is clear, bring about this curious result :—

(*b*)

involving a most puzzling and useless complication for the reader. The three upper parts of the harmony at (*a*) obviously form a series of "chords of the sixth," and the combinations in Example (*b*) which are marked × are, with the notation there given, little more than meaningless from any harmonic standpoint.

9. It may be argued that these upper parts are nothing more than three streams of chromatic passing-notes upon Tonic harmony, and that, as such, the "Melodic" notation at (*a*)

would in any case be possible.   But, in the following versions, the passing-notes really become integral harmonic factors :—

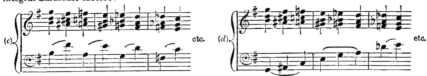

and a passage is produced in which the bonds of key, or tonality, are for the moment loosened—to return to a greater definiteness later on.   Of such a loosening of the bonds of tonality we have a wonderfully fine example in Wagner's " Die Walküre " :—

WAGNER.—" Die Walküre."

10.   But we may go a step further ; may not passages such as those given below be thought of as coming equally within the limits of one key, viz., the key of C ?—

(i) *Major triads :*

(*e*) *On Leading-note.* ELGAR.—" In the South."

(ii) *Minor triads :*

(*f*) *On raised 1st.*
R. STRAUSS.—" Nachtgang."

(*g*) *On lowered 3rd.*

(*h*) *On lowered 7th.*

SCHUMANN.—Concerto in A minor.

If so, then surely we are face to face with the fact that a more freely-written chromatic scale becomes necessary, even for *harmonic* purposes. For it is clear that the chords marked × in Examples (*b*), (*c*), (*d*), (*e*), (*f*), and (*g*) require notes not to be found in the Harmonic chromatic scale of their own special keys (viz., C♯, A♯, D♯, D♮, A♮, and G♭).

The late Professor Prout, in his *Harmony : its theory and practice* (17th edition), describes the chords indicated (*x*) and (*y*) in the following extracts (amongst others) as " False Triads " :—

AUBER.—" Le Dieu et la Bayadère."

(*x*)

(Key D major.)

SCHUBERT.—Sonata (Op. 42).

(*y*)

etc.

and as being in reality 13ths disguised by False Notation1 thus :—

and

etc.

$\left(\substack{13 \\ 9 \\ V_g}\right)$ $\left(\substack{13 \\ 9 \\ II_g}\right)$

a theory which it is difficult for the ear to accept, or even to realize, though the intellect might acknowledge its ingenuity.

11. The fact really is that triads may be formed on every degree of the chromatic scale, and used within the key, without causing modulation.   And a similar use of Fundamental discords upon these degrees is, of course, not impossible, as the following examples seem to shew :—

ELGAR.—"Gerontius."

(*a*)

$\left(^{7}_{3}\text{VI}_{\flat}\right)$

(*b*)   (Key D.)   etc.

$\left(^{7}_{3}\text{VII}\right)$

M. RAVEL.—Sonatina.

etc.

Key A (?)   Key F ♯ major.

*** Successions of chords of the major 9th, like the above, are a not infrequent (and somewhat irritating) mannerism of the composers of the modern French school and their imitators.

12. But it is hardly profitable, perhaps, to speculate further here along these lines. For the moment it is sufficient to say that the theory of the " Harmonic " chromatic scale is serviceable enough for the *more usual* chromatic chord-formations (which are made singularly clear to the student by its means), and that in the case of passing-notes, passing-chords, and chromatically-altered chords the more elastic " Melodic " notation affords the necessary notational freedom. After all, the use of *any* system of notation is to clarify, not to disguise, and the choice of the precise form it should take at any given moment must always, in the long run, be made upon grounds of expediency, and not of theory.

13. Moreover, so many so-called " chords " are the result of the side-by-side movement of independent melodic strands that any attempt to explain them upon a " natural " basis—*i.e.*, according to Nature's harmonic series*—is doomed to failure, if carried too far ; for as Helmholtz rightly says :—" the system of scales, modes, and harmonic tissues does not rest solely upon unalterable natural laws, but is . .   also the result of æsthetical principles, which have already changed, and will still further change with the progressive development of humanity." (Helmholtz—*Sensations of Tone.*)

---

* As was done by the late Alfred Day, and others.

APPENDIX D.

THE ECCLESIASTICAL MODES.

1. ALTHOUGH it is impossible within the limits of the present volume to enter with any degree of fulness into the important and far-reaching subject of the history and uses of the medieval scale-system,* a few words as to their influence on later composers seem to be necessary.

2. The so-called Ecclesiastical Modes which were the precursors of our modern scales were twelve in number, six *Authentic* modes, and six *Plagal* modes.

N.B.—The slurs indicate the position of the semitones, which, it will be noted, varies in every case.

3. The Authentic and Plagal forms of each Mode were distinguished from one another by the range or compass of the melody. If this lay, roughly speaking, between the " Final " (indicated above by the letter F) and its octave, it would be in the Authentic form; if between the note a 4th below the " Final " and the 5th above it, in the Plagal form.

---

* For further information on the matter, the student is referred to (i) The article thereon in Grove's Dictionary of Music and Musicians (revised edition) (ii) Appendix A in Prout's " Harmony " (17th edition); (iii) " Etude sur l'harmonie moderne," by René Lenormand ; (iv) Chapter XXII of " Modern Academic Counterpoint " by Dr. C. W. Pearce ; (v) Chapter XIII of " The Organ Accompaniment of the Church Services," by Dr. H. W. Richards.

4. The "Final" (as its name implies) was the note upon which a melody written in **any** particular mode concluded; the Dominant of the mode (indicated by the letter *D* in the examples in Sec. 2) was "that note of the melody more prominent than the rest, round which the other notes circle." It must not be confused with the word *Dominant* in its more modern application as the 5th degree of a scale.

5. The Modes can be used by present-day composers in three principal ways :—

(i) *A melody itself modal in character may be harmonized strictly in the style of the period at which it was the familiar form of musical expression*, in which case the harmonies should include no unprepared discords, and should be confined to the notes contained in the mode itself, *e.g.*—

3rd (Phrygian) Mode.

Elgar has an effective instance of the use of the 9th (Æolian) Mode (transposed a semitone down) :—

ELGAR.—"Dream of Gerontius."

(ii) *A similarly "modal" melody may be treated with a greater freedom of harmonic resource, (provided always that it is in keeping with the character of the melody itself)*. Many of Bach's harmonizations of the old Lutheran Chorals are typical instances of this method; the following rendering of the last two lines of a Choral in the 3rd (Phrygian) mode is peculiarly striking :—

BACH.—"Herzlich thut mich verlangen" (concluding bars).

Rébikoff—to come down to the present day—has produced a peculiarly desolate and mournful effect, suggestive of a Russian pastoral scene, by means of a melody in the 9th (Æolian) mode, harmonized by a succession of bare 5ths :—

W. RÉBIKOFF.—"Ländliche Scene" (Op. 10).

(iii) *A " modal " flavour may be given to the music by some special form of cadence usually identified with the Modes, e.g.—*

6. Further, the skilful use of diatonic triads (especially in root-position) may create more or less of the Ecclesiastical atmosphere commonly associated with the Modes, even though both melody and harmony may clearly belong to the more modern scale-system :—

(*See also* the middle section (in E ♭ major) of Chopin's Nocturne in G minor, Op. 37.)

Wagner produces an intensely devotional effect by similar means :—

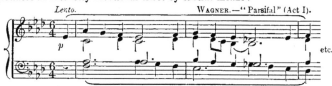

and Debussy uses Secondary 7ths to create a pseudo-modal impression in his Suite for the Pianoforte :—

7. To harmonize successfully according to the strict rules of the medieval Modal system requires long and patient study of a special kind, the consideration of which is outside the scope of the present volume. Such study has its natural and legitimate objective in the accompaniment of Plain song, in which the use of modern (and especially chromatic) harmonies would result in what the late Mr. W. S. Rockstro described as "an abomination which neither gods nor men can tolerate"*. Apart from Church use, strict modal harmony must in these days necessarily be more or less of an exotic, and it is unthinkable that musicians will revert to it *as a system.* Many of the characteristic effects, however, of modal writing will doubtless be increasingly employed to enlarge the range of melodic and harmonic possibilities, and thus notably to increase the resources of the composer's art. Scale-systems are, after all, merely the *media* by means of which the ideas of different generations of writers most naturally find their outlet, the framework of the musical structure, so to speak. The idioms of a language—musical or any other—change with the passage of time and the development of thought, and it is reasonable to assume that the future will see new scale-systems as firmly established and as universally accepted as are those with which we are familiar to-day. Progress in art is not to be found in the mere revival of former habits of thought and turns of expression, however beautiful (and even novel) they may seem to us after a long period of disuse or neglect ; but the development of the historic sense in our age has led to the re-discovery of many things in themselves deeply interesting, which have been overlaid by an accumulation of more recent interests. These "finds" of the historian are clearly a heritage for the present day, and no artist of wisdom will neglect them in his desire to widen the boundaries of his art, but will put them under contribution for his purpose as occasion arises, if they seem to supply the suitable investiture for his ideas.

---

* Witness, for example, the kind of harmonization indulged in by some Anglican organists in their treatment of so-called Gregorian chants !

APPENDIX E.

THE STRING QUARTET.

1. As many of the exercises in the present volume are intended to be worked as Trios and Quartets for bowed-instruments, a few words are here appended upon the compass of each of the component parts of the usual String-Quartet, and upon the important matter of *bowing* and the method of its indication in writing.

2. THE VIOLIN, whose four strings are tuned thus :—

has, for ordinary purposes, the following compass :—

with all the intermediate sounds of the chromatic scale.   Good players can carry the compass a few notes higher, but the student should regard  as the upward limit for his present purpose.

THE VIOLA has its strings tuned a perfect 5th lower than the Violin, thus :—

with a workable compass of—

(including, as in the case of the Violin, all the intermediate sounds of the chromatic scale). The part for the Viola is always written with the Alto (C) clef, unless the music lies in the higher part of the instrument, when the Treble (G) clef is used.

THE VIOLONCELLO (or '*Cello*) is in pitch an octave lower than the Viola, its four strings being tuned :—

and its usual compass ranging from—

The Bass (F) clef is used for all but the highest notes, when the Tenor (C) clef is substituted, in order to avoid unnecessary ledger-lines.

As in the case of the Violin, the upward compass of the Viola and the Violoncello is often extended by players possessing an advanced technique.

3. Comparing a quartet of bowed-instruments with a quartet of voices, it may be said that, roughly speaking, the 1st and 2nd Violins correspond to the treble and alto voices, the Viola taking the place of the tenor, and the 'Cello that of the bass voice respectively. It need hardly be said that the range of each " string '-part is far less restricted than is the case with voices, where the vocal compass has necessarily to be carefully adhered to in all cases. Further, in actual practice the above-named distribution of the parts does not hold good for long together ; " crossing " frequently takes place, and it is often the case that the 'Cello (for example) may be found playing a melody in its upper register while the Violins and the Viola are adding parts underneath, or that the 1st Violin may be " singing " on its rich and expressive fourth string while the Viola adds a counterpoint above it—and so on.

4. It is very essential that the special kind of " bowing " desired should be carefully marked in each part. It is important to remember that, unless a clear indication is given to the contrary, every note will be played *detached, i.e.,* with a separate stroke of the bow for each, a *legato* rendering being thus out of the question, *e.g.*—

If a *legato* is required, two or more notes are included in one (upward or downward) movement of the bow, the actual number of notes to be thus included being shewn in the copy by a slur, *e.g.*—

5. If too many notes are taken in one " bow," the bow itself has to move so slowly across the string that the tone rapidly weakens in volume, and at the end of the stroke becomes extremely attenuated. It will be understood, therefore, that the bowing in Ex. (*a*) below would be practically impossible, that in Ex. (*b*), however, being quite feasible and effective, owing of course to the difference of speed * and amount of tone required in the two cases :—

* Obviously, many more notes can be included in one bow at a high rate of speed than at a slow one.

6. It will be seen from the foregoing remarks that the slur, in string-writing, has an entirely different signification from that which it possesses in vocal music, or in music written for the Pianoforte or Organ. The main point to be observed is that in the case of bowed instruments the slur is used, not to determine actual *phrase-lengths* (save in rare instances), but merely to indicate the changes of bow. A passage such as the following might conceivably be " phrased " for the Pianoforte by means of a slur extending over its whole length :—

but as an indication of bowing in the case of the Violin, the slur over the four bars of *Andante* would be absolutely meaningless. The extract appears as follows in the work from which it is taken :—

Schubert.—Quartet in A minor (Op. 29).

N.B.—No break of the " legato" would be caused by any good player at the moment of changing from an upward to a downward movement of the bow (or *vice versâ*) in a " cantabile " passage such as the above.

7. For a consideration of the many subtle varieties of bowing possible to a first-rate player the student must be referred to a treatise on Violin-playing or on Orchestration ;* one or two of the more familiar forms of passage met with in string-writing may, however, be mentioned here :—

(i) *Groups of two slurred notes, either (a) with the accent or (b) against it :—*

Haydn.—Symphony in D.   Beethoven.—Symphony No. 9.

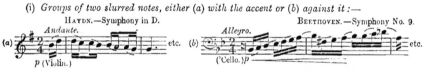

(ii) *Combinations of slurred and detached notes :—*

Mozart.—Quartet in C major.

(iii) " *Staccato Volante*"—*played in one bow (indicated thus . . . .) :—*

Mozart.—Quartet in D major.

(iv) *Groups of two or more notes played in the same bow, each note being more or less emphasized or stressed (indicated thus ◠ ◠ ◠) :—*

Dvořák.—Quintet in A (Op. 81).

* See *A practical guide to Violin-playing*—H. Wessely, and *The technique of the modern Orchestra.* —Ch. Widor. (Joseph Williams, Ltd.)

8. The strong accent of a bar usually coincides with a *down*-bow* :—

except :—(i) in the case of certain phrasings " across the accent," *e.g.*—

when the down-bow is taken on a normally weaker part of the bar ; (ii) when a *slurred* passage of fairly rapid notes reaches its completion on a strong accent, *e.g.*—

in which case the down-bow frequently falls upon the note *following* the normally accented part of the bar.

9. The strings are at times plucked with the fingers instead of being played with the bow ; this effect is called *pizzicato* (*i.e.* pinched), and is shewn in the player's part by the abbreviation, *pizz.*, the word *arco*† being employed to indicate that the use of the bow is to be resumed. In quartet-writing and chamber-music in general the *pizzicato* is rarely used for long at a time, but at special moments may often be extremely telling :—

N.B.—The parts are compressed on three staves to save space.

10. For the many effects to be obtained by " double-stopping," the *tremolo* and " double-bowing," the student is referred to any modern treatise on instrumentation ; it is obvious that such matters cannot be dealt with adequately within the scope of an Appendix such as this, the object of which is necessarily and of set purpose severely limited.

---

* A down-bow, *when specially required*, is indicated thus :— ⊓ ; an up-bow as follows :—V
† Or *coll' arco* (*i.e.* with the bow).

APPENDIX F.

MISCELLANEOUS EXERCISES.

PRELIMINARY NOTE.

1. As, in the scheme of the present volume, the experimental use of the various musical idioms with which the student becomes acquainted takes a foremost place, he has from the very first been expected to try his hand at inventing (both at the Pianoforte and away from it) phrases and sentences embodying the various chord-progressions dealt with in the several chapters.

2. In such invention the learner's rhythmical sense, his feeling for balance of phrase, and his ability to think with some degree of continuity are put to the proof. It is in the last resort upon *rhythmic* interest that success (either in improvisation or in pre-considered composition) depends, and, in the endeavour to secure this to some extent, no better practice can be found than in playing or writing answers to given phrases.

3. At first the given phrase (which may be quite short) should be balanced by one of the same length. For example we will take the first two bars of one of the earliest exercises on the Primary triads (Ex. 5 on page 79), and add a different termination :—

Of course, the musical value of the above as it stands is slight, but the little sentence is at least shapely and rhythmical. It should be compared with the following, in which the breaking up of the added two bars into two one-bar "rhythms" (like the first phrase), is particularly tiresome :—

The conclusion to be drawn from this is, naturally, that the answering phrase should not slavishly reproduce the rhythmic pattern of the first, but—while preserving its general feeling— should contribute some degree of variety of outline.

4. A common fault with students (and others), in continuing a melody, is that of immediately repeating its initial notes *at the commencement of the second phrase.* For example, many a beginner (supposing he had invented four bars something like the following) :—

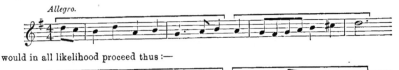

would in all likelihood proceed thus :—

to the great detriment of his tune. Either of the succeeding versions of the second phrase would be better :—

where the opening portion of the tune is reproduced in *Sequence,* or :—

in which the figure of four quavers (in bar 3 of the original phrase) is twice used at a different pitch, to carry on the tune, a degree of both unity and variety being thereby secured.

5. When a certain amount of facility in answering a given phrase by another of equal length has been obtained, an attempt should be made to *extend* the new phrase, so as to make it rhythmically weightier and more important, and thus to arrive at a higher degree of continuity. This extension may be carried out in several ways,* the chief of which are illustrated below. We will first take a four-bar phrase, and add four more bars to complete a normal eight-bar sentence :—

Next, we will postpone the termination of the sentence by an Interrupted cadence at (×), and then add two more bars to bring the music to its necessary conclusion :—

---

* This subject is discussed and exemplified in considerable detail in the Author's *Form in Music.* (Joseph Williams, Ltd.)

An Inverted cadence might be used equally effectively, in place of the Interrupted one :—

Finally, we will take the opening two bars of the second phrase and carry them up in sequence to a higher point of climax at (*y*), the music then subsiding upon a twice-repeated Tonic cadence. It will doubtless be noticed that the idea of sequential repetition is again made use of as the music dies away upon the initial rhythm of the whole tune, ♫ ♩ ♩ ♩.

6. Much practice is of course needed to develop a musical thought in an attractive and interesting manner, but the student will be aided greatly in his task by the careful analysis of such works as the Sonatas and Symphonies of Beethoven, Brahms, Tschaïkowsky and others, and the music-dramas of Wagner, where such " thematic development " is seen in its highest form.

EXERCISES.

A. Take the first phrase only of several of the simpler melodies in this volume, and **add** one or more responsive phrases (as indicated in the foregoing remarks), harmonizing the whole in a manner suitable to the nature of the particular melody itself.

B. Harmonize the following phrases suitably, completing each example as indicated.

(Add *two* phrases of four bars each to complete. Touch the keys of C minor and E♭ major and then close in B♭ major.)

(Add eight more bars, to end in G major; then return to the given phrase, and add another eight bars to close in C major.)

write a C.M. Hymn-tune. Modulate to the Dominant key in the 2nd line; touch C♯ minor and F♯ minor in the 3rd line, and return to the Tonic key in the last line of the tune.)

(Add four more bars ending with an Interrupted Cadence in G major, and then bring to a conclusion by means of two (or four) more bars closing with a Perfect Cadence.)

(F♯ minor.)

.(Add four more bars to close in A major, then use the 1st phrase, transposed into B minor, returning to F♯ minor by the addition of a concluding phrase. This final phrase might be a normal one of four bars extended by sequential treatment to eight, or even twelve, bars. (*See* Sec. 5 above.))

(Key D major.)

(Continue the above by adding a second phrase ending in B♭ major. Begin the third phrase thus:—

the fourth phrase to end in G minor. Add a few bars of Coda on a Tonic pedal.)

C. (i) Beginning thus :—

write a short piece in two parts. . Construct it in simple Binary form, the first section of which should be 8 bars in length, closing in key C with a double-bar. The second portion of the piece may modulate rather more freely, and may run to 12 or 16 bars, concluding in the Tonic key. Reproduce the closing bars of Part I (transposed) at the end of Part II.

(ii) Beginning thus :—

write a Minuet for the Pianoforte, in Simple Ternary form as follows :—

Part I (8 bars) closing in F ♯ minor.

„ II (12 to 16 bars), developing the idea of Part I, and touching the keys of E minor, D major, and G major. Lead back to re-entry of original phrase in Tonic key as—

„ III (8 bars), closing this time in the Tonic key. Short Coda to end.

D. Add a Pianoforte accompaniment to the following melodies. Write the melody itself on a separate staff, as in the case of a vocal solo, or a composition for Violin and Pianoforte.

*** Remember that many simple melodies require very little accompaniment; therefore do not overlook the great value of *rests*. Carefully consider the character of each melody before beginning to harmonize it.

E. Add parts for 2nd Violin and Viola to the following. Continue the piece for at least eight or twelve more bars, and close in the Tonic key :—

F. Elaborate the following succession of chords in the two ways suggested below. The chords may be of any length, but their order must be preserved :—

FINAL NOTE.

A useful form of exercise may be devised by taking chord-successions (such as those given in Roman numerals throughout this volume), and using them in connexion with previously prepared rhythmic schemes, as the basis either of short improvisations at the Pianoforte, or of more considered compositions. For example, if the following (purposely simple) succession of harmonies were taken as a basis (the semi-colon representing the separation of a complete musical sentence into two separate phrases), several little pieces could be constructed upon rhythms similar to those indicated below :—

The following examples are possible workings of the foregoing schemes:—

N.B.—The use of chord-successions in connexion with varied rhythms, in a manner similar to that suggested above for the student's experiments in Pianoforte improvisation, has (the Author believes) been a feature of the teaching of extemporization by Mons. Jaques-Dalcroze, Dr. Yorke-Trotter, Mr. Ernest Read and others. These remarks upon the subject would not be complete without cordial acknowledgment of the Author's indebtedness to these well-known teachers in this respect.

APPENDIX G.

GLOSSARY OF TECHNICAL TERMS AND EXPRESSIONS REFERRED TO, BUT NOT EXPLAINED, IN THE COURSE OF THE TEXT.

Anacrusis.—In poetry, "an upward beat at the beginning of a verse, consisting of one or two unaccented syllables introductory to the just rhythm." (Chambers' Etymological Dictionary). In music, an unaccented note, or a group of unaccented notes preceding, and leading up to, the first metrical accent of a phrase, *e.g.*—

Bass (*Bass-note*).—The lowest note in any harmonic combination, however high or however low the entire combination may be.

Bass voice.—The lowest male voice. Average compass :—

Cadence (or *Close*).—The completion of a rhythmical period. Cadences are usually classified under four headings, as follows :—

    (a) *The Perfect Cadence* (or *Full Close*)*—when a phrase terminates with the chord of the Tonic, preceded by that of the Dominant (V—I).

    (b) *The Imperfect Cadence* (or *Half Close*)—when a phrase terminates with the chord of the Dominant (preceded by any other harmony), producing the effect of " temporary arrest."†

    (c) *The Interrupted Cadence*—when a phrase ends with a progression from Dominant harmony to some other chord than that of the Tonic. A familiar instance is that of (^{7}V—VI.)

    (d) *The Plagal Cadence*—when a phrase ends with the chord of the Tonic, preceded by that of the Subdominant (IV—I).

Canon.—A form of composition in which a theme or melody announced by one voice (or part), is imitated (*i.e.*, reproduced) by another voice, or by other voices. This reproduction is carried out, in almost all cases, at quite a short distance of time after the first voice has begun—perhaps at a bar's distance. (*See* Chapter II (B), exercise (vi).)

Canto Fermo.—(*lit.* a "fixed song.") A melody (usually written in semibreves) chosen for the purpose of contrapuntal elaboration.

Choral (or *Chorale*).—A Lutheran hymn-tune.

Chord.—Two or more sounds in combination.

Chromatic.—Contrary to a given key-signature : opposed to Diatonic. A chromatic *scale* is one proceeding entirely by semitones. A chromatic *interval* is one not found in any diatonic scale. A chromatic *chord* is one having one or more of its notes inflected by an accidental, but not causing a change of key. (The major 6th and 7th of a minor scale are, however, diatonic). A chromatic *semitone* is a semitone, the two notes of which bear the same letter-name, *e.g.*, F to F♯.

Close position.—When the upper notes of a chord lie close together, at some distance from the bass, *e.g.*—

                                (*See* Extended, or Open, position.)

---

* Sometimes called the *Authentic Cadence.*

† As a matter of fact, there are many other forms of Cadence which produce the effect of " temporary arrest," and it seems reasonable to extend the term *Imperfect Cadence* to such progressions, (*e.g.*, I—IV : I—VI, etc.)—*See* the Author's " Form in Music," pp. 11, 12.

Contrapuntal.—A term applied to a species of writing in which the element of Counterpoint (*q.v.*) is prominent.

Counterpoint.—The art of adding one or more *melodic* parts against one that is given. A part so added is often spoken of as a *Counterpoint* to the original melody.

Diatonic.—In accordance with a given key-signature : opposed to Chromatic. A diatonic *scale* is one proceeding by tones and semitones in some definite order. A diatonic *interval* is one that can be found in a diatonic scale. A diatonic *chord* is one formed entirely from the diatonic notes of the scale. A diatonic *semitone* is a semitone, the two notes of which bear different letter-names, *e.g.*, F to G♭.

Double Counterpoint.—Invertible Counterpoint : *i.e.*, a melody which will serve equally well above or below the melody to which it is added.

Enharmonic.—*lit.* consisting of intervals smaller than the semitone. The distinction, however, between sounds of the same pitch in the tempered scale, but having different names (*e.g.*, G ♯, F x, A ♭♭) is also said to be *enharmonic*.

Extended Position.—(*See Open Position.*)

Ground Bass.—A recurring bass-passage, each repetition of which receives varied treatment.

Harmonics.— Sounds given out by a vibrating string or column of air, in addition to its fundamental tone, or "generator."

Interval.—The difference in pitch between two sounds. Intervals may be considered (i) melodically, *e.g.*—

or (ii) harmonically, *e.g.*—

Inversion.—(i) *Of an interval :* the changing of the relative position of the two sounds composing the interval, *e.g.*—

(Perf. 5th.)   (Perf. 4th.)

Inversion.

(ii) *Of a chord :* the placing of any note of a chord, other than its root, in the *bass*, or lowest part (*see* Chapter XI, Sec. 2).

Key.—A series of sounds, forming some particular scale, in which each sound bears a definite relationship to (i) a central sound called the Tonic, or key-note, (ii) every other sound of that scale.

Mode.—(i) A term sometimes used to denote a particular aspect of a key, *e.g.*, its *major mode*, or its *minor mode.* Thus C major and C minor are often spoken of as the two opposite *modes* of the key of C.

(ii) An old Ecclesiastical scale. The position of the semitones in such scales varied in every instance. (*See* Appendix D.)

Motion.—The progression of a melodic part or line in relation to another, or others. There are three kinds of Motion, viz., Similar, Contrary and Oblique (*see* Chapter II, Sec. 3).

Open Position.—When the notes of a chord lie at *approximately* equal distances from one another, *e.g.*—

(*See Close Position.*)

Overlapping of parts.—This is said to take place (i) when a higher part proceeds to a lower note than that sounded by a lower part in the previous chord, or (ii) when a lower part proceeds to a higher note than that sounded by a higher part in the previous chord, *e.g.*—

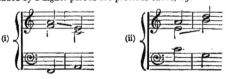

The prohibition against overlapping is more applicable to strict vocal harmony than to harmony for instruments, and even then it is frequently disregarded, *e.g.* —

Overlapping is unobjectionable between different positions of the same harmony, *e.g.* —

Part.—A sound, or a series of sounds, allotted to a single voice, or to an instrument producing only one sound at a time.

Part-writing.—The distribution of parts in relation to one another.

Phrase.—A musical period, or "rhythm," with some form of cadential termination, which is its rhythmic climax or culmination.

Pitch.—The height or depth of a sound. Pitch may be (i) *absolute* (or *fixed*), according to some definite standard, (*e.g.*, $\equiv$ = 522 vibrations per second), or (ii) *relative, i.e.*, it may be higher or lower than that of another sound, with which it is for the moment being compared.

Polyphonic.—(*lit.* "many-sounding"). Music is said to be polyphonic when it consists of several parts, of individual and independent melodic interest. (*See Contrapuntal.*)

Progression.—Movement, either melodic or harmonic.

Root.—The sound from which a chord is derived, and from which it takes its name. (*See* Chapter IX, Sec. 1.)

Scale.—A series of sounds in alphabetical order, having a definite relation to a central sound called the Tonic, or key-note.

Scale-degrees.—The following names are usually applied to the various degrees of any diatonic scale :—
1st, Tonic (or key-note); 2nd, Supertonic; 3rd, Mediant; 4th, Subdominant; 5th, Dominant; 6th, Submediant; 7th, Leading-note.
In *Sol-fa*, the following are the degree-names for the major and minor scales respectively :—
Major scale : Doh, Ray, Me, Fah, Soh, Lah, Te, Doh'.
Minor scale (harmonic form); Doh, Ray, Maw, Fah, Soh, Law, Te, Doh'.
   „   „   (melodic forms): Doh, Ray, Maw, Fah, Soh, $\left\{\begin{array}{l}\text{Lah, Te,}\\ \text{Law, Taw,}\end{array}\right\}$ Doh'.

Score.—" An arrangement of all the vocal and instrumental parts of a composition one above the other on the same page. Scores are of different kinds :—(1) *Close* or *compressed score, i.e., Short score (q.v.).* (2) *Full score,* one in which all the parts (for orchestra, chorus, etc.) are written on separate staves. (3) *Pianoforte* or *Organ score,* one in which the vocal parts are written on separate staves, the orchestral accompaniment being condensed. (4) *Open score, i.e., Full score (q.v.).* (5) *Short score,* an arrangement of a composition upon two staves, as for the Organ or Pianoforte: also, four parts written upon two staves. (6) *Vocal score,* (*a*) one in which each voice-part is written upon a separate staff, (*b*) another name for a Pianoforte or Organ score." (From "Dictionary of Musical Terms," by Arthur J. Greenish—Joseph Williams, Ltd.)

Time.—The grouping of a series of regular pulses into sets by means of periodic accent.

Tonality.—Key, in the widest application of the term ; including not only the relationship of the sounds within any one key to another and to their key-note, but the relationship of key to key, implied by the shifting of the key-centre, so as to cause what is described as Modulation. (*See* Chapter XIX.)

Transition.—A passing, or merely momentary, modulation, sometimes spoken of as a Transient modulation.

SUPPLEMENTARY EXERCISES TO BOOK I.

CHAPTER II. Section A (pages 10-12).

Add a melodious part (note-against-note) for 2nd Violin below the following melody :—

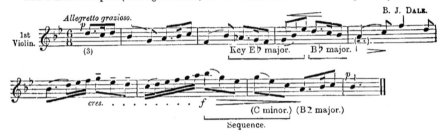

CHAPTER II. Section D (page 15).

Add a similar melodious part below the following :—

CHAPTER II. Section E (pages 15-16).

Add a similar melodious treble part *above* the following :—

CHAPTER IV. Section A (page 29).

Add a right-hand part moving in quavers throughout.

CHAPTER IV. SECTION B (page 29).

Add an Alto part below the following, moving in quavers throughout, except at the end of each phrase, when a minim should occur simultaneously in the two parts:

CHAPTER IV. SECTION E (pages 32–33).

Add a melodious Viola part, of similar character to that of the given part, above the following 'Cello part. (A crotchet followed by a quaver, thus—♩ ♪ should be accompanied by three quavers, thus—♫♪, and *vice versá.*

Add a melodious part (of similar character to that of the given part) *below* the following melodies :—

MELODY AND HARMONY.

Add a similar part *above* the following 'Cello part.   Write for the Viola, on the Alto staff.

CHAPTER V.   SECTION F (page 39).

Add a part in quavers above the following, consisting principally of tied notes.   Include as many instances of suspensions as possible.   An *occasional* passing-note may be used.

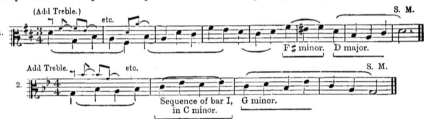

Add a Treble in *crotchets* above the following, introducing suspensions where suitable.

CHAPTER V.   SECTION H (page 39).

Add another part (in which the notes vary in length), similar in style to the one given, *below* the following.   Introduce tied notes (or rests) where suitable.

Add a similar part (for Viola) *above* the following :—

CHAPTER VII   (pages 46–47).

The following exercises may, at the option of the teacher, precede or accompany the Preliminary Exercises in 3-part melodic writing given on pages 47–50. Each of the subjects given below is intended to be accompanied by *two* other definitely melodic parts, in which the notes should be of identical length with those of the given part.

N.B.—Each subject should be used (in turn) as a Bass, a Treble, and a middle part (Alto or Tenor). To this end it should be transposed so as to suit the particular voice required. The hints as to three-part melodic writing given in Chapter VII. Sec. 6 (pages 50–51) should be carefully studied before working the exercises given below.

CHAPTER VII. Section B (pages 49–50).

Add a middle part in continuous quavers (except where otherwise indicated). The third quaver in each bar must be a suspension (which need not necessarily be *tied*). Suspensions may be used also at the first quaver of some of the bars.

HARRY FARJEON.

Add a middle part to the following, mostly in quavers and crotchets. Tied notes and suspensions will rarely be available, but an occasional accented passing-note may be found effective :—

HARRY FARJEON.

CHAPTER VII. Section C (page 53).

Add one part in half-pulse notes, and one part mainly in pulse-notes, to the following, in the manner shewn in the example on p. 52. Use each subject in turn as a Bass, a Treble, and a middle part, transposing it in every case to suit the particular voice. The quicker-moving part should be a different one in each instance.

N.B.—The following exercises may be preceded by the use (in the manner now proposed) of the six subjects by the Author of this volume, given on page xi.

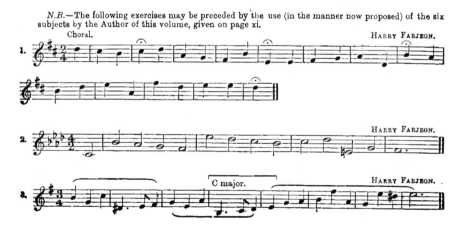

4.

N.B.—Work the foregoing subjects also in the manner indicated on page 53 (II.).

CHAPTER VII. Section E (page 57).

Add two florid parts to the following, placing the subject in turn in Bass, Treble, and Alto.

1.

(or, optionally.)

Add parts for Viola and Violoncello below the following melody. Take care to make the added parts melodically interesting, by developing some figure or figures in either the subject itself or in one of your own parts. Mark the bowing.

2.

*** The two foregoing exercises may be used equally well for *four*-part writing, as indicated in Chapter VIII (II.), page 61.

MODAL MELODIES.

(See Appendix D, page 277.)

The following 'modal' melodies, by Mr. Harry Farjeon, may be worked in two, three, or four parts (or even with a pianoforte accompaniment). The melodies should be kept in the treble part.

MODE I.—DORIAN.

Lento.

1.

Mode III.—Phrygian.

Andante.

2.

Mode V.—Lydian.

Con moto.

3.

Mode VII.—Mixo-lydian.

Allegro.

4.

ANALYTICAL INDEX.

By SYLVIA E. CURREY, L.R.A.M.

₊ *The initials f.n. after the number of a page indicate that the particular subject is referred to in a foot-note on that page.*

	PAGE	PAR.
ACCENTED passing-notes (Appoggiaturas)—		
Above notes of chord	150	7
of Dominant seventh	151	8
Approached by leap	149	4
Chromatic ...	149	5
Early notation of ...	148	f.n.
In combination	151	8
In two-part melodic	28	(f)
writing	42	6
Resolving upwards	149	5
	150	7
Sounded with note of resolution	149	6
Accentual position—		
Of cadential six-four chord	94	7
Of successive positions of one harmony	82	note to 6
Of suspensions	34	4
	135	6
Accompaniment of a voice or solo instrument	269, 270	
Added sixth, Chord of ...	183	10
	188	second f.n.
	13	f.n.
Aeolian mode ...	162	4
	277	2
Anacrusis, defined	295	
Anacrusis, Treatment of	63	note (a)
Anticipations ...	159	10
Appoggiaturas (see *Accented passing-notes*)		
Appoggiatura treatment of	150, 151	
chord of Dominant ninth	202-204	
Arco ...	284	9
Augmented fourth in two-part	40	2, 3
writing ...	41	4
Augmented interval—		
In melody ...	5	3
In minor key, Avoidance of	14	14, 15
In Tonal sequence...	259	5
Augmented triad—		
Defined	64	2
Formed by chromatic	195	2
alteration of chords	196	3
	239	8, 9
In Tonal sequence ...	259	5
On Mediant of minor key	114	7
Augmented sixth, Chord of—		
Formation of	241	1, 2
Inversions	244	7
"Italian," "French," "German"	242	3
Less usual forms of	244	8
On minor sixth of scale	242	3
On minor sixth of scale, resolutions	242	4
On minor second of scale ...	242	3

	PAGE	PAR.
Augmented sixth, Chord of—*Continued*—		
On minor second of scale, resolutions	243	5, 6
On Subdominant of major key	244	9
Authentic cadence	295	f.n. to "Cadence"
Authentic Modes	277	2, 3
Auxiliary-note below harmony-note ...	18	note to (a) 4
BASS (Bass-note), defined	295	
Bass voice, defined	295	
Binding-tone	67	10
Binding-tone, Release of	68	11
Bowing (see under *Violin*)		
Broken-chord formations	95	f.n.
	267 et seq.	
CADENCE (or Close)—		
Defined	295	
Feminine ending ...	93	3 and f.n.
	146	16
Imperfect ...	295	
In two-part melodic writing	10	10
Interrupted...	295	
Inverted	122, 123	7
Masculine and Feminine endings contrasted	94	B
Perfect ...	295	
	65	6
Plagal ...	295	
	65	6
Cadential six-four chord—		
Accentual position...	94	7
At an Imperfect cadence ...	93	3
Before a Perfect cadence ...	92	2
Defined	93	4
Doubling	93	5
Figuring	93	note to 4
Treatment ...	93	6
Canon, defined ...	295	
Canon, Example in form of	44	9, ii
	13	
Canon, Exercises in form of	32	E2
	45	E
Canto Fermo, defined ...	295	
Changing-notes ...	30	4
	158	note to 9
Choral, defined ...	295	
Choral with three florid parts added (Bach) ...	60	
Chord, defined ...	295	
Chords of sixth in succession ...	84-86	11-13
Chromatic, defined	295	

	PAGE	PAR.
Chromatic alteration of chords—		
Chromatic alteration explained	195	1, 2
Of Dominant harmony {	196	3
	241, 242	1, 2, 3
Of Subdominant secondary seventh	221	9
Of Subdominant secondary seventh (example) ...	222	10
Of Subdominant triad {	196	f.n.
	197	III.
Of Submediant triad ...	197	f.n.
Of Supertonic chromatic chord of seventh ...	242	3
Of Supertonic secondary seventh	197	IV.
Of Supertonic secondary { seventh, first inversion {	221	f.n.
(" Added sixth ")... (	244	9
Of Supertonic triad (in		IV. and
major key)	197	f.n.
Of Supertonic triad (in minor key)	197	V.
Of Supertonic triad (major)	239	8
	195	2
Of Tonic triad ... {	196	3
	239	8
Chromatic Triads—		
On Dominant (augmented triad)	196	3 (I.)
On minor second of scale ...	197	V.
On minor sixth of scale ...	197	f.n.
On Subdominant	197	III.
On Supertonic (major triad)	224, 225	4–6
On Supertonic (diminished triad)	197	IV.
On other degrees of chromatic scale	273–275	
Chromatic chord of seventh on Supertonic—		
Inversions	226	8
Omission of root	227	10
Resolutions...	226	7
Treatment of seventh ...	226	7, 8, 9
Chromatic chord of ninth on Supertonic—		
Inversions	233	3
Resolutions...	232	2
Treatment of ninth ...	232	2
Chromatic chord of eleventh on Supertonic	238	5, 6
Chromatic chord of thirteenth on Supertonic	239	8
Chromatic chord of seventh on Tonic—		
Inversions	229	12, 13
Resolutions...	230	14
Treatment of seventh ...	230	notes to (i, ii) 14
Chromatic chord of ninth on Tonic—		
Inversions	233	3
Resolutions...	233	ii
Treatment of ninth ...	232, 233	2
Chromatic chord of eleventh on Tonic	238	7

	PAGE	PAR.
Chromatic chord of thirteenth on Tonic	239	8
Chromatic discords on other degrees of chromatic scale—		
Chords of augmented sixth	241–244	
Fundamental discords ...	276	11
	18	note to (a) 4
Chromatic passing-notes {	149	5
	158	9
	178	12
	195	1, 2
Chromatic pivot-chords... ...	247-249	
Chromatic scale—		
Harmonic form	271	3
Melodic form	272-274	4–9
Need for freer notation for harmonic purposes ...	273-276	
	295	
Close position, defined ... {	66	note to 8
Common chord, defined ...	64	2, 3
Compass in vocal writing ...	10	11
Compass of Strings	281, 282	1, 2
Concordant intervals	9	6
Concordant triads, defined ...	64	3
Connection of Tonic and Dominant triads	66, 67	8, 9, 10
Connection of Tonic and Subdominant triads	66, 67	8, 9, 10
Consecutive fifths, defined ...	10	8
Consecutive fifths, diminished {	121	note to 5
and perfect in succession · {	122	note to 6
Consecutive fifths, in florid melodic movement	27	(d)
Consecutive fifths, in suspensions, Avoidance of	36	8
Consecutive fourths with bass {	84	f.n.
	102	f.n.
Consecutive octaves, defined ...	10	7
Consecutive octaves, in florid melodic movement	27	(d)
Consecutive octaves, in suspensions. Avoidance of	36	8
Consecutive unisons, defined ...	10	7
Consecutives allowable {	154	note to (b)
(sevenths, octaves, etc.) {	265	5
Contrapuntal, defined	296	
Contrary motion, defined ...	8	3
Contrary motion, in florid two- {	27	3 (c)
part writing ... ... {	28	(f)
Counterpoint, defined	296	
Crossing of parts	10	9
	56	note to example 2
Crossing of parts in music for Strings {	62	note to example II.
	282	3
DECREES of scale, Natural tendencies of	5	3(c)and f.n. to this
Delayed resolution of Dominant seventh ... ... {	41	4
	124	10, 11
Diatonic, defined	296	
Diatonic chords of seventh (see Secondary chords of seventh)		

	PAGE	PAR.
Diatonic chords of ninth (see *Secondary chords of ninth*)		
Diminished fifth in two-part writing	40	1, 2, 3
Diminished interval in melody	5	3 (a)
Diminished seventh, Chord of	205	7
Diminished triad—		
Defined	64	2
In Tonal sequence	259	5
On Supertonic of minor key	{ 105	5, 6
	114	f.n.
On Supertonic of major key (chromatic)	197	IV.
On Leading-note of major or minor key	112, 113	4
Discords in two-part writing—		
Between two moving parts	55	(2)
Essential	40-42	
Unessential	{ 17	2, 3
	34	4
Dissonant intervals	17	f.n.
Dissonant triad	64	2, 3
Dominant, in Ecclesiastical Modes	278	4
Dominant triad—		
Character of	65	6
Followed by Subdominant harmony	{ 74	1, 2
	86	14
Preceded by Subdominant harmony	{ 74, 75	1-3
	85	13
Dominant seventh, Chord of—		
As modulating chord	168	7
Figuring	127	15
Inversions	120	1, 3
Inversions, Use of	{ 121, 122	5-7
	124	9
Omission of fifth	123	8
Omission of root	124	f.n.
Resolution delayed	{ 41	4
	124	10, 11
Resolution on Subdominant harmony	126, 127	13
Resolution on Submediant harmony	{ 120	3
	124	8
Resolution on Tonic harmony	120	3
Resolution with rising seventh	121, 122	6
Taken in sequence ("Transitional")	168	f.n.
With appoggiaturas	150, 151	
With suspensions	135	7
Dominant ninth, Chord of—		
Decorated with appoggiaturas	211	11
Inversions (major ninth)	205, 206	8
Inversions (major ninth), avoidance of consecutives	206	9
Inversions, freer treatment of seventh	207	10
Inversions, minor ninth	{ 204	6
	205	7
Ninth as appoggiatura	{ 150, 151	
	202, 203	
Ninth resolving on root	202	3
Ninth resolving on third	203	3 (ii)

	PAGE	PAR.
Dominant ninth, Chord of— *Continued*—		
Ninth resolving on fifth or seventh	203, 204	4
Ninth as essential note	204, 205	5, 6
Resolved on Tonic chord	204	5
Dominant eleventh, Chord of	215	2
Dominant eleventh, Chord of, Inversions (secondary sevenths)	216	3
Dominant thirteenth, Chord of—		
In minor key	219	*note to* 5
Inversions (secondary sevenths)	220-222	8-10
Movement of thirteenth when accompanied by seventh	222	11
Position of thirteenth when accompanied by seventh	222	11
Thirteenth as appoggiatura	218	4
Thirteenth as essential note	219, 220	5, 6
Dorian mode	277	2
Double counterpoint, defined	296	
Double pedal	261	10
Double suspensions	144, 145	12, 13, 14
Doubling—		
In succession of chords of sixth	85	12
In triads (direct)	67	9
In triads in first inversion	{ 83	7, 8
	105	6
	122	f.n.
In triads in second inversion	93	5
Of discords, in pianoforte idiom	266	
Of Leading-note	67	*note to* 9
Of Leading-note (exceptions to above rule)	259, 266	
Of melody, in pianoforte accompaniment	269	9 *and* f.n.
Downward compass of violin, viola, violoncello	32, 33	f.n.
ECCLESIASTICAL Modes	277	
Eleventh, Chord of (see *Dominant eleventh, Chromatic chord of eleventh*)		
Enharmonic, defined	296	
Enharmonic modulation—		
By means of augmented triads	{ 253	10
	254	11
By means of chord of augmented sixth	252	8, 9
By means of chord of diminished seventh	249-251	
Essential discords	{ 204	5
	211	11
	215	1
	218	3
	219	5
	232, 233	2, 3
	238	6
	239	8
Essential discords in two-part writing, Treatment of	40-42	

	PAGE	PAR.
Expedient false notation (see *False Notation*)		
Extended position, defined ...	296	
Extension of phrase	286, 287	5
	220	7
	234	4
	239	10
FALSE Notation	244	*note to* 9
	271	2
	273	7
	275	10
False Relation	169	*note*
"False Triads"	275	10
	93	*f.n.*
Feminine ending... ...	102	*f.n.*
	126	13
	146	16
Fifths, Consecutive, defined ...	10	8
(see *Consecutive fifths*)		
Fifth, Interval of, in two-part melodic writing	9	6
Figuration	267-269	
Figured bass—		
Defined	vii	12-14
	84	10
Of chord of Dominant seventh	127	15
	143	10
Of suspensions ...	144	11
	147	
Of triads	84	10
	93	4 *and note*
Use of lines of continuation	101	*note*
Final, in Ecclesiastical Modes ...	277, 278	3, 4
Florid melodic movement ...	17 *et seq.*	
Florid melodic movement, Hints with regard to	26-28	3
Florid melodic movement, treat- m n of four notes to one ...	30	4
Florid tmelodic movement, use of leaps	26, 27	3 (*b*)
Florid melodic movement, use of Imitation	54	*note* (2)
Florid melodic movement, use of melodic minor scale ...	23, 43, 44	
Four-part melodic writing ...	59 *et seq.*	
Fourth, Interval of, in two-part melodic writing ...	36	10
	42	6
Fourths with bass, Consecutive	84	*f.n.*
	102	*f.n.*
French sixth	242	3, 4
	244	7
Fundamental sevenths, defined	179	*note to* 1
Fundamental sevenths	276	11
GERMAN sixth	242	3, 4
	244	7
Ground Bass, defined	296	
HARMONICS, defined	296	
Harmonic minor scale ...	13	12
Harmonic chromatic scale ...	271	3
Harmonization of melodies—		
Cadence (see *Cadence*)		
Importance of good bass ...	80	1

	PAGE	PAR.
Harmonization of melodies— *Continued*—		
Use of accented passing-notes	154, 155	
	80	1, 2
Use of inverted chords	81	4
	82	6
Use of modulation ...	177, 178	
Use of suspensions ...	140, 141	
Harmonization of Choral, by Bach	60	
	278	5 (ii)
Hypo-Aeolian and other Plagal Modes	277	2
	54	*note* (2)
	55	*note* 1
IMITATION	56	*note to ex.* 2
	62	*note*
Imperfect cadence, defined ...	295	
Implied and expressed modulation	177, 178	
Interrupted cadence, defined	295	
	106	7
Interval, defined	296	
	55	*note* 1
Inverse movement ...	57	*note to example* 3
Inversion of interval, defined ...	296	
Inversion of chord, defined	296	
	80	2
Inverted cadence	122, 123	7
Inverted pedal	262	11
Ionian mode	277	2
Italian sixth	242	3, 4
	244	7
KEY—		
Defined	296	
Determined by Dominant seventh followed by Tonic chord	166	*note to* 4
Nearly-related keys ...	165	2, 3
Not defined by a single chord	166	4
	224	2
LEADING-NOTE—		
	67	*note to* 9
Doubling	259	
	266	
Falling (in Bach)	69	*f.n.*
In minor key	13	12
In minor key, How to approach ...	14	15
	75	3
In Tonal sequence ...	259	5
Use of, in melody	5	3
Leading seventh, Chord of ...	205	8
Leaps, Use of, in melody ...	4, 5	
Leap to perfect fourth in two-part melodic writing ...	27	*second f.n.*
Lydian mode	277	2
MAJOR thirds on fourth and fifth degrees in succession ...	9	*f.n.*
Major triad, defined	64	2

	PAGE	PAR.
Masculine ending	94	B
Mediant triad, in major key ...	113	5, 6
Mediant triad, in minor key ...	114	7
Melodic chromatic scale ...	272–274	4–9
Melodic construction	4, 5	
Melodic minor scale	13	12
Melodic minor scale, in {	150	note to 7
" Appoggiatura ninth " {	202	note to 2
Melodic minor scale, in florid {	23	5, 6
two-part writing ... {	43, 44	
Melodic minor scale, in for- {	161, 162	
mation of chords ... {	192, 193	
Melodic minor scale, treat- {	43	7
ment of major sixth.... {	161, 162	2
Melodic minor scale, treat- {	43	7
ment of minor seventh {	161, 162	2, 3, 4
Melody, defined	1	2
Minor scale, Forms of	13	12
Minor scale, defined	64	2
Mixed (or Modulating) sequence	258	2
Mixolydian mode	277	2
Mode, defined	296	
Modes, Ecclesiastical	277	
Modes, Ecclesiastical, Use of, {	278–280	
in modern music ... {		
Modulation—		
By pivot-chord {	166	5
{	167	6
By pivot-chord (chromatic)	247, 248	3
{	167	5
{	168	7 and f.n.
By pivot-note ... {	173	8
{	174	note to II
{	177	10
{	248	4
Enharmonic	249 et seq.	
Expressed and implied ...	177, 178	
Nearly-related keys ...	165	3
On a pedal	261	9 and f.n.
Transient	168	7
Use of six- four chord of {	167	note to 6
new key ... {	173	8
{	175	9 and note
Motion, defined	296	
Motion, similar, contrary, {	8	3
oblique ... ... {	9	4
NEAPOLITAN sixth	197	note and f.n.
Nearly-related keys	165	2, 3
Ninth, Chord of (see Dominant		
ninth, Secondary chords of		
ninth, Chromatic chord of ninth)		
Numeral notation ... {	vi, vii	9–11
{	68	note to C
{	81	note to 4
Oblique motion defined ...	8	3
Oblique motion to octave or		
unison	127	14
Octave, Use of, in two-part melo-		
dic writing	9	6
Octaves, Consecutive (see Con-		
secutive octaves)	10	7
Open position, defined	296	

	PAGE	PAR.
Ornamental resolution of Domi-		
nant seventh	124	10, 11
Ornamental resolution of passing		
notes	158	9 (b) and note
Ornamental resolution of Sus-		
pensions	135	5
Overlapping of parts	296, 297	
Overlapping of parts, in two-part		
writing	10	9
PART, defined	297	
Part-writing, defined	297	
Passing-notes—		
Accented ... ... {	28	(f)
{	148–151	
Approached by leap ...	158	9 (a)
Auxiliary-note	18	note to 4
Changing-notes ... {	30	4 (iii)
{	158	note to 9 (b)
Chromatic ... {	18	note to 4(a)
{	149	5
{	158	9
{	178	12
{	195	1, 2
Defined	17	3
In two-part melodic writing	17–32	
Progression of second pass-		
ing-note	20	note
Quitted by leap	158, 159	9 (b) and (c)
Resolution delayed ...	158	9 (b)
Usual treatment of {	17	3
{	18	4
Passing six-four chord	96	8
Passing six-four chord, Treat-		
ment of	97	9
Pedals—		
Defined	260	7
Decorated	262	13
Double	261	10
Effect of Dominant or Tonic		
pedal	260	8
Effect of pedal on other		
degrees of scale	260	2nd f.n.
Inverted	262	11
Modulation on	261	9 and f.n.
Treatment	261	9
Perfect cadence, defined ...	295	
Perfect cadence, accentual posi-		
tion of final chord	68	C
Perfect cadence, omission of fifth		
from Tonic chord	69	12
Perfect fourth in two-part melo-		
dic writing	42	6
Phrase, defined	297	
Phrygian mode	277	2
Pianoforte idioms—		
Decoration and figuration...	267–269	
In accompaniment of {	269	9
vocal or instrumental {		
solo	270	10, 11
In arrangement of chords ...	263, 264	1
In chord-progression ...	264(3)–266	

	PAGE	PAR.
Pianoforte idioms—*Continued*—		
	264	*note to (b)*
	265	*f.n.*
In doubling ...	266	*(c)*
	269	9 *and f.n.*
	270	10
In treatment of discords	266	*(d)*
	270	10
In varying density of har-	263	1
mony	265	5
Picardy third	71	*note (a)* G
Pitch, defined	297	
Pizzicato	284	9
Plagal cadence, defined	65	6
	295	
Plagal Modes	277	2, 3
Polyphonic, defined	297	
Preparation of dissonant fifths	114	*note and f.n.* 7
Preparation of secondary sevenths	180	4 *and f.n.*
Preparation of suspensions ...	133	2
Primary triads (enumerated) ...	65	4
Progression, defined	297	
Progression, Aspects of ...	2	
QUARTET of Strings, Examples of	59, 62, 63	
Quartet of Strings, Instruments of	281, 282	
REAL sequence	257	2
Related keys (see *Nearly-related keys*).		
Release of binding-tone	68	11
Resolution of discords in two-part writing—		
Of diminished fifth and aug- mented fourth	40, 41	2, 3, 4
Of second and seventh ...	41, 42	5
Responsive phrases, Addition of	6	*f.n.*
	285–287	
	29	*note to* A
	32	*(b)*
	33	*first f.n.*
Rests, Use of, in melodic writing	37	11
	54	*note (4)*
	59	
	63	*(c)*
Retardations, defined ...	35	*note to* 5
	134	*f.n. to* 3
Rhythm	1	
Rhythmic figure in melodic writing	54	*note (4)*
	63	*note (b)*
Root, defined	297	
SCALE, defined	297	
Scale-degrees, defined	297	
Score, defined	297	
Second proceeding to unison ...	28	*(e)*
Second inversion of triads (see *Six-four chord*)		
Secondary triads, explained ...	104	1, 2
Secondary triads, in first inver- sion	114	8
Secondary triads, in second in- version	115	9

	PAGE	PAR.
Secondary chords of seventh—		
Defined	179	1
Formed on melodic minor	189	*f.n.*
scale	192, 193	
Inversions	180	5
On Mediant of minor scale	181	6
On Subdominant ...	189, 190	
	220(8)–222	
On Submediant	189, 190	
	181	6
	183	10, 11
On Supertonic ...	188	1, 2
	189	3
	216	
Prepared	180	4
Resolved on chord having root a fourth above ...	179	3
Taken in sequence ...	182	9
Secondary chords of ninth—	212–214	
Sequence—		
Defined	11	*note, ex.* 4
	257	1
In florid melodic move-	30	4
ment	32	*first f.n.*
Licences in course of	259	5
Mixed (or Modulating) ...	258	2
Of Dominant sevenths ...	168	*f.n.*
Of Secondary sevenths ...	182	9
Real, defined	257	2
Tonal, defined	257	2
Seventh, Chord of (see *Dominant seventh, Secondary chords of seventh, Chromatic chord of seventh*)		
Similar motion, defined ...	8	3
Similar motion to fifth, between extreme parts	77	5
Similar motion to octave,	77	5
between extreme parts	125	12
Similar motion to unison ...	125	12
Six-four chord—		
Accentual position	94	7
	97	9 *and f.n.*
Approach to	97	10
Cadential	92 *et seq.*	
Followed by another six- four chord	102	*f.n.*
Passing	96, 97	
Strings, Writing for	281–284	
Subdominant triad—		
Character of	65	6
Followed by Dominant	74, 75	1, 2 3
harmony	85	13
Preceded by Dominant	74	2
harmony	86	
Submediant triad ...	106	7
	111	1, 2
Submediant triad, doubling ...	106	8
Supertonic triad	104, 105, 111	
Supertonic triad, in minor key	114	*f.n.*
Supertonic chromatic triad ...	224, 225	
Supertonic chromatic chord of seventh	226, 227	
Supertonic chromatic chord of ninth	232 *et seq.*	

	PAGE	PAR.
Supertonic chromatic chords of eleventh and thirteen	238, 239	
Suspensions—		
Accentual position	{ 34 / 135	4 / 6
Defined	34	3, 4
Double	{ 144 / 145	12 / 13,14
Figuring	{ 143, 144 / 147	
In two-part melodic writing	35–37	
In three-part melodic writing	{ 49 / 54	B / note (3)
Over chord of Dominant seventh	135	7
Preparation	{ 133 / 135	2 / 4
Resolution delayed	135	5
Resolved upwards	{ 134 / 145	3 and f.n. / note to 14
Sounded with note of resolution	137	note to (c)
Suspended fourth	133	2 (b)
Suspended Leading-note	134	3
Suspended ninth	133	2 (a)
Suspended sixth	134	(c)
Triple (Suspension of whole chord)	{ 145 / 146	15 / 16
Syncopation in two-part writing	34–37	
Thirteenth, Chord of (see Dominant thirteenth, Chromatic chord of thirteenth)		
Three-part melodic writing—		
Distance between parts	51	ii
Omission of note of triad	50, 51	6
Passing-notes in two parts at at once	52	note
Use of Imitation	54	note (2)
Tie, Use of, in florid melodic movement	36	8, 9, 10
Tie, Value of, in three-part writing	54	note (3)
Tierce de Picardie	71	note (a)
Time, defined	297	
Tonal sequence	257	2
Tonal sequence, Licences in course of	259	5
Tonality, defined (See also Key)	297	
Tonality, Vagueness of	{ 44 / 111 / 162 / 168	note to 7 / 1 and f.n. / 3 / f.n.
Tonality, Vagueness of, example by Grieg	177	10

	PAGE	PAR.
Tonality, Vagueness of, example by Chopin	249	5
Tonality, Vagueness of, example by Wagner	274	9
Tonic triad	66	7
Tonic triad, Character of	65	6
Tonic triad, Omission of fifth	{ 69 / 123	12 / 8
Tonic chromatic chord of seventh	229–230	
Tonic chromatic chord of ninth	232 et seq.	
Tonic chromatic chords of eleventh and thirteenth	238, 239	
Transition, defined	297	
Triad—		
Consonant, defined	64	3
Defined	64	1
Dissonant, defined	64	3
Doubling	67	9
Primary	{ 65–69 / 74 et seq.	
Secondary	104 et seq.	
Triads, Weak and strong progressions of	{ 86 / 112	14 / 3
Triple suspensions	{ 145 / 146	15 / 16
Tritone	5	f.n.
Two-part melodic writing—		
Distance between parts	10	f.n.
Treatment of minor key	{ 14 / 23	
Use of interval of fifth	9	6
Use of interval of fourth	36, 37	note to 10
Unessential notes, defined	{ 17 / 34	2 / 4
(See also under Passing-notes and Suspensions.)		
Unison, Use of, in two-part writing	9	6
Unison, Oblique motion to, from second	{ 28 / 127	(e) / 14
Unisons, Consecutive	10	7
Violin—		
Bowing, How to indicate	282–284	
Compass	281	2
Pizzicato	284	9
Viola, Compass of	281	2
Violoncello, Compass of	282	2
Vocal Melody—		
Characteristics of	4	2
Compass for the four voices	10	11
How it differs from instrumental melody	4	f.n.
Voice-parts, Arrangement of	{ 51 / 72	ii / 14

Printed in Poland
by Amazon Fulfillment
Poland Sp. z o.o., Wrocław

17457574R00188